PRESERVING SUMMER'S BOUNTY

PRESERVING SUMMER'S BOUNTY

Marilyn Kluger

M. Evans and Company, Inc.
New York

Portions of this book previously appeared in *Gourmet* magazine, some in slightly altered form. Copyright © Marilyn Kluger 1971, 1975, 1977, and 1978. Reprinted by permission of *Gourmet*.

Library of Congress Cataloging in Publication Data

Kluger, Marilyn.
  Preserving summer's bounty.

  Bibliography: p.
  Includes index.
  1. Canning and preserving. I. Title.
TX603.K49   641.4   78-31114

ISBN 0-87131-266-2 HARDCOVER

ISBN 0-87131-388-X PAPERBOUND

M. EVANS AND COMPANY, INC.
216 East 49 Street
New York, New York 10017

DESIGN BY Ronald F. Shey

DRAWINGS BY Mary Azarian

Manufactured in the United States of America

9 8 7 6 5 4 3

Contents

Contents

For my father
Charles Marshall
whose stories are my wellspring
of memories

Acknowledgments

My sincere thanks to all who have given me help during the writing of this book. I am grateful to Marcelle Allen and Sandra Simons, Cooperative Extension Specialists of Purdue University, who checked the manuscript for accuracy, and to my friend, Alla McConathy, who also read the manuscript and made valuable suggestions.

Thanks to all who helped me pinpoint elusive information; Jane Heramb, Vanderburgh County Extension Agent; pharmacist Bill Reine; and the librarians of the Evansville Public Library.

I especially appreciate the efforts of Victor Chapin and Nancy Uberman in my behalf, and the continuing support and encouragement of my special friends and mentors, Vardine Moore, Ellen Wedeking, and John Schaffner.

Foreword

Although my kitchen does not yield the magnitude of home-preserved foods that my mother's did, every summer finds me caught up in a round of canning, freezing, drying, pickling, and jellying. As soon as the sprawling vines in our half-acre garden bring forth crisp cucumbers and zucchini and the tomato, cabbage, and okra plants are bountiful, I look up the heirloom recipes and gather my own special favorites. The home freezer is defrosted and made ready for the first packages of strawberries and red pie cherries. I buy extra supplies of sugar, vinegar, spices, jar lids and rings, and canning and freezing jars. I have the gauge of the pressure canner tested, and eventually all is in readiness.

Once the garden produce begins, all comers to our door are greeted by the sharp spicy scents of vinegary brews and the sweet fruity fragrances arising from preserving kettles. Rows of sparkling glass jars upturned on the drainboard are the usual sight, and the overspilling panful of peelings perpetually needs to be carried out and thrown over the fence to the chickens. Day after day the nostalgic fragrance of preserving wafts into the very cracks and crevices of the kitchen, where it seems to linger even after the garden has spent itself.

But there are reasons besides the pleasure of evoking

memories of other summers and flavors that I carry on the preserving tradition. There is the security of knowing that jars of food canned in my own kitchen contain only healthful, pure, and clean ingredients. Because we preserve only freshly picked vegetables and fruits of the finest quality from our carefully cultivated garden or those from trusted sources, our home-produced fare provides the best nutrition possible from canned, frozen, and dried foods. In terms of dollars and cents, food preservation in a home kitchen requires a minimal outlay, especially when all or part of the produce is grown by family members. In terms of time and effort invested, the undertaking is costly, but I, like many others, find the manufacture of my own unique brand of pickles, preserves, jellies, jams, relishes, and sundry other foods to be immensely satisfying.

Why not join me in a season of preserving summer's bounty? This book is a sharing of the methods and recipes I use for preserving foods at home and a gleaning of the timeless procedures and handed-down recipes relied on by my mother and grandmothers, those skillful, energetic cooks who are always my inspiration in the summer kitchen.

Newburgh, Indiana   *Marilyn Kluger*

PART I

Canning Fruits
and Vegetables

A REMEMBRANCE
OF CANNING SEASON

When I recall my country childhood, the events of the 1930's are the ones that come to mind. To me, those remembered years were the happiest of times—not the hard times they were to many who look back on that decade. For my family, the thirties were a time of plenty.

That we lived a life filled with abundance in a time of scarcity and deprivation was simply because our home was on a small farm in southern Indiana. In such a place, there was little uncertainty about securing the necessities of life. An industrious family on a well-managed farm could take care of its own needs. That was the way of life my grandparents and parents had chosen, and it kept us in comfort and plenty during those years.

My father often pointed out to us how great a part of our necessities came from our own land and our own labors. Sometimes he would lean back in his chair during a particularly satisfying meal and take inventory of the foods on the table. Frequently he could attribute all of them to our own efforts and acres, and from the heavy oak table in the kitchen we could actually see where much of our food grew. The garden lay along the south side of the house, separated from it by a double row of fruit trees, including the Georgia Belle peach, which bore white-fleshed fruits, and the Red Delicious apple. From the same window we

3

could see the barn beyond the garden where the milk cows and beef steers were stabled, and behind the barn was the feedlot where the pigs were kept. The kitchen's east window faced the poultry house against the background of more fruit trees, for our house was built at the edge of an orchard of two hundred trees. Beyond the fence lay fields that yielded quail and small game, and bordering them were the wild plum, crab apple, and persimmon trees, a wild orchard from which we gathered fruits from trees Dad had not tended. In the woods were the tall shagbark hickories and majestic black walnuts that showered down nuts in the autumn, and wild grapevines twined over smaller trees nearby.

We actually sat in the midst of our fields of plenty. The kitchen table was a veritable cornucopia for the harvest from our acres. In the center, piled in a crunchy mound on the ironstone meat platter might be quail Dad had hunted, or smoky fried ham slices cut from the muslin shrouded ham hung in the smokehouse. The biscuits keeping warm on the lowered oven door were made with flour ground from our own wheat at the mill in a neighboring town. The shortening that made tender, flaky biscuits and crisp-fried quail was white leaf lard rendered from fat hogs we had butchered. The clabbered milk in the biscuits and the sweet milk in the gravy came from our Jersey cows. The butter was from our own churn, and the greenish gold sorghum that trickled slowly from a heavy glass pitcher was made by Uncle Emmett from cane grown in a small plot down by the creek. The baked apples were Stayman Winesaps that were grown in Dad's orchard, and they were stuffed with black walnuts from my grandfather's woods. Honey from my grandmother's hives, eggs from our hens, and tart wild-plum jelly from Mother's cache of home-canned foods in the cellar completed a typical array of foods produced on the farm by my family.

My mother, like all tireless countrywomen of that day, felt duty bound to can, jelly, preserve, pickle, dry, salt down, or otherwise "put up" all the surplus of vegetables and fruits from the orchard and garden, so that her family would eat well during the winter. Every summer she was caught up in the round of food preservation that began in

4

early spring with the first ripe berries and did not end until the last batch of fruited mincemeat was put down in a stone jar under a pool of brandy.

At the end of the preserving season the cellar shelves were a spectacle of plenty. Mother had at least five hundred canning jars and all were filled when cold weather came. Row upon row of colorful jars lined the walls from floor to ceiling and the rough board shelves sagged gently under the weight of the flavorful burden. It was an awe-inspiring sight, even to me, to whom had fallen the boring secondary chores of snapping beans, pitting cherries, "topping and tailing" gooseberries, shelling peas, peeling peaches, pulling onions, stemming grapes, silking corn, picking berries, digging potatoes, and pulling weeds out of the vegetable rows in the garden. I could understand Mother's quiet pride and her feeling of accomplishment at having stored away the plenty of summer for winter's dearth. Her laden cellar shelves testified to her industry and bore out her philosophy of waste not, want not.

Since we lived almost directly across the road from my grandparents, my mother and grandmother often combined their efforts and made family projects of preserving the sudden abundances of peaches, corn, apples, and beans that would have overwhelmed one woman working alone. Sometimes a neighbor or an aunt came to stay for a few days to help with the canning, and at the height of the orchard harvest, even my father and grandfather left their farm work to help peel the fruit that had to be canned, or dried, or made into jellies, butters, and preserves.

It was pleasanter when there were extra hands to lighten my mother's work load during the canning season, not only because I was usually freed of my duties and allowed to swing under the tall maples with a visiting cousin, but because the monumental chore of putting up the surplus produce took on the air of a sociable with the ladies gathered in the kitchen, laughing and talking as they peeled and sliced and chopped. Somehow the pleasant babble of swapping recipes and the small gossip drifting out of the open window softened the grim fact that only hard daily work provided the security of well laden cellar shelves and full cupboards at the end of the summer.

Canning Fruits and Vegetables

Growing, harvesting, and preserving the winter's provisions in the quantities that were needed to feed our family was an effort to which we all were dedicated from the moment the first asparagus stalk appeared in the garden border until the last turnip was laid in the root cellar. The time devoted to preserving summer's bounty was so defined that it was referred to as "canning season"—as if it were a fifth season of the year.

The advent of the season of canning, pickling, and preserving precipitated a flurry of activity not to be matched by any other seasonal task of the farmhouse. As soon as spring gardens produced their first tender offerings, my mother swung into action. Down from the top shelf of the pantry came the dark blue, white-flecked enamelware canner and the heavy, steep-sided jelly kettle. Out of the depths of cupboards and drawers were mustered tin canning funnels, rectangles of paraffin, wooden spoons, boxes of rubber jar rings, and other scattered paraphernalia associated with the preserving rites. Dark earthenware jars, much in need of scouring, scalding, and airing, were carried out of the smokehouse anteroom into the sunshine. The kraut cutter was brought down from the attic and the food grinder assembled. In the cellar, baskets of clear and aqua colored glass canning jars—pints, quarts, half-gallons—were gathered together. These were carried up to the summer kitchen. Scrubbed in dishpans of steaming, sudsy water, rinsed under streams of clear water from the kitchen pump, and stored upside down in sparkling readiness for those fast approaching days when worktables would be eternally laden with overflowing vessels—colanders heaped high with red cherries, tin pails mounded with glossy blackberries, pans spilling over with cucumbers and tomatoes, and baskets burgeoning with green beans, peaches, and apples.

Throughout summer and fall the pungent odors of preserving wafted from the kitchen and pervaded the farmhouse. Even on the hottest days, smoke curled upward from the chimney as fires raged under the canning kettles. It seemed that every lid lifted filled the air with sweet fruit scents or sharp savory gusts of vinegar and spices, for

A Remembrance of Canning Season

Mother was of German ancestry and her table was always embellished with sweets and sours.

The spicy fragrances escaping from the kitchen kettles were often distinctively tomato-scented. Three long rows of tomatoes planted down the middle of the garden were the prolific source of the main ingredient for Mother's catsup, chili sauce, relishes, tomato sauce, tomato juice, and whole canned tomatoes. No other garden vegetable was as useful to Mother's menus in the summer or so necessary in canning our winter's supply of vegetables and relishes. And no other garden vegetable required so much of our effort in return for its generosity. It seemed that there was always one chore or another concerning tomatoes that needed doing from the very moment the hearty infant plants were bedded in the garden soil in early May (when the pin oak leaves are as big as a mouse's ear), until the last green tomatoes were salvaged from doomed vines in October, just before the frost.

The tomato rows in the garden formed boundaries for my summer days as a child. I could obtain my release from the garden chores only after I had weeded or watered or hoed or sheltered or suckered or stalked or picked tomatoes. Morning after morning, I was dispatched to the garden to do whatever the tomatoes required.

But my bondage to tomatoes had its rewards. A garden in summer is a place where miracles can be attended day by day. Tiny fragrant pea blossoms form into limp green pods which gradually swell into fatness and soon are ready for picking. Green tendrils reach out at the bottom of a fence and stretch upward daily until suddenly the plant sprawls all along the top wire and green cucumbers hang like pendants from the vines. In a matter of days, yellow trumpets of blossom change into miniature squashes, then small squashes turn into huge squashes. The changes and transformations that occur in the garden world are swift and miraculous.

My father's habit was to walk out to the barn every morning by way of the garden. When he came in to breakfast, he always had something or other to report that would pique our curiosity.

"The corn grew three inches last night," he would comment; or "There is a big tomato about half way down the center row that will be ripe by noon today"; or "That fat watermelon is beginning to sound hollow."

Hearing such observations made the oatmeal and eggs and biscuits fairly vanish from our plates. My brothers and I each wished to be first out to the garden to make the morning discoveries.

"Whoever finds the ripe tomato gets it!"

"Watch out for that mean bumblebee! He's working on the pumpkin blooms."

"The beans are almost ready! Look! Look!"

Green bean bushes match tomato plants in their generosity but they are more enthusiastic in their giving. A row of green beans is ready all at once, by the bushelful. Then, no sooner has the crop of green beans been canned or pickled or cooked for the table than tender new beans again appear on the bushes. By July, two long rows of beans in a garden can wear out the enthusiasm of even the most dedicated food preserver and bring an ache to the back of even the hardiest bean picker.

"I can't look at another bean!" my mother would say when she had reached that point—and still another basket of beans would be lugged in from the garden.

But the basket of green beans would sit on the porch table just long enough for Mother to get the kitchen in order for another round of canning. She was never one to let good food go to waste. Then she would pick up the basket of beans, not without a sigh, and take it to the porch swing where she always sat with a commodious pan in her lap, swinging gently while she broke the beans.

It took five deft motions to snap each bean, two to break off the ends, followed by three crisp snaps to break the bean into pieces. That was a lot of work for each bean! But I think Mother welcomed the chance to sit in the wide swing and snap beans. It was a relaxing activity compared with other work, something her hands could do without the help of her mind. I liked to be there on the shady porch when she was swinging gently and snapping beans, or shelling peas, or stemming strawberries. Those were the times when Mother could listen to me, or when she sang hymns and old songs, or when she told funny stories about teaching school. It was cool and breezy and pleasant on the porch. There were always flower boxes on the ledges, with drifts of purple and pink and white petunias blooming in them. Sometimes when we were very quiet, ruby-throated hummingbirds came to the flower boxes and hovered over the petunias, sipping nectar.

Many of the golden hours of summers gone by were spent on that vine covered porch. Sometimes whenever I remember us sitting there together, snapping beans, stemming grapes, seeding cherries, I can recall the gentle squeaking of the white-painted porch swing blending with the soft, soothing harmonies of Mother's hymns as clearly as if it were yesterday. Those flashes of memory are as brilliant as the plumage of hummingbirds that came to the porch, and as sweet and fleeting as the fragrance of petunias spilling over the flower boxes.

While the front porch with its swing was the site of much peeling and seeding and sorting, in preparing the garden's bounty for table use and for canning, the back porch was nearer the kitchen and became its necessary extension in summertime. When the wood- and coal-burning range was fired up full force on canning days, the kitchen was too hot for comfort. So we moved almost all of our kitchen-centered activities, except cooking, to the screened-in back porch for the duration of the canning season. We prepared foods, ate our meals, and washed the dishes in the open air, as it were, because three sides of the porch were screened. It was cool and pleasant, with summer breezes blowing across the porch, and an ideal arrangement, except when rains came from the north or east. Then we pushed the table and chairs toward the innermost wall to keep them from getting wet and returned to the kitchen to do our work until the rain stopped.

The ice box was always kept on the back porch. In the wintertime, we never bothered to keep ice in it at all. Those foods that required cold temperatures were simply placed in the ice box, sans ice. In winter, the whole porch was an ice box, in effect, because it was as cold as the outdoors. The food could be placed where it would keep cold, or even freeze. We actually kept very little food on hand that needed refrigeration. We had a daily supply of fresh milk and eggs, morning and evening. When we were to have chicken for dinner, one was butchered on the spot. Perishable prepared foods were never kept from one day to the next. If food was not eaten at the meal for which it was cooked, or perhaps for supper on the same day, it was fed to the bird dogs. We always ate fresh foods or freshly prepared foods. Leftovers were not our style of eating.

But in summer, the ice box was used to chill the milk, cream, and butter, to keep the eggs and meat fresh and safe, to ice the watermelons, and to set gelatin desserts. And having the big block of crystal-clear ice in the top of the ice box meant that we could chip chunks off it for iced lemonade and, best of all, that we could make ice cream in the hand-turned crank freezer.

Mother seemed always to know just when we would most appreciate a freezerful of homemade ice cream. When my brothers and I came in for our noontime dinner after a long morning of picking peaches under a blazing summer sun and spied the extra fifty-pound block of ice slowly melting and making a puddle of water near the basement drain, the rest of the day took wings and sped by. The afternoon was miraculously shortened by the promise of the reward awaiting us at the end of it. Suddenly we were quicker and nimble fingered as we picked the remaining bushels of ripe fruit. Now there was a cooling mirage in the midst of the sweltering peach grove to spur us onward—the image of a glass dessert dish mounded high with soft, delicate, tongue-frosting homemade ice cream. No prospect was more inspiring to contemplate than that of making and joyfully consuming a freezer of ice cream. Our eager anticipation of the summer evening to come all but banished the discomforts of the humid July weather and the aggravation of our itching skin irritated by peach fuzz.

When we finally gathered under the spreading branches of the Red Delicious apple tree at the side of the house ready to take our turns cranking the handle of the White Mountain ice-cream freezer (with dusk falling and the katydids and crickets beginning their rasping chorus, with the moon on the rise and the giant bull frog tuning up in the barnlot pond, with the shy whippoorwills calling softly in the distance), our appetites and indeed all our senses were pitched at their highest peaks.

Mine was the first turn of cranking the wooden ice cream freezer because the handle rotated easiest before the creamy vanilla-flavored and peach-enriched custard began to thicken. When the liquid contents of the gallon-size canister began to solidify and freeze, turning the handle required the strength of my brothers' arms.

Finally, after a time that seemed as endless as had the morning in the orchard, the handle of the ice cream freezer would hardly turn at all. It was then that my older brother sat firmly on top of the freezer, with a burlap sack between his seat and the crushed ice, to hold the ice tub down solidly while my father gave it the last few strong turns that ensured the proper consistency of the ice cream. When the dasher was at last drawn out, with a delectable firm mass of rich, smooth ice cream clinging to its wooden ribs, the moment itself was one to be savored along with the peachy flavor of the frosty blend.

Mother's ice cream was rich and smooth because it contained lots of cream from our best Jersey cow. Sometimes she used Junket rennet tablets or a cooked custard base in making ice cream, but usually it was just a simple mixture of cream, eggs, sugar, and Watkins vanilla extract. When peaches or other fruits were in season, she added those mashed ripe fruits to the mixture. Here is Mother's recipe:

Country-Style Homemade Ice Cream

Beat 4 to 6 eggs until light and fluffy. Add 2½ cups sugar, 4 cups light cream, ½ teaspoon salt, and 2 tablespoons vanilla extract. Stir until sugar is dissolved. Pour ice cream mixture into 1-gallon canister of ice-cream freezer. Add 2 cups sweetened, crushed ripe peaches or strawberries, or several mashed ripe bananas. Add enough additional light cream to fill the canister three-quarters full, or about 2 cups. Freeze until firm in ice-cream freezer.

Of all the good foods we ate on the farm, none was so irresistible a treat as the fresh peach ice cream that rewarded our day spent on top of the ladder picking peaches.

Because Dad had an orchard, peaches were a staple item in our diet, summer and winter. From the ripening of the first delicate white peaches in July to the last golden-fleshed Hale Havens in September, there was a steady procession of delicious fresh peach dishes across our table. For winter use, Mother dried, preserved, and canned quantities of the fruit. She might put up as many as two hundred quart jars of peaches during a summer, which meant that we were sure to see peaches on the table every other day, at least. But our family never tired of them, fresh or canned. Mother's canned peaches were so choice that a simple peach half covered with rich cream was, in itself, a satisfying dessert. Although she was a skillful canner, Mother had an advantage when it came to canning peaches. Of the wealth of fruit right outside our kitchen door, she chose only those peaches of the best quality and the fullest flavor and that were at the perfect state of ripeness. These were sped immediately from tree to jar, with hardly a pause between picking and preserving. Every particle of their golden perfection was captured in each canning jar.

My favorite canned peach was the tiny, red-fleshed Indian peach, a clingstone variety. Mother always canned those small fruits whole with a delicate spicing of cinnamon and clove and barely more than a hint of vinegar in their sweet syrup. Her pickled peaches were milder than those canned by my aunts and grandmothers, in deference to our family's taste. They were not served as a garnish for meats, as most pickled peaches are today, but as a spicy fruit dessert to accompany sponge cake or sugar cookies. And each tiny pickled Indian peach was the perfect mouthful for a child!

This is the recipe used by Mother to pickle and spice Indian peaches and other clingstone varieties of peaches, such as the white-fleshed Champion that grew beside the well south of the house.

Pickled Peaches

Plunge ripe clingstone peaches into boiling water, then into cold water, and slip off their skins. In a large saucepan, make a syrup of 1 cup sugar, 1 cup water, 1 to 2 tablespoons vinegar, ½ stick cinnamon, and 2 cloves for each quart of whole peeled peaches to be canned. Bring the syrup to a boil, add the peeled peaches, and bring to a boil again. Boil the peaches only until they are tender enough to pierce with a broomstraw.

Lift the cooked peaches out of the boiling syrup with a slotted spoon, pack into hot jars, and cover with boiling syrup, leaving ¼-inch head space. Adjust lids and process jars in a simmering water bath for 10 minutes to ensure seal. Cook only 1 or 2 quarts of peaches in the syrup at a time.

As the different varieties of peaches ripened in Dad's orchard, Mother canned or pickled or dried or made jams and butters of them until she had put up enough jars for the coming year. But peaches were not the only summer fruit preserved for our winter use. The canning of fruits began with the reddening of the first strawberries in our one-acre patch, followed by the tart red pie cherries, apricots, red and black raspberries, gooseberries, plums, pears, quinces, grapes, and apples. In addition to the cultivated fruits, we had an abundance of wild fruits in the fields and fence rows around the farm. We gathered "wild goose" plums, mulberries, elderberries, "sarvis" berries, crab apples and wildings, red haws, pawpaws, persimmons, wild fox grapes, tiny wild strawberries, and bucketful after bucketful of glossy, dark, wild blackberries.

Of the summer fruits that we preserved on the farm, wild blackberries were second in importance in our provisions. Only peaches were canned in greater quantity. Mother always canned at least a hundred quarts of blackberries and fifty smaller jars of blackberry jams and jellies. Besides those, she also canned half-gallons of blackberry juice for drinking and for making fresh jelly later on. We picked bucketful after bucketful of glossy, dark berries dur-

ing the entire month of July. Those mornings spent berry-
ing were peaceful interludes away from the farmhouse. But
after we returned from the briar thickets, faces heat-
flushed, fingers stained and scratched, chigger bites already beginning to itch, and pails full, the serious business
of canning blackberries got under way.

My chore was to help make ready for the afternoon's
canning while Mother served a midday meal to my father
and brothers. I carried the buckets of blackberries out by
the cistern to be near the water supply while washing the
fruit. Three large enamelware pans were filled with cold
water from the pump, for Mother's rule was that the berries be quickly rinsed through three waters. The berries
were turned into the first pan of water, then promptly
lifted out and placed in the next pan of water before they
could become waterlogged, then finally rinsed in the third
pan, leaving behind trash and small insects that were in
the berries.

From then on, the blackberries were Mother's province.
While she looked them over and sorted out the imperfect or
overripe berries, I cleared the kitchen for the canning project. After the dinner dishes were put away, I washed the
aqua-colored Mason jars in hot, sudsy water; my hands
were small enough to fit down inside the jars to get them
clean. After a rinse in clear water from the cistern, the jars
were placed in hot water in the canner and boiled for 20
minutes on the kitchen stove. Mother was very particular
about cleaning and sterilizing her canning equipment, and
to this she attributed much of her success in "keeping" the
jars of food she canned.

When the sterilized jars were safely removed from the
boiling water and had cooled enough to be handled, I
slipped a rubber ring over the rim of each jar, making sure
its surface lay flat against the glass ledge below the threads
where it belonged. Then we filled each jar with glistening
damp blackberries, leaving just enough head space to cover
the berries with simple syrup that Mother had stirred to a
boil on the kitchen range. Then we wiped the rims of the
jars clean with a damp cloth—if a drop of the sticky syrup
remained, the jars would not seal. No step in the canning
procedure was carelessly done. Before she screwed down

the zinc lids and tightened them with her strong hands, Mother passed a finger around the rim of each jar to be sure none had been chipped when we filled the jars with berries.

Finally the blackberries we had picked that morning were all packed into quart jars, ready to be arranged inside the canning kettle on its rack. Next, enough hot water was poured in the canner to cover the jars to a depth of more than an inch over their lids. Then, before the canner was placed over the front burners of the range, Mother lifted the stove lid and fed more coal lumps and dry wood to the fire so that it would burn hotter and bring the water in the canner quickly to the boiling point. Then, after 15 minutes at a lively boil, Mother removed the hot jars, one by one, from their boiling water bath. Before she set each jar of canned berries on a folded dish towel to cool, she completed the seal by gripping the zinc lid with a canning wrench and turning it, slowly and firmly, until it was tight.

With the day's canning finished, Mother took her mending and retreated from the hot kitchen to the comfort of the porch swing. All afternoon the rows of dark jars cooled in the kitchen. It was not until the next morning, after Mother turned each jar upside down briefly and examined the lid to make sure it was sealed, that we carried the newly-canned fruit to the cellar.

When I think of those unending hot July mornings we spent in the berry patches filling the erstwhile milking pails to the brim with gleaming sweet blackberries and the afternoons we spent in the steamy kitchen making jelly and canning the morning's pickings, the summer days gone by seem as vivid and recent as yesterday.

Every day's canning added another seven or fourteen or twenty-one jars to the growing store of canned fruits and vegetables in our cellar. At the end of the canning season, the rough board shelves that reached from floor to ceiling against one wall of the cool cellar held hundreds of filled jars of canned foods. It was truly a spectacle of plenty! There, before our eyes, were our meals for an entire year.

After a season of preserving summer's bounty, we *knew* where our winter meals were coming from!

Choosing and Using Canning Equipment

If you plan to preserve a part of summer's bounty of fruits and vegetables by canning, you need certain special canning equipment in addition to regular kitchen utensils that you may already have on hand. For efficiency, assemble all the essential equipment in one area before beginning a canning project.

ABSOLUTELY ESSENTIAL is

. . . . *a water-bath canner for processing acid foods,* including certain sweet acid fruits, fruit juices, jams, fruit butters, marmalades, conserves, preserves, relishes, some tomato products, vinegared and pickled vegetables and fruits. In short, all canned products *except jellies and low-acid foods* can be processed in the boiling-water bath (BWB) at 212°F for the time specified for each food.

. . . . *a steam-pressure canner for processing all low-acid foods,* such as most vegetables, all meats, poultry, seafood, and the few varieties of low-acid tomatoes (see p. 76) at a temperature of 240°F (10 pounds pressure at sea level to 2,000 feet above) for the time specified for each food.

16

AVERAGE PH VALUES FOR SOME COMMON FOODS

pH	
0	
2.9	Vinegar
3.0	Gooseberries
3.2	Rhubarb, dill pickles
3.3	Apricots, blackberries
3.4	Strawberries; lowest acidity for jelly
3.5	Peaches
3.6	Raspberries, sauerkraut
3.7	Blueberries
3.8	Sweet cherries
3.9	Pears
4.2	Tomatoes (4.0 to 4.6)
4.4	Lowest acidity for processing at 212° F
4.6	Figs, pimientos
5.0	Pumpkins, carrots
5.1	Cucumbers
5.2	Turnips, cabbage, squash
5.3	Parsnips, beets, snap beans
5.4	Sweet potatoes
5.5	Spinach
5.6	Asparagus, cauliflower
5.8	Meat, ripened
6.0	Tuna, carrots
6.1	Potatoes
6.2	Peas
6.3	Corn
7.0	Meat, unripened
14.0	

Acidity — Neutral — Alkalinity

Source: *Handbook of Food Preparation,* American Home Economics Association 2010 Massachusetts Ave. N.W. Washington, D.C. 1975.

WHY

Foods processed in a water-bath canner can be heated to a temperature of 212°F., or boiling, which is adequate to sterilize food inside the jars and to destroy yeasts, molds, and bacteria that may be present in acid foods and that will cause spoilage if not destroyed by heat.

All low-acid foods must be processed in a steam-pressure canner at a temperature higher than that reached in the boiling-water bath (BWB) in order to prevent the survival and growth of *Clostridium botulinum* spores which produce the rare but deadly botulism toxin. A steam-pressure canner is designed to heat food to a temperature of 240°F (10 pounds pressure) and sustain it for a time that is adequate to kill botulism spores and other bacteria which are capable of surviving a boiling-water bath.

THE WATER-BATH CANNER

Buy a special canner intended for the purpose of processing filled jars in boiling water for canning. It consists of a large, deep metal kettle with a tight lid and a rack that holds the jars. It must be deep enough to hold pint or quart jars on a rack ½-inch above the bottom of the kettle with enough space above the tops of the jars to allow water covering the jars to boil freely without splashing out, at least 2 to 4 inches above the jar tops.

Since a quart jar is 7 inches tall, that means the canner must be at least 11½ inches tall to meet the minimum requirements. Out of curiosity, I measured my two BWB canners and found one to be only 9 inches tall (it is fine for processing pint jars) and the other to barely be within the requirements. So shop around before you buy a new BWB canner, and get one that is roomy enough not to cause problems.

Water-bath canners are commonly made of graniteware or enamelware, aluminum, or stainless steel. Enamelware canners are relatively inexpensive and are practical for other uses. In addition to processing filled jars during

18

canning, they are recommended for holding foods in salt, vinegar, or lime solutions during canning preparations and can be used for pre-cooking large quantities of acid foods, such as catsups, before processing. One care must be exercised—enamelware canners are not extremely durable and the enameled finish can be chipped easily during normal use. A moderate chipping of the finish of the canner does not spoil it for processing filled jars during canning. But if the canner becomes badly chipped, it should no longer be used to prepare loose salty or acid foods, because the inner metal that is exposed could leach out into the contents of the vessel.

Aluminum water-bath canners are lightweight, durable, and inexpensive but the metal darkens and discolors unattractively with use, especially in hard water. To counteract the harmless staining caused by minerals in the water, add ¼ cup of vinegar to the water in which the jars are processed. To remove the stains from aluminum kettles, boil in them a solution of water and cream of tartar for 5 to 10 minutes, using 1 to 2 tablespoons of cream of tartar to each quart of water.

Aluminum vessels also react chemically with acids or salts in loose foods being prepared in them and pitting in the surface may appear eventually. Pitting is harmless to the food and, once formed, there is no way to remove the pits. Simply scour the utensil lightly with a soap-filled steel wool pad after each use.

Stainless steel water bath canners are lightweight and virtually indestructible, and they retain their shiny attractive appearance with little maintenance throughout long service. Only an occasional polishing with baking soda is needed to keep stainless steel shining.

Stainless steel containers are safe to use with salt, lime, acid, and lye mixtures, as are graniteware or enamelware containers. Although canners made of stainless steel are comparatively expensive initially, they are a good buy in the long run, both for processing filled jars during canning and for cooking loose foods in large portions.

Caution: Do not use copper, unlined iron, zinc, or chipped enamelware kettles for precooking loose acid foods before canning. Enameled cast-iron kettles, such as Le Creuset, are fine because the enameled finish keeps the iron from coming in contact with the food.

IMPROVISING A WATER-BATH CANNER

It is possible to improvise a water-bath canner and make-do with Grandmother's wash boiler, a lard can, or some other large, deep, kettle with a tight lid, but you need to be handy to devise a rack that effectively holds the jars ½ inch above the bottom of the vessel and keeps them from jostling around inside when the water begins to boil vigorously. I recommend getting off to a good start by outfitting the canning kitchen with proper equipment. Shy away from the makeshift in canning equipment.

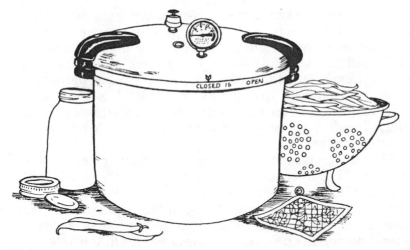

Dial pressure gauge-type pressure canner

THE STEAM-PRESSURE CANNER

All low acid foods must be processed in a steam-pressure canner (also called a pressure canner) at a temperature of 240°F (10 pounds pressure) for a specified length of time. Low-acid foods include all vegetables except tomatoes, rhubarb, and pickled vegetables.

The steam-pressure canner is a heavy kettle with a lid that can be locked down or clamped on to make it steam tight so that pressure is allowed to build up inside the canner.

Close-up of a dial pressure gauge

There are two types of steam-pressure canners available for home use. One type has a dial pressure gauge on the lid to indicate the pounds of pressure inside the sealed canner, and a petcock which, when open, allows steam and air to escape from inside the kettle and, when closed, permits the pressure to mount inside the kettle. It also has a safety valve or fuse that blows out whenever pressure builds too much inside the canner, and an interior rack to hold the canning jars inside.

The other type of steam-pressure canner available for home use has a weighted gauge on the lid that controls the pressure inside the kettle. It also has a safety valve. The air vent is closed by placing the weighted gauge over it as soon as the air is exhausted. This gauge makes a jiggling sound during the processing as excess pressure is released.

To comply with the current published standard for safety set by the Underwriter's Laboratories for pressure

Weighted gauge-type pressure canner

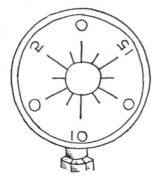

Close-up of a weighted gauge

cookers and canners, the major companies manufacturing pressure cookers and canners have recently redesigned their models to prevent covers from being removed while pressure is present. At this writing, the safety-improved models of Mirro-Matic and Presto pressure cookers and canners are on the market. Any of the models of Mirro-Matic pressure canners manufactured since the autumn of 1977 or any of the models of Presto pressure canners manufactured since the autumn of 1978 will feature the protective device. Both companies have incorporated locking devices into their designs which ensure that the covers of the pressure cookers cannot be opened before internal pressure is safely reduced.

Consult and follow the manufacturer's directions for operating the pressure canner.

The steam-pressure canner should be made of heavyweight metal, usually cast aluminum, and fitted with a rack to keep the jars off the bottom of the canner, or a basket to keep them evenly spaced.

Pressure canners are available in various sizes. The small size holds 4 quart or 7 pint jars. The standard size pressure canner holds 7 quarts or 10 pints. Larger pressure canners are available, holding as many as 16 quarts or 24 pints, but these are difficult for one person to handle when fully loaded. The space available on the stove must be considered before buying an extra-large pressure canner.

Pressure saucepans are not generally recommended for processing foods for canning, but they may be used to process small batches of pints or half-pint jars if pressure can be maintained at 10 pounds and 20 minutes are added to the processing time. The extra time is necessary because the pressure saucepan was not made for canning and it cools and heats more rapidly than pressure canners.

MAINTENANCE AND CARE OF PRESSURE CANNERS

The weighted gauge pressure canner needs only to be thoroughly cleaned, including the gauge, after each use. The air vent can be kept unblocked by inserting a piece of wire through it. If the gauge needs cleaning, use a toothpick to dislodge particles of food that might be stuck in the gauge openings. Keep the rubber gasket clean and free from grease. Do not store the pressure canner with the lid clamped in place. The weighted gauge cannot get out of kilter so it does not require testing.

The dial gauge pressure canner requires regular special maintenance because the dial gauge can become inaccurate. If the gauge is incorrect, the processing may not be adequate and all bacteria, including botulinum, may not be killed. The dial gauge should be checked each season before the pressure canner is used for processing low acid foods.

The manufacturer of your pressure canner or your county's Cooperative Extension Service can tell you where to have the gauge checked. Sometimes clinics or special sessions are arranged by the home extension agent for testing dial gauges.

If you use a pressure canner a lot or find it inconvenient to take it where necessary for testing the gauge, it may be more practical for you to buy your own maximum thermometer for checking the dial gauge yourself. Directions for its use in testing the dial gauge will accompany the thermometer.

If it is determined during testing that your dial gauge reads 5 pounds too high or too low, you must buy a new gauge for the pressure canner. If the error is less than 5 pounds, you can compensate for the inaccuracy by raising or lowering the pressure used for processing according to the following chart:

ADJUSTMENTS FOR INACCURATE DIAL GAUGES WHEN PROCESSING AT 10 POUNDS PRESSURE ADJUSTED FOR ALTITUDE:*

If the gauge reads high—

1 pound high, process at 11 pounds
2 pounds high, process at 12 pounds
3 pounds high, process at 13 pounds
4 pounds high, process at 14 pounds
5 pounds high, buy a new gauge

If the gauge reads low—

1 pound low, process at 9 pounds
2 pounds low, process at 8 pounds
3 pounds low, process at 7 pounds
4 pounds low, process at 6 pounds
5 pounds low, buy a new gauge

Keep the booklet that accompanied your pressure canner close at hand and refer to it for specific instructions for using and maintaining the utensil. Keep the petcock of the dial gauge pressure canner clean by drawing a string through it and keep the safety valve opening free from obstructions in the same way.

ADJUSTING PROCESSING TIME FOR HIGHER ALTITUDES

All times given in the charts and recipes in this book are based on processing times for altitudes of less than 1,000

---

* This information is taken from "Home and Garden Bulletin No. 8," published by the United States Department of Agriculture.

feet above sea level for the boiling water bath and less than 2,000 feet above sea level for the pressure canner.

If you live at a higher altitude, you must increase the processing time for the boiling water bath or adjust the pressure of the pressure canner according to the information below.

If you do not know what the elevation of your area is, you can obtain the correct figure from the surveyor's office of your county, from library sources, from the Cooperative Extension Service of your county, or from the United States Soil Conservation Service office in your area.

ADJUSTING TIME FOR BOILING-WATER-BATH PROCESSING AT HIGH ALTITUDES

Add 1 minute for each 1,000 feet above sea level when processing time is under 20 minutes. Add 2 minutes for each 1,000 feet above sea level when processing time is over 20 minutes.

ADJUSTING PROCESSING PRESSURE FOR STEAM PRESSURE CANNER AT HIGH ALTITUDES*

At Altitude of —	Process at Pressure of —
Less than 2,000 feet	10 pounds
2,000 to 3,000 feet	11½ pounds
3,000 to 4,000 feet	12 pounds
4,000 to 5,000 feet	12½ pounds
5,000 to 6,000 feet	13 pounds
6,000 to 7,000 feet	13½ pounds
7,000 to 8,000 feet	14 pounds
8,000 to 9,000 feet	14½ pounds
9,000 to 10,000 feet	15 pounds

If your pressure canner has a weighted gauge rather than a dial gauge, use 15 pounds pressure at all altitudes above 2,000 feet. Do not use the raw-pack method for canning vegetables at altitudes above 6,000 feet when using the pressure canner.

*Some of the information in this chart is excerpted from *Ball Blue Book*, Edition 30, copyrighted by Ball Corporation, Muncie, Indiana 47302.

SELECTING JARS FOR CANNING

Use only perfect glass jars manufactured expressly for canning or those intended for both canning and freezing purposes. These jars have been tempered to withstand the temperatures necessary to preserve food by home methods.

Jars are available in half-pint, pint, 1½-pint, quart, and half-gallon sizes. Most jars have either wide mouths or regular mouths, but closures are still made by one company (Bernardin) for the old-style narrow mouth jars ("63" closures). Most jars are of the regular Mason-type, having round straight sides that curve inward at the shoulder of the jar and narrow to form the neck of the jar. Jars also come in tapered shapes, with a narrow bottom flaring out to form a wide-mouth opening. Other wide mouth jars have fairly straight sides and a cylindrical shape. Some old jars that you may have and new Canadian jars that are available in northern states are almost square-shaped. All standard jars have openings and rims that match up with standard closures so that a perfect seal can be formed when one brand of jar is used with a closure manufactured by another company.

Jars may be used year after year as long as they are not chipped, cracked, or otherwise damaged.

Caution: Do not re-use commercial packers' jars for home canning. The jars that contained foods bought at the grocery such as pickles, mayonnaise, instant coffee, baby food, peanut butter, and the like are not safe for home canning. These jars were manufactured by different standards than those manufactured for home canning and freezing and are known as "packers' ware." They are intended to be used only once by the packer of the food sold in them.

Not only does the glass of packers' ware jars differ in its resistance to heat and cold, resulting in unexpected breakage, but the rim, neck, and screw bands of the jars are not designed to match up with standard jar closures, so you can never be assured of a perfect seal. Sometimes the mouth and threads appear to be the same as standard closures, and indeed, home canners who reuse these jars sometimes obtain a perfect seal. However, the practice of reusing commercial jars for home canning is fraught with peril. Why invite trouble?

If you must appease your sense of economy, save the nicest packers' ware jars and recycle them for storing dried foods, homemade vinegars, or for refrigerator storage jars.

Cooked jellies that will be sealed with a layer of paraffin may be stored in straight-sided packers' ware jars with wide mouths that make removal of the paraffin possible. This is safe because these jars do not have to be processed at high temperatures or sealed with a standard closure. But be careful when you pour the hot jelly into the jar, taking precautions not to subject the glass to an abrupt temperature change.

PREPARING JARS FOR CANNING

Examine glass canning jars carefully for nicks, cracks, sharp edges, or chips that could prevent an airtight seal or result in breakage during processing. Run your finger around the rim of each jar to detect any dips or imperfections that might not be visible. Do not use any jars with such defects for canning. Discard them or use them for storing dried foods or other purposes.

Wash the jars in hot soapy water using a stiff bottle brush to reach the bottoms and inner curves. Rinse the jars thoroughly in the hottest water available and keep them hot until used by leaving them in a pan of hot water. If you are not going to pack the jars immediately after washing them, invert the rinsed jars to drain on a rack, being careful not to chip the rims. Invert the drained jars on a clean tray and cover them with a clean towel until ready to use. Reheat the jars (see below) before packing them with hot or raw food.

It is adequate to wash canning jars in a dishwasher in very hot water. If the jars have been stored in a place where they have become quite dirty, you may want to give them a preliminary washing with the bottle brush, to ensure loosening all of the soil, before putting them in the dishwasher.

If you are using a boiling water bath or the steam-pressure canner to process the food, it is not necessary to sterilize jars that have been washed clean and rinsed well because both the jars and the food inside them will be sterilized during processing. Only food being canned by the open-kettle method—and that means only jellies—need be packed in sterilized jars. Jars in which dried foods are stored should also be sterilized.

However, there are other times when sterilization of jars in addition to the most careful cleansing seems prudent. Jars that have contained spoiled food should be sterilized before they are re-used. Jars that have become extremely dirty should be sterilized in addition to being given a routine thorough cleansing. Jars that are used to store milk in the refrigerator should be sterile.

If sterilization of the porcelain-lined zinc lids or metal screw bands seems necessary in addition to the usual thorough washing and rinsing, follow the procedure for sterilizing jars, which follows.

The new flat self-sealing lids with sealing compound and new rubber rings need only to be briefly immersed in a separate pan containing boiling water just prior to applying the closures to jars according to directions of the manufacturer.

TO STERILIZE JARS

Wash and rinse jars as directed above and invert them inside a deep kettle on a rack. The water bath canner is ideal for this purpose. Cover the jars with water, bring to a boil and boil the jars for at least 15 minutes. Remove the jars from the boiling water and let them drain in the canner rack until cool enough to handle.

If you are sterilizing the jars just prior to the canning project, let the jars remain in the hot water to keep them hot, or leave the jars in the canner rack to drain while suspended just above the steaming water until you are ready to pack them with prepared hot or raw food.

Minerals in your water may cause a film to form on jars during sterilization. This is unsightly but does not affect the quality of the food being canned in the jars. To counteract the effect of hard water, you may add ½ cup vinegar to the water in which the jars are sterilized.

REHEATING JARS BEFORE PACKING

If desired, jars may be cleaned and prepared the day before canning is to be done, but the jars should be reheated before packing them with hot or raw food.

Jars that are to be filled with hot pre-cooked food must be hot when filled to prevent breaking or cracking them. It is desirable to have jars hot when they are being filled with raw or cold fruits and vegetables, too, because the canning liquid poured into the jars to cover the food will be hot or boiling.

To reheat the cooled clean jars safely before packing them with hot precooked food or hot canning syrup, you do not need to boil the jars. You only need to gradually heat the jars so that they are near the temperature of the food you will be packing in them.

You can place the jars in the dishwasher, rinse them briefly, and let them go through the dry-cycle.

Or rinse them with hot water at the sink.

Or place them in a pan containing warm to hot water and put it on the stove on low heat.

Or place the clean jars in the rack of the water bath canner in which you are heating several inches of water prior to the canning procedure.

If the jars are inverted on the rack above the shallow hot water, or in a pan of hot water, the hot liquid may be drawn up into the upside-down jars. In this case, you simply lift up each jar with the canning tongs and let the water run out.

PACKING PREPARED FOODS INTO CANNING JARS

There are two methods of packing prepared foods into canning jars before processing. Foods may be packed into the hot jars after they have been heated or precooked, by the hot-pack method, or while they are unheated or cold and uncooked, which is the raw-pack method. Not too long ago the Raw-Pack method was often called the cold pack and the water-bath canner was called a cold packer, but the terminology has changed.

HOT PACK

Pack prepared precooked food rather loosely into canning jars, leaving head space as recommended for each food (See the section on head space below.) Transfer the hot mixture to hot jars directly from the kettle in which the food was precooked, leaving the kettle on the heat if possible, so that the food is at or near the boiling point when packed.

Cover the top of the cooked food with syrup, juice, or cooking liquid from the kettle, expelling any trapped air bubbles from the jar (see instructions below) and leaving the amount of head space recommended for the food so that no portion of it is exposed to air in the head space, which might cause the food to darken.

RAW PACK

Pack prepared uncooked food firmly into clean, hot canning jars, leaving the proper amount of head space for each food after expelling air bubbles from the contents of the jar (see instructions below).

Only starchy foods, which expand during processing, such as shelled beans, corn, soy beans, limas, peas, etc., should be packed loosely into the containers, leaving 1-inch head space, as well.

Fill the jar and cover the food completely with syrup, juice, or water. The amount of liquid required to fill the jar varies from about ½ cup to about 1½ cups, depending on the food being canned.

REMOVING AIR BUBBLES FROM PACKED JARS OF FOOD

When the jars are packed, run a long, thin, nonmetal spatula around the jar between the food and the sides of the jar to release any trapped air bubbles that might prevent liquid from completely covering and surrounding the food packed in the jars. If space is created by expelling air bubbles from the food in the filled jars, add more liquid to bring it back to the desired level before closing the jar for processing. This is your last chance to add the correct amount of liquid to the prepared food in the jar.

If for some reason there is not enough liquid on the food after it is processed, it is too late to do anything about it. Food will not spoil because there is too little liquid in the jar but it will soon discolor at the top of the jar. Just remember to use those jars as soon as possible after canning.

Removing air bubbles from jar

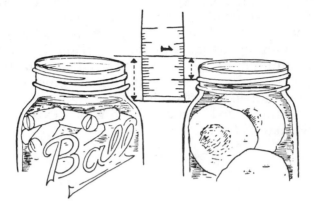

HEAD SPACE

A small amount of space should be left between the top of food packed into the jar and the closure. This is called head space, and it varies according to the food being canned. Follow the specific directions accompanying the recipe for the food you are canning. If your recipe omits a recommendation for head space, you may refer to these general directions:

> For vegetables (except tomatoes), meats, and soup mixtures: 1-inch head space.
>
> For tomatoes, fruits, berries, and beets: ½-inch head space.
>
> For butters, marmalades, preserves, conserves, jams, pickles in large pieces, applesauce, and fruit purees: ¼-inch head space.
>
> For jellies, ground relishes, and chopped or sliced pickles: ⅛-inch head space.

Jars should be filled to the recommended level to ensure the best possible preservation of the food being canned. Follow the canning instructions exactly. If the recipe recommends ½-inch head space, do not leave 1-inch head space. Too much head space may leave more air in the jar than is necessary and cause darkening (oxidation) of the food at the top of the jar. Conversely, if the jars are filled too full, liquid may be forced from them during processing, leaving the jars less than full of liquid when processing is completed. Loss of liquid during processing does not cause canned food to spoil, but the food exposed above the liquid may darken unattractively.

Most commonly used closure: two piece screw band and flat self sealing lid

Glass lids and rubber ring plus wire-clamp fasteners

CLOSURES FOR CANNING JARS

Standard jars require either a two-piece screw band and a flat self-sealing lid closure or a two-piece closure consisting of a rubber ring and porcelain-lined zinc cap. The screw bands and zinc caps can be used again and again, as long as they are clean, not dented, or bent out of shape, or rusty, but *new* rubber rings and *new* self-sealing flat lids must be used in each canning procedure.

If you have a supply of old jars with glass lids and wire-clamp fasteners that are in perfect condition, you can use them for canning as long as you use a new rubber ring under the glass lid each time you use such a jar for canning.

Lately, there have been some new jars of this type on the market, especially since the Bicentennial year, but it

Porcelain-lined zinc cap with rubber ring closures

remains to be seen if they were only a specialty item or if they will continue to be available. These old-fashioned-looking jars evoke a certain nostalgia for those of us who appreciate reminders of days gone by and are perfect for the special home-canned foods you want to give as gifts.

These three types of closures have been in continuous use for a long period. The two-piece screw band and flat self sealing lid is by far the most commonly used jar closure today.

There are other jar closures on the market such as the two-piece plastic screw band and self-sealing lid with the "magic button" vacuum detection feature, but it is not practical to include in this book directions for using them. So if you are using jar closures other than the standard two-piece screw band and flat self-sealing lid, the two piece porcelain-lined zinc cap and rubber ring, or the glass lid and wire-bail with rubber ring, do not use the directions given here. Consult the directions of the manufacturer of your closures for the method of applying closures and sealing jars.

CLOSING GLASS CANNING JARS

All glass canning jars and their closures must be flawless in order to obtain a perfect seal after proper processing. Select zinc lids or metal screw bands and wash and dry them before beginning the canning project. Remember: metal screw bands and zinc porcelain-lined lids can be reused if they are in perfect condition but *new* rubber rings or *new* self-sealing caps must be used for each canning project.

PROCEDURE FOR TWO-PIECE METAL SCREW BAND AND SELF-SEALING LID CLOSURE

When you are ready to pack the clean, hot jars with prepared food, place the flat metal lids, which come with a special sealing compound applied to them, in a shallow pan, and cover them with hot or boiling water, according to the manufacturer's recommendation. Leave them in the hot or boiling water to soften the sealing compound until all the jars are packed and sealed.

Fill and complete the closure of only one jar at a time.

Fill each jar with prepared food, using a canning funnel. Leave the recommended head space and remove any air bubbles from the jar. Immediately wipe the rim and screw threads of the jar with a clean, damp cloth to remove any spilled food, which could prevent a perfect seal.

Lift the self-sealing lid from the hot water with tongs, shake the excess water from the lid, and carefully apply it to the clean rim of the packed jar. While holding the cap in place with the index finger of one hand, screw the metal band down firmly with the other hand so that it is "hand-tight." Do not use a jar wrench or tighten the screw band so much that it cuts through the soft sealing compound. Make sure you have the lid centered on the jar with the sealing compound next to the rim of the jar.

Place the packed jar in the rack in the canner and proceed at once to pack and close the next jar. Continue without interruption until all the jars are packed and closed.

Process the jars of food according to the directions for the food.

At the end of the processing time, turn off the heat. If you are using the water-bath canner remove the jars with the jar lifter, and place them upright on a folded cloth or a rack to cool.

If the jars were processed in the pressure canner, do not remove them until the pressure canner has been decompressed.

Important: *Do not tighten the screw band after removing the processed jar from the canner.*

Cool the jars 12 to 24 hours in a draft-free place with at least one inch of space between the jars. Do not cover the jars during cooling.

Shortly after removing the jars from the canner, you will hear a pleasant ping as each jar seals and the center of the flat, self-sealing caps becomes slightly concave.

The next day, when the jars are completely cool, check each jar to see that each is sealed (see p. 40). Remove the screw bands and store the canned food in a dark, dry, cool place.

PROCEDURE FOR PORCELAIN-LINED ZINC CAP AND RUBBER RING CLOSURES

Drop the new rubber rings in hot water before applying them to the neck of the jar. Apply the rings to all of the hot jars just before beginning the packing procedure but do not fill all the jars at once or complete all the closures at once. *Fill and close only one jar of food at a time.*

Fill each hot, clean jar with prepared food, using a canning funnel. Leave the recommended head space and remove air bubbles from the jar. Immediately wipe the rim and screw threads of the jar, and the rubber ring with a clean damp cloth to remove any spilled food that could prevent a perfect seal.

Immediately apply the porcelain-lined zinc cap.

Tighten it as much as possible by hand, then loosen it by ¼ inch.

Set the filled jar on the rack in the canner and pack the next jar at once in the same manner.

After processing the jars according to the directions for the food being canned, turn off the heat under the canner.

If you are using the water bath canner, remove each hot jar at once, using a jar lifter, and tighten the zinc cap as much as possible, using a canning wrench, to complete the seal.

If you are using a pressure canner, *do not remove the jars until the canner is decompressed*. Then remove each jar with a jar lifter and tighten the zinc cap as above.

Set the jars upright on a folded cloth or rack to cool for 12 to 24 hours. Allow 1-inch space between each jar for air circulation but do not cool jars in a draft or cover them with a cloth while they are cooling. Do not tighten the caps after the jars have cooled or disturb the closure in any way after it has been tightened or you may destroy the seal, which formed when the jar was hot.

The next day, test the jars for a perfect seal (see page 40) and store them in a cool, dry, dark place until used.

PROCEDURE FOR GLASS CAP–RUBBER RING–WIRE BAIL CLOSURE

Fit a new rubber ring on the ledge at the top of each hot clean jar. Dip the new rubber rings in hot water before applying.

Fill only one jar at a time with prepared food, using a wide-mouth canning funnel. Leave the recommended head space for the food being canned and remove any air bubbles from the jar. Wipe the jar rim and the rubber ring clean with a damp cloth. Put on the glass lid so that it fits into the groove at the top of the jar. Put the longer wire on top of the lid *but do not fasten down the short wire*.

Place each jar in the canner as soon as it is filled and proceed with filling the next one without delay.

Process the jars of food according to the directions for the food.

Remove jars from the water-bath canner as soon as the

processing time is finished. Remove jars from the pressure canner after the pressure has decompressed. After processing and as soon as each jar is removed from the canner, push the short wire down tight to complete the seal.

Set the jars on a folded cloth or cooling rack, with one-inch space between them, and allow to cool for 12 to 24 hours in a draft-free place. Do not cover the cooling jars with a cloth or disturb the closure after fastening down the short wire.

The next day, test for a perfect seal (see below). Store the jars in a cool, dry, dark place.

TESTING FOR SEAL

TWO-PIECE METAL SCREW BAND AND SELF-SEALING LID CLOSURE

Remove the screw band after the jars have cooled for 12 to 24 hours. The center of the lid should be slightly depressed, or concave, in the center because the vacuum inside the jar pulled the lid down in the center as it cooled. If the lid makes a clear ringing sound when tapped with a metal spoon, the jar is sealed. A dull sound when the lid is tapped, may indicate that the jar is not sealed. However, it could also mean that food inside may be touching the jar lid. Turn the jar sidewise and rotate it to check for leakage. If there is no leakage and the self-sealing lid cannot be lifted off, the jar is airtight.

A slight pinging sound may be heard as each jar seals during cooling.

PORCELAIN-LINED ZINC CAP AND RUBBER RING CLOSURE

After the jar has cooled for 12 to 24 hours, tilt it to the side and roll it slowly to check for leakage. If there is none, the jar is airtight.

GLASS CAP–RUBBER RING–WIRE BAIL CLOSURE

After the jar has cooled for 12 to 24 hours, tilt it to the side and roll it slowly to check for leakage. Do not disturb the wire bail. If there is no leakage, the jar is airtight.

CANNING IN METAL CANS

This book does not include directions for canning in metal cans since so few people, proportionately, have the equipment necessary for tin-can-canning. Metal canning in the home requires all the equipment needed for canning in glass jars as well as a can sealer and new cans and lids. The special equipment needed for canning in metal cans is available today, but hard to find.

If you need detailed information on processing foods in tin cans, refer to the Home and Garden Bulletin Number 8 published by the United States Department of Agriculture. It can be purchased for 45 cents from Consumer Information Center, Pueblo, Colorado 81009.

PROCESSING FRUITS AND ACID VEGETABLES IN A STEAM CANNER

Two companies are now manufacturing steam canners intended for use in processing fruits and acid vegetables for canning. Directions are not included in this book for steam canners, but they are included with the purchase of the vessel. *It should be stressed that these steam canners cannot be used for processing low-acid vegetables or meats.*

OTHER EQUIPMENT NEEDED FOR CANNING

In addition to the boiling-water-bath canner and the steam-pressure canner, there are other special items that are needed for efficient canning, as well as appliances and utensils found among the regular kitchen equipment.

Glass canning jars, of course, along with appropriate closures, including new jar rings and new self-sealing lids, will be needed. A jar lifter, canning tongs, canning wrench, wide-mouth canning funnel, a ladle, and a slotted spoon are invaluable. A vegetable blancher with its own perforated inner basket, large and small sieves, colanders, large stainless steel or Pyrex mixing bowls, and a large, heavy kettle are all essential.

Measuring cups and measuring spoons, including a one-quart measure, will be needed, as well as a kitchen scale for weighing quantities of fruits and vegetables. If you have a scale that weighs ounces, it, too, will come in handy in using certain recipes.

An accurate timer will be needed; the stove timer will do, or, for processing longer than 1 hour, an alarm clock. A 3-minute egg timer or a stopwatch is needed for timing under 5 minutes.

Sharp knives and a cutting board, trays, rimmed cookie sheets or large, shallow pans, kitchen shears, vegetable peelers and corers, a juice reamer, a four-sided grater, long-handled wooden and metal spoons, and a good supply of clean dish cloths, dish towels, and pot holders will be needed.

A long, narrow plastic spatula to release the bubbles in the jars when packing them is helpful; if you do not have one made expressly for the purpose, use the handle of a bowl scraper. Cheesecloth, a jelly bag, jelly thermometer, labels for jars, a food grinder for chopping vegetables and fruits, a food mill for making purees, and an electric blender will all be used, if available. Other labor savers are a cabbage shredder made for cutting kraut, a vegetable slicer for making thin, uniform slices, a corn slicer for removing kernels from cobs, a French-bean slicer, an apple peeler, a cherry pitter, and a pea sheller—if you have these, hours will be saved. And the ultimate luxury is to have one of the new food processors that chop, mince, slice, grind, grate, and shred—in seconds!

A WORD ON GETTING ORGANIZED

To give yourself the best possible chances for an enjoyable, not to mention successful, canning session, there is no substitute for being organized in preparing for and carrying out the project. Here are some hints.

1. Plan your canning projects in advance. Do not attempt to "work in" the canning of a half-bushel of ripe peaches if it looks like you have one of those hectic days coming up. Make arrangements to free yourself of usual responsibilities that will interrupt the canning procedure. Get a babysitter, send the teenagers off to have hamburgers for lunch, switch days if it is your turn to drive in the car pool, have someone take your telephone messages, do not have repairmen or cleaning help underfoot to supervise when you are trying to work efficiently and swiftly. Make all of the conditions as pleasant as possible so that you enjoy canning as a homemaking task.

2. Collect all the supplies, special equipment, and utensils you will need beforehand. An unexpected trip to the grocery can upset your schedule. Make sure the pressure canner is operating as it should well in advance of the canning season. Repairs and new parts often require a week or two of waiting. In the meantime, the green beans may have gone by their season.

3. Read the recipes and review the procedures you will use before beginning each project to refresh your memory.

4. Do not attempt to do a preserving project while you are preparing dinner—you will need the stove and sink space—or while canning undertake anything that will divide your attention. Schedule the canning or preserving project for the best time of day for you or allow an entire day to prepare several canner loads in succession.

5. Clear out the kitchen so you have the best possible clean area in which to work. You need clear counter and sink space for preparing fruits and vegetables, all the range burners free for canning kettles and equipment, and an area for cooling the canned jars, as well as ample storage for the foods when finished. Put away for the duration of the canning season the decorative objects that you have around on the counters and tables—the sparkling and colorful rows of jars filled with canned fruits and vegetables will give your harvest kitchen the look of abundance and beauty.

Food Safety

FOOD SPOILAGE ORGANISMS—BACTERIA, MOLDS, AND YEASTS

BACTERIA

Bacteria are microorganisms that exist in the soil, water, air, and on all surfaces with which they come in contact. Because bacteria are so prevalent everywhere, all food products become contaminated with some of the bacteria.

Certain bacterias, such as those in yogurt, cheeses, pickles, and vinegar, are useful in food preservation but others cause food spoilage or illness.

Brief boiling of acid foods at 212°F destroys bacteria that may be present in them and cause food spoilage. Others found in low-acid foods require processing during canning at a much higher temperature (240°F) for a specified time to destroy them.

Some bacteria are particularly heat resistant. While the actively growing bacteria may be destroyed by boiling, their spores may survive to grow and later cause spoilage or illness if the food is not subjected to a high temperature (240°F) for a sustained time.

The most infamous of the heat-resistant bacteria that may be found in low-acid foods is *Clostridium botulinum*

44

which is capable of producing lethal toxin if its spores are not destroyed by adequate heat during processing of canned foods. Botulinum spores can grow in an airless environment, which means they can multiply in a sealed jar of food that has not been adequately processed.

Another group of bacteria that have great heat resistance are the thermophiles. These grow best at a temperature range of 100°F to 180°F, and cause flat-souring and gas formation in canned foods. Growth of the thermophiles is encouraged when canned foods are not cooled promptly and properly.

Since bacteria thrive and multiply rapidly under various favorable conditions, one aim of successful and safe food preservation is to create counteracting conditions which destroy harmful bacteria or inhibit their growth. Besides canning, drying, heating, freezing, salting, and the use of chemical agents are all methods used in home food preservation to destroy or control bacterial growth.

In canning foods, boiling them at 212°F for a time prescribed for each food will destroy bacteria, molds, and yeast that exist in acid foods. Bacteria that may exist in low-acid foods and can survive boiling temperature, such as the dangerous bacteria *Clostridium botulinum*, are destroyed by processing the canned food in a steam-pressure canner at 240°F (10 pounds pressure at sea level) for a scientifically determined length of time prescribed for each low-acid food. If the processed jars of food are then properly sealed so that no new spoilage organisms can enter, the canned foods are safe from bacteria, molds, and yeasts that cause spoilage.

AN EXTRA SAFEGUARD AGAINST BOTULISM POISONING Properly processing low-acid foods for the correct length of time in the steam pressure canner kills the particularly heat-resistant spores of *Clostridium botulinum* and prevents botulism poisoning.

However, as an extra safeguard, should the organism not be destroyed because of an unknown failure (such as an undetected inaccuracy of the pressure gauge of the pressure canner), *always follow these rules when preparing home-canned low-acid foods for the table:*

1. *Never taste a low-acid home-canned food straight from the jar.* One spoonful of food containing the botulism toxin could be fatal. Botulism toxin has no odor. Food containing botulism toxin has no unusual appearance. Botulism spores can grow in an airless environment so they can live on in a properly sealed jar and produce poison in food that was not heated enough to kill the bacteria during processing.

2. *Always bring home-canned low-acid foods to a rolling boil, then boil for 15 minutes in a covered pan before tasting or eating the food.* Allow 20 minutes for corn, greens, poultry, meat, and seafood. The USDA recommends, "If the food looks spoiled, foams, or has an off-odor during heating, destroy it." If there are leftovers which you wish to eat at another meal, store the food in the refrigerator until wanted, then reboil the food before eating it.

MOLDS

Molds are caused by microscopic spores that float through the air and fall on food or other organic material and begin to grow when conditions are favorable. Molds grow well in moist dark warm places where the temperature ranges from 50 to 100°F, but they will grow on refrigerated products, as well. Freezing renders molds inactive but does not kill them.

When mold develops on food, it is easily seen with the naked eye. It is a fluffy mass that appears in various colors. Acid, sweet, and neutral foods all develop molds. Some molds, such as those molds added to cheeses for curing them, are harmless, but others can cause illness as well as deterioration of the food affected.

Molds are easily destroyed by brief boiling at 212°F. Properly processed and sealed canned foods are safe from mold development. If mold should be found in a jar of food that has been opened, the seal was not tight and the food should be thrown out. After the jars are opened, the food can be recontaminated by mold spores and the cycle can begin all over again, in due time.

If mold is found under the paraffin seal on a jar of jelly, the jelly should be thrown out. It was formerly thought that the mold could be scraped off jelly and the rest of it would be harmless to eat. New findings have revealed that this is not so. (Molds can accumulate in the system and cause illness.)

YEASTS

Yeasts require moisture, sugar, and air for growth. They cause fermentation in foods and change sugar into alcohol and carbon dioxide. This is desirable if one is making wine but disastrous when the fermentation is unintentional and forms in an improperly sealed jar, wasting the food. Yeasts that are present in the atmosphere must be kept out of pickling brines when making cucumber pickles and sauerkraut, but you may wish to attract them when you are making starter for sourdough bread. Sweet foods such as fruits and juices will ferment if kept too long at room temperature in an open container. Refrigeration slows down the development of yeast and freezing inhibits it, but cold does not kill yeast, as evidenced by frozen bread dough that rises when the yeasts are reactivated by warm air outside the freezer.

Boiling at 212°F will destroy yeasts in foods being canned and prevent their growth when the foods are properly sealed in jars. However, boiled food can become recontaminated with new yeasts if inadequately protected after boiling, because of a faulty seal on the canning jar for instance, and yeast growth can begin anew.

OTHER SPOILERS—ENZYMES

Enzymes are chemical substances found in all plants that bring about favorable changes in fruits and vegetables up until the time the desired stage of ripeness is reached. After the peak of ripeness, enzymes go on with their action and cause eventual decomposition of food.

The greatest damage by enzymes to foods being canned is the loss of color, texture, flavor, and "freshness" between the time the foods are harvested and canned. For that reason it is desirable to work quickly, speeding the food from garden to jar to prevent unnecessary loss of quality. An old maxim worth following is "two hours from garden to jar."

Proper heating (from 140° to 212°F) stops enzyme action in foods being prepared for preservation. The boiling temperature used for processing foods in the boiling water bath is adequate to stop enzyme action in foods being canned. Brief blanching in boiling water or by steam is needed for some vegetables and fruits that will be dried, canned, or frozen.

Since cold slows down the action of enzymes while heat (even that of a warm room) of 85° to 120°F speeds up enzyme action, if the harvested foods cannot be prepared and preserved at once, it is best to hold them in the refrigerator until they can be attended to.

Perhaps the most dramatic illustration of enzymatic change in vegetables is the flavor of sweet corn that is cooked in boiling water *immediately* after picking it as compared to the flavor of sweet corn that has been picked several hours or days before cooking it. The same loss of flavor is obvious in fresh peas. Anyone who gardens puts the kettle of water to boil before going out to the garden to gather the corn for dinner.

UNSAFE CANNING PROCEDURES

In the light of what is known today, the memories of some of the canning procedures that have been used during the last forty years make me shudder. Not only was the mincemeat canned in the trusty old "cold packer" in a boiling water bath (albeit for hours!), but so were corn and green beans and other low-acid foods. Then there was the kraut fermented in canning jars, the fried sausage balls put down in hot melted lard, the ketchups bottled and sealed with wax in reused bottles saved from bought ketchups, and the jars of fruit processed in the oven. Our bounteous farmstead cellar surely must have held unknown dangers at one time or another. But, fortunately, our family was protected by my mother's excellent knowledge and careful practice of canning principles and by her watchfulness over her store of carefully canned goods. At the first hint of spoilage, the first buldging zinc cap, the faintest off-odor or off-color, she threw out the jars of canned foods. And we never ate or tasted home-canned low-acid foods that had not been boiled for 15 to 20 minutes before they were tasted. Those were the days of the "cooked-to-death" green beans and the pots bubbling away on the stove long in advance of dinner, and for good reason.

OPEN KETTLE

Until recently, the open kettle method of processing foods for canning was popularly used to can pickles, relishes, jams, preserves, catsups, acid fruits, and other foods. *Today the open kettle method is recommended only for canning cooked jellies.*

In the open kettle method the food is first cooked in an open kettle and put directly into jars and sealed without further processing. The open kettle method was never safe for low acid foods because the food is not cooked to 240°F, which is necessary to kill the bacteria that may exist in low-acid foods. It was used mainly for processing acid fruits and foods for many years before it fell into disrepute.

One reason for avoiding the open kettle is that a proper seal may not be obtained. Another reason is that there is a possibility that spoilage organisms may enter the cooked food while it is being transferred from cooking kettle to canning jar. A third strike against the open kettle method is that the jar and lid can be improperly sterilized and contaminate the canned food.

OVEN CANNING

Oven canning is not safe for food preservation because the food inside the jars heated in the oven does not become hot enough to destroy the harmful bacteria. It is also dangerous because the hot jars may explode in the oven or when they are removed.

I remember my mother canning certain foods in the oven of our kitchen stove. She was always nervous when she gingerly handled the jars in the oven, for fear that one would explode and endanger anyone nearby with flying

49

glass. Fortunately, so many jars broke in the oven that she soon abandoned the then popular method and went back to her standard methods of processing canned foods.

MICROWAVE OVEN CANNING

Early instruction books accompanying microwave ovens included directions for canning but these were soon dropped because the process has not been perfected. Identical jars of food processed in a microwave oven do not all reach the required temperature.

OTHER METHODS TO AVOID

From time to time we hear of fad methods of processing particular foods for canning. *Do not be tempted to try any of these methods.* Use only the methods approved by the United States Department of Agriculture; in short, the boiling-water bath for acid foods, the steam-pressure canner for low-acid foods, and the open kettle only for canning jellies.

Do not use aspirin as a substitute for processing, do not process in the dishwasher or electric slow cooker, and do not use any outdated methods from ancient cookbooks that recommend defunct procedures such as inverting a canning jar over a lump of burning sulfur.

STORING CANNED FOODS

Most directions for storing canned foods call for storage in a cool, dark, dry place until used. A temperature range often suggested is from 35° to 70°F, which allows a lot of leeway. The "cool" place could be interpreted as the refrigerator, which is about 35°F but obviously is not large enough to store canned foods, or any room in the house, which is 68°F. or lower, summer or winter, with automatic heat and air conditioning.

So where will we store our carefully preserved foods? And more importantly, where will we *not* store them? The damaging factors in storage that cause properly canned foods to lose quality between the time of storage and use are excessive heat or cold, moisture, and light.

The ideal place to store canned foods is in a dark, dry, cool basement or cellar where the temperature is constant, summer and winter, between 50° and 65°F. But lots of cellars are cool, dark, and *damp*. And lots of us do not have basements—we have heated utility rooms. So, not having a basement, or a faulty one, we have to look around to find the best place available.

If you have a friend or relative who will store your food for you in a basement, you have a solution. You can bring home several dozen jars at a time. Short storage under less than ideal conditions will not result in significant loss of quality.

If you cannot arrange for basement storage, look for a dark closet in your house that has decent air circulation and does not become overheated, and relegate it to food storage. But do not use upper shelves of kitchen cabinets because it is always hotter near the ceiling. Do not use shelves above the stove or near a heat register. Excessive heat causes rapid loss of food quality.

Maybe you could use an unheated upstairs room for canned food storage for part of the year, or a semi-heated garage attached to the house. If the storage area becomes cold enough to freeze food during extreme weather, move your jars into a warmer place then, or blanket them temporarily. Freezing does not cause spoilage unless it breaks the jar or the seal, but it causes food to soften, or lose its texture. If the storage area, such as the space back of attic walls, serves in winter but becomes too hot in the summertime, move the food to another place when the weather changes.

If the food cannot be stored in dark closets or on shelves in a darkish basement, it should be put into cardboard cartons (use those you bought the canning jars in) for storage. This will make handling easier if you have to transfer the food from one place to another. Or rig up a roller-type window shade that can be drawn down from the top shelf, or install a shower curtain in front of open shelves that are in direct light. Too much light will cause canned foods to fade in color.

If you are planning to preserve a considerable portion of your food by canning, you really ought to have a proper place to store it. If there is no basement storage for your canned foods, or no improvised place that is satisfactory, perhaps you should plan to build or remodel an area to provide the right conditions for your foods.

HOW LONG CAN CANNED FOOD BE STORED?

Properly processed and sealed canned foods that are properly stored will keep for years. However, there will be a gradual loss of color, texture, and flavor.

It is recommended that canned foods be used before the next season's harvest, or in about one year. But if any jars of food are left over when the new crop is canned, they can be used as needed during the second year as long as they are properly sealed and show no signs of spoilage.

Always inspect all jars of canned food for any of the following signs of spoilage before cooking or eating them.

Bulging tin cans
A bulging lid
Leakage
Spurting liquid when opened
Off-odors when jar is opened or food is cooked
Mold (throw out the contents of the entire jar; do not just scrape off the moldy part.)
Fermentation or a sour smell
An unsealed lid
Foaming
Any unusual appearance

WHAT TO DO WITH SPOILED FOOD

If home-canned food is not properly sealed, spurts or leaks liquid, is in a bulging tin can, looks spoiled, smells bad in the jar or during cooking, foams, is off-color, or is suspect for any other reason, *dispose of the food at once* so that it cannot be consumed by humans or animals. Bury it, put it down the garbage disposal, or burn it. Wash and sterilize the canning jar before using it for any other purpose.

GOOD PRACTICES IN CLEANLINESS AND FOOD SAFETY IN THE KITCHEN

The following precautions may seen elementary to some cooks but since they may be of value to others, I will list them here nevertheless. Not all good cooks keep clean kitchens and many are oblivious to the risks involved. Some, myself included, become lax about standards from time to time.

So why not review recommended cleanliness and food safety practices and make resolutions to improve our standards, if needed?

Remember that many of the mysterious short-lived "bugs" and no-name viruses that beset people begin in the kitchen and are food-borne. The next time you or someone in your family has an inexplicable stomach upset, look at this list.

1. Keep the kitchen scrupulously clean, including floors, counters, cabinets, refrigerator, range, and other appliances. Do not let food that should be thrown out accumulate in the refrigerator. Do not install carpeting in a kitchen where food preservation is a major activity; it is a dirt trap in a busy kitchen. An important aspect of preventing food spoilage and contamination is preventing microorganisms from getting into the food.

2. Wash food *clean* before preparing, preserving, or eating it. Some of the most stubborn and potentially dangerous bacteria are soil borne, including *Clostridium botulinum*. It is reckless to eat fruit or vegetables without washing them or to eat food that has touched an unclean surface. Most people are careful about this when visiting a foreign country but ignore the precaution when at home. Scrub or wash, and thoroughly rinse fruits and vegetables several times in pure clean water. Do not let food stand or soak in the soiled water in which it was washed and do not let the dirty wash water drain off over the food after washing it. Lift the vegetables and fruits out of the soiled water, then drain the water out of the pan or sink. Wash poultry, meats, seafood, mushrooms, and fragile fruits under running water.

3. Wash your hands with hot water and soap, rinse them in clear water, and dry them on a clean towel before beginning any food preparation. Keep fingernails short and clean. Do not use the dish towel to dry your hands. Use paper towels or keep a hand towel tucked in your belt, à la Julia Child. Rewash your hands each time you handle something besides food, such as your clothing or hair, a handkerchief, a child, a pet, or furniture. Bacteria are on every surface. It is all right to use your hands for mixing certain ingredients together as long as your hands and fingernails are clean and you do not have an open cut on your hands. Be especially sanitary if someone in the household is sick with a contagious illness. Keep out of the kitchen if you yourself are not well.

4. Do not let prepared food remain outside the refrigerator for any unnecessary time. Did you know that a total of 4 hours is the maximum a jar of mayonnaise can be allowed to remain at room temperature without risking the formation of harmful bacteria in it? This means that each time you use the mayonnaise you must put it back into the refrigerator immediately after using it or you could easily use up the safety margin before you use up the mayonnaise.

5. Do not cover hot food while it is cooling because covering slows down the cooling and encourages the growth of the thermophilic bacteria. Contrary to popular belief, it is safe to cool ordinary amounts of hot food in the refrigerator. If you must quickly cool a large amount of food, place it in several shallow containers instead of one large, deep container so that the center of the food cools rapidly and turn up the temperature control to compensate for the possible increase in temperature inside the refrigerator when the large amount of hot food is put inside. Or, cool the hot foods first by setting the containers with the hot food in them into another container holding ice or ice water.

6. Always cover cooled food stored in the refrigerator. Do not store jarred food without lids, or bowls of food without covers or plastic wrap or foil. When the tops are uncovered, the food is ready to receive air-borne spores of yeasts and molds.

7. Use clean well-laundered dish cloths and towels. Keep

the sink clean and use clean dishes and utensils for food preparation.

8. Use scrupulously clean utensils for preparing raw meats and milk products. Do not use a knife or cutting board for preparing raw meat and then use it to prepare other foods without washing it. Wash, scalding if necessary, the equipment used to prepare these foods.

9. Wear clean clothes and keep your hair covered or tied back. A clean apron or smock worn over your other clothing is a good idea. Do not comb your hair in the kitchen.

10. Do not sweep the kitchen floor or dust the furniture while food is being prepared. Household dust carries bacteria. Shut out dust entering the kitchen from outside sources during dry summer weather when the air is dusty, or nearby roads are dusty. Outside dust is powdered earth and earth is loaded with bacteria.

11. Do not allow moldy foods, peelings, or breads to remain in the refrigerator or the kitchen, as they release spores into the air that could fall on other food and contaminate it. Dispose of garbage immediately and do not let trash cans become overloaded. Do not let mildew form under sinks and in other likely places. Wash these areas with water containing chlorine bleach to destroy the mildew. Do not let trash cans collect soil and odors.

12. Keep rodents, flies, roaches, and other insects out of the kitchen. These intruders contaminate exposed foods. Do not use household sprays around uncovered food, even if the can says the ingredients are safe to use near food. Treat your kitchen to exterminate insects and rodents when exposed food or drinking liquids are not in the area.

13. Do not try to save or use for preserving foods that have moldy spots, even if you cut away the bad parts. Do not try to economize by buying overripe foods for making relishes or catsups. Overripe and partially molded food is already on the road to decomposition. Preserve only the best-quality foods you can obtain.

Canning Fruits

METHOD OF PROCESSING

Prepared fruits properly processed in a boiling-water bath at 212°F for a time specified for each fruit are adequately protected against spoilage caused by molds, yeasts, and bacteria that exist in acid foods, such as fruits.

See the BASIC INSTRUCTIONS page 18 for detailed instructions for preparing the canning equipment and using the water-bath canner.

METHODS OF PACKING FRUITS FOR HOME CANNING

Fruits may be packed by the hot-pack method or the raw-pack method, as explained on page 31.

Most raw fruits should be packed firmly into the jars, because they will shrink during processing. If fruits, especially ripe, juicy fruits, are packed too loosely, they will float at the top of the jar. Hot fruits should be packed into jars fairly loosely when they are at or near the boiling temperature.

When fruits are precooked for the hot pack method,

drop them into boiling liquid to avoid overcooking them. For soft, juicy fruits such as peaches and berries, only the briefest boiling is allowable if they are to stay firm.

Applesauce and fruit purees require hot packing after longer boiling to reduce the fruit to the desired softness.

SELECTING FRUITS FOR CANNING

Choose only fresh, firm, perfect, ripe fruit. Do not pick or buy underripe, overripe, or soft fruits for canning. Full flavor and sweetness have not developed in underripe fruits; fruits that are too ripe are already losing quality and acidity. Choose only those that are at their peak of quality.

Some varieties of fruits are better suited to canning than others. Qualities such as firmness or juiciness determine how the product should be prepared for canning. For example, some apples cook up easily and should be used for sauce; other varieties keep their firmness and could be canned in quarter shapes. Read the nursery catalogs, inquire at the orchard where you buy your fruits, or ask your home extension agent to recommend varieties for your intended use.

Buy or pick only as much fruit as you can handle at one time, perhaps enough for one canner load at a time.

Make every effort to prepare and can the fruits within a few hours after picking or buying them. Find an orchard nearby or transport the fresh fruit in a portable ice chest. When you reach home, prepare the fruits for canning at once or store them in the refrigerator in the interim. But do not let them languish in the refrigerator or on the counter, losing freshness. Have the preparations for canning finished when you go out to get the produce.

Sort fruits for canning according to size so that all pieces are uniform and will cook equally during processing. The filled jars will also look prettier if the fruits are of the same size.

PREPARING FRUITS FOR CANNING

Keep the fruits cool until you are ready to prepare them. Wash them all thoroughly to remove sprays, waxes, or organic soil, which contains stubborn bacteria that may contribute to spoilage.

Wash fruits before paring, scalding, or stemming.

Do not let fruits stand in water and become waterlogged. Water-soluble vitamins and flavor will leach out.

Handle fruits gently. At their peak of ripeness, fruits are fragile and bruise easily. Bruises hasten decomposition.

Add an antidarkening agent to peeled light-fleshed fruits, which have a tendency to darken after peeling or cutting, such as apples, peaches, apricots, and pears. The antidarkening agents (which are antioxidants) usually contain ascorbic or citric acid and help to preserve the color and flavor of the fruit.

USING ANTI-DARKENING AGENTS

Antidarkening agents are food substances that may be added to certain fruits and vegetables that tend to oxidize quickly and darken during preparation or storage. The antidarkening agent helps to preserve the natural color of the food and preserves flavor, as well.

The antidarkening agent may be referred to as an antioxidant, a fresh-fruit preserver, a color keeper, or color preserver. The most effective color preserver is ascorbic acid, which is vitamin C. The antidarkening agent may be pure ascorbic acid, a combination of ascorbic acid and citric acid, lemon juice, vinegar, or salt water.

The antidarkening substance is sprinkled directly on the fruit; added to the juice or liquid used for holding, preparing, or preserving the fruit; or mixed with the sugar or sweetened syrup used on the fruit. Use the correct amount of the appropriate substance or mixture for the fruit you are preparing, as directed in the recipe or on the chart on next page.

ANTIDARKENING TREATMENTS

Agent	Methods and Proportions to Use
Ascorbic acid U.S.P. (vitamin C)	a. ½ teaspoon per quart of syrup b. ½ teaspoon per 2 cups granulated sugar c. ½ teaspoon in 1 cup to 1 quart water, for dipping fruit after peeling d. ¼ to ½ teaspoon to each quart sliced fruit, dissolved in a little water and sprinkled on the fruit e. 1 tablespoon citric acid and 1 teaspoon ascorbic acid to 1 gallon water for dipping fruit
Lemon juice	a. 2 tablespoons undiluted juice sprinkled over 1 quart fruit b. 2 to 3 tablespoons juice to 1 gallon water, for dipping fruit
Citric acid	a. 1 teaspoon to 1 gallon water for dipping fruit b. 1 tablespoon citric acid and 1 teaspoon ascorbic acid to 1 gallon water for dipping fruit
Vinegar and salt	a. 2 tablespoons salt and 2 tablespoons vinegar in 1 gallon water for holding fruit briefly—not more than 20 minutes. Rinse before packing.
Commercial mixtures such as Fruit Fresh (These may include a combination of ascorbic and citric acids, sugar, and silicon dioxide)	As directed on tin or package, usually— a. 1 teaspoon mixture to 1 cup syrup b. 1 to 3 teaspoons mixture to 1 cup sugar c. 2 teaspoons mixture to 1 quart cut fruit

ADDING SWEETENING TO FRUITS

Sugar may be added directly to juicy fruits that will be packed hot because they will make sufficient juice when they are simmered with about ½ cup sugar to each quart of fruit.

Other prepared fruits may be covered for canning (or freezing) with sweetened syrup, extracted juice, or water. The sweetening may be of sugar, syrup, or honey.

You may substitute light-colored, mild-flavored honey or light corn syrup for up to one-half of the sugar in a recipe. You may also substitute dark syrup, sorghum, brown or raw sugar, or molasses for part of the sugar in the recipe if you do not object to the flavor of the sweetening in the fruit. Dark syrups and sugars may cause a slight darkening of the fruit.

Honey seems sweeter than sugar, so you may need to adjust the amount of sweetening to taste when you use honey.

Allow from 1 to 1½ cups syrup, extracted juice, or water for each quart of raw-packed fruit.

TO MAKE SUGAR SYRUP Combine sugar and water, in the proportions given in the accompanying chart, in a large, heavy pan. Bring to a boil, stirring only until the

Kind of Syrup	Water	Sugar	Yield
Very light (For when only light sweetening is desired.)	4 cups	1 cup	4½ cups
Light (For soft fruits, such as sweet cherries and berries.)	4 cups	2 cups	5 cups
Medium (For most fruits—peaches, pears, apples, plums, berries, and acid fruits.)	4 cups	3 cups	5½ cups
Heavy (For larger sour fruits or those wanted to be extra-sweet such as cranberries, gooseberries, rhubarb.)	4 cups	4¾ cups	6½ cups

60

sugar dissolves. Boil until the liquid clears, and skim if necessary. Keep syrup hot until used, but do not boil down.

This syrup can be made in advance and stored in the refrigerator until needed, but must be reheated for use.

Fruit juice may be substituted for all or part of the water in the syrup recipe.

Ascorbic acid, commercial color preservers, or lemon juice may be added to the cooked syrup, if desired.

OMITTING SUGAR IN CANNED FRUITS

Sugar or other sweetening is not necessary to keep properly processed canned fruits from spoiling, so it can be omitted altogether when there are reasons why one wishes to can fruits without sweetening.

Perhaps someone in the family is on a restricted diet, or sugar is scarce during canning season, or so expensive that the home-canner may not be able to afford the purchase of large amounts of sugar, all at once, during the round of canning.

Omitting the sweetening from canned fruits presents no special problems although sugar does help to preserve color, flavor, and texture to some degree. Sugar or a noncaloric sweetener can be added to the canned fruit after it is opened for use.

If you wish to substitute an artificial sweetener for the sweetening when canning fruits, consult the directions of the manufacturer of the product recommended for your special-dieter's use.

Some fruits canned with artificial sweeteners develop an off-taste when heated so it is sometimes preferable to add the artificial sweetener after opening the canned fruit.

If you decide to omit the sweetening when canning fruit, pack the fruit in its own extracted, unsweetened hot juice, in other hot juice, or in boiling water. Follow general directions as given for canning the fruit with sugar.

TO EXTRACT JUICE FROM RIPE PREPARED FRUITS
Crush some of the fruits in a large pan, then heat to sim-

mering (185° to 210°F) over low heat. Crush and stir the fruits as they simmer, until tender. Strain the juice and use it to hot-pack fruits.

PROCESSING FRUITS IN A BOILING-WATER BATH

Fruits that have been properly prepared, then properly processed in a boiling-water bath at 212°F for the recommended time, are adequately protected against spoilage caused by molds, yeasts, and bacteria.

Though detailed information on the boiling-water bath and the use of canning jars is given earlier in the book, for the reader's convenience, these step-by-step instructions, which pertain to fruits only, are gathered here.

1. When ready to begin packing the prepared fruit into hot canning jars, place the rack in the water-bath canner and pour 4 to 5 inches of warm water into the canner. Place the canner on the stove and adjust the heat to keep the water *hot if using the raw-pack method, boiling or near boiling if using the hot pack.*
2. Pack the jars one at a time with the prepared fruit, using the canning funnel and following the specific directions for each fruit.
3. Cover packed fruit with hot or near-boiling liquid (water, syrup, juice, or pickling solution), leaving the proper head space.
4. Remove the canning funnel. Insert non-metal spatula to release any trapped air bubbles between jar and fruit. Add more canning liquid, if necessary, to correct the head space.
5. Clean rim and top of jar, including rubber ring, if used, to remove any particles of spilled food.
6. Close jars.
7. As soon as each jar is packed and closed, place it on the rack in the shallow hot water in the water-bath canner.
8. When all jars are packed, closed, and placed inside the water-bath canner, pour in enough hot or near-boiling

water to bring the level of the water in the canner to a depth of 1 to 2 inches above the tops of the jars. *Do not pour boiling water directly on the glass jars.* Cover the canner.
9. Turn the heat to high. Begin counting the processing time when the water in the canner comes to a full boil. Keep the heat adjusted so that the water maintains a hard boil all during the processing. *Keep the tops of the jars covered by at least 1-inch of boiling water all during the processing time.* If necessary, add more *boiling*, not cool, water to keep the water at the proper level.
10. Process the jars of fruit for the full time specified for each fruit in the recipe. Adjust processing time for altitude, if necessary, as explained on pages 25–26.
11. When the processing time is finished, turn off the heat and remove the jars from the canner at once, either by using a jar lifter or by lifting the canner rack.
12. Place the jars upright on a folded pad of cloth or on a cooling rack away from drafts. Complete seals if the jars are not self-sealing (see instructions on pages 37–41).
13. Let jars cool undisturbed for 12 to 24 hours, then test for seal (see instruction on page 40.)
14. Remove the screw bands from sealed jars with two-piece closures of screw bands and self-sealing lids. *Do not force the screw bands off.* (Sometimes they will not come off without destroying the seal.) If they will not come off easily, try briefly covering the screw bands with a hot, damp cloth to loosen them, or simply store the jars with the screw bands in place.
15. Wipe the jars with a damp cloth and label them. Store canned fruits in a cool, dry, dark place.

INSTRUCTIONS FOR PREPARING AND PROCESSING SPECIFIC FRUITS

Fruit or Prepared Food	Packing Method	Preparation	Minutes in Boiling-Water Bath	
			Pints	Quarts
Apples	Hot pack	Wash, pare, core, and slice or cut into pieces. Place pieces in an antidarkening solution at once. Use 2 tablespoons salt and 2 tablespoons vinegar in 1 gallon water, or an ascorbic acid solution. If the salt solution is used, rinse fruit afterward and do not let it remain in solution more than 20 minutes. Drain the pieces, then boil gently for 5 minutes in light or medium sugar syrup. Pack hot apples in jar and cover with hot syrup leaving 1/2-inch head space. Adjust lids and process.	15	20
Apple sauce	Hot pack	Wash, quarter, and core apples. Pare only if desired. Simmer in a small amount of water until tender; stir and mash while cooking. Put through food mill to make sauce. Sweeten to taste, or about 1 cup sugar to 1½ quarts sauce. Reheat to boiling. Pack in jars, leaving 1/4-inch head space. Adjust lids and process.	10	15

Apricots		*See Peaches.*		
Berries, firm Blueberries Currants Elderberries[1] Huckleberries (also Strawberries)[2]	Hot pack	Wash fruit and drain. Add ½ cup sugar for each quart and let stand for 2 hours in a cool place. Bring to a boil in a covered pan, stirring gently or shaking pan to prevent sticking, until the berries are heated through. Fill hot jars with heated berries, then fill jars with boiling water or very light syrup, if necessary, leaving ½-inch head space. Adjust lids and process.	10	15
Berries, soft Blackberries Dewberries Loganberries Raspberries Youngberries (*not* strawberries)	Raw pack	Use for soft berries. Wash fruit in cold or ice water. Drain. Fill hot jars, shaking berries down while filling. Cover berries with boiling medium or light syrup, leaving ½-inch head space. Adjust lids and process.	10	15
Cherries	Raw pack	Wash in cold or ice water, drain, and pit, if desired. If pits are left in cherries, stick each one with a needle to keep skins from bursting. Fill hot jars with cherries,	20	25

[1] Add 1 tablespoon vinegar or lemon juice to each quart of elderberries to add flavor.
[2] The color of strawberries tends to fade when they are canned.

Fruit or Prepared Food	Packing Method	Preparation	Minutes in Boiling-Water Bath	
			Pints	Quarts
		shaking down for a full pack. Cover with boiling syrup, using very light, light, or medium one for sweet cherries; a medium or heavy syrup for sour cherries. Leave 1/2-inch head space. Adjust lids and process.		
	Hot pack	Wash in cold water or ice water, drain, and pit, if desired. If pits are left in cherries, stick each one with a needle to keep skins from bursting. Add 1/2 cup sugar to each quart of fruit, more if cherries are sour. Add a little water to unpitted cherries only. Cover and heat until cherries are heated through. Pack hot, leaving 1/2-inch head space. Add boiling water or very light syrup if needed to make enough liquid to cover fruit. Adjust lids and process.	10	15

Product	Pack	Procedure		
Cranberries and Gooseberries	Raw pack	Wash, stem, and sort berries. Drain. Pack hot jars with raw berries. Cover berries with boiling heavy or medium syrup, leaving ½-inch head space. Adjust lids and process.	15	20
Cranberry sauce, jellied		Prepare cranberries as above. Boil 4 cups cranberries in 2 cups water until all the skins pop open. Press berries through a sieve or food mill. Add 2 cups sugar to pulp and juice. Boil rapidly about 5 minutes or to the jelly-point (when a drop jells on a cold plate), or to the temperature of 220° to 222° F on a jelly thermometer. Pour hot jelly into hot wide-mouth jars leaving ¼-inch head space. Adjust lids and process.	10	—
Cranberry sauce, whole-style	Hot pack	Wash, stem, and sort cranberries. Drain. Boil 4 cups sugar and 4 cups water together for 5 minutes. Add 8 cups cranberries. Boil, without stirring, until all the skins pop open, about 5 minutes. Fill hot jars with hot sauce, leaving ½-inch head space. Adjust lids and process.	10	—

INSTRUCTIONS FOR PREPARING AND PROCESSING SPECIFIC FRUITS

Fruit or Prepared Food	Packing Method	Preparation	Minutes in Boiling-Water Bath	
			Pints	Quarts
Fruit juices	Hot pack	*Extracting juice:* Wash fruit and drain. Peel and remove pits, if necessary, and cut into pieces. Peeling is not necessary for most fruits. Place fruit in a kettle. Crush berries, grapes, and small fruits to start the flow of juice and add small amounts of water as needed. Apples and hard fruits need to be covered with water for cooking. Heat fruit to simmering and cook gently until the fruit is soft, about 10 minutes for soft fruits, 20 to 25 minutes for hard fruits. Avoid hard, excessive boiling, which destroys flavor, color, and pectin. Strain the juice through a jelly bag or a cloth-lined colander. For clear juice, use several layers of cheesecloth or a flannel cloth. *Canning juice:* Add sugar, if desired, 1 to 2 cups per gallon of juice. Reheat juice to simmering (190° F). Fill hot jars with hot	10	10

		juice, leaving 1/2-inch head space. Adjust lids and process.		
Fruit purees[3] Peach Apricot Berry Apple Grape Pear Plum Rhubarb	Hot pack	Wash ripe fruit, drain. Peel and remove pits, if desired; cut fruit in pieces, or partially crush berries and soft fruit. Simmer fruit until soft, adding water if necessary to keep fruit from sticking. Sieve or put through a food mill. Add sugar to taste. Reheat puree to simmering (190° F). Pack hot into hot jars, leaving 1/4-inch head space. Adjust lids and process. Option: Add ascorbic acid to those fruits which tend to darken.	10	15
Gooseberries		See *Cranberries*.		
Grapes, Concord, unripe	Raw pack	Unripe Concord grapes, picked while still green in color and before the seeds harden, may be canned for use in pie making. To prepare, wash, drain, and stem the unripe grapes. Pack into hot jars and cover with boiling-hot medium or heavy syrup. Leave 1/2-inch head space. Adjust lids and process.	20	25
Nectarines		See *Peaches*.		

[3] Use canned fruit puree for special diets, for feeding small children, in recipes calling for pureed fruit, or for making into fruit butters or dried fruit leathers at a later time.

INSTRUCTIONS FOR PREPARING AND PROCESSING SPECIFIC FRUITS

Fruit or Prepared Food	Packing Method	Preparation	Minutes in Boiling-Water Bath	
			Pints	Quarts
Peaches, apricots, and nectarines	Raw pack[4]	Wash in cold water, drain, and peel (dip peaches and apricots in boiling water, then in cold water, to loosen skins), or omit peeling apricots. Halve and slice, pit, and scrape cavities if fibers remain. Apricots and clingstone peaches may be left whole and canned with pits. Use antidarkening treatment while preparing fruit. Drain. Pack into jars, cavity side down, layers overlapping. Leave 1/2-inch head space. Cover with boiling medium or light syrup. Adjust lids and process.	25	30
	Hot pack	Prepare as above. Bring medium or light syrup to a boil, drop in a few fruits at a time, and cook gently until fruit is just heated through. Pack hot fruits in hot jars, arranging as directed above. Cover with boiling syrup, leaving 1/2-inch head space. Adjust lids and process.	20	25

70

| Pears[5] | Hot pack | Stem, wash, pare, and core ripe pears. Follow the antidarkening treatment given for apples. Make sure all grittiness at core is cut out. Halve or quarter pears. Make a medium or light syrup, bring it to a boil, drop the pears in the simmering syrup, and simmer for 5 minutes. Pack fruit in jars and cover with boiling syrup, leaving 1/2-inch head space. Adjust lids and process.

Options
• Add 2 sticks of cinnamon and red food coloring to the syrup. Remove cinnamon before packing.
• Add 2 strips of orange or lemon peel to syrup. Remove before packing.
• Add green food coloring and oil of peppermint, a drop at a time, until desired flavor and color are achieved.
• Add 1/4 cup red hots (Cinnamon Imperials) candy to give color and cinnamon flavor to the syrup.
• Use pineapple juice in making canning syrup. | 20 | 25 |

[4] Use raw pack for fully ripe fruits or for varieties that lose their shape easily when boiled.

[5] Bartlett pears are the best kind for canning. They must be picked when mature, then allowed to ripen off the tree. Place them indoors in a cool place (60° to 65° F) until ripe. The flesh should yield to the thumb, but they must not be mushy soft. Kieffers and other varieties may also be canned, if properly ripened.

INSTRUCTIONS FOR PREPARING AND PROCESSING SPECIFIC FRUITS

Fruit or Prepared Food	Packing Method	Preparation	Minutes in Boiling-Water Bath	
			Pints	Quarts
Plums	Raw pack	Wash in cold water, drain. Prick skins with needle if leaving whole. Halve and pit freestone plums, if desired. Scald and peel, if desired, but plums are usually canned unpeeled. Pack in hot jars and cover with boiling medium or heavy syrup. Leave 1/2-inch head space. Adjust lids and process.	20	25
	Hot pack	Prepare as above. Heat syrup to boiling, add a few plums at a time and leave each batch in the syrup only until fruit is heated through. Remove from boiling syrup with a slotted spoon and pack in hot jars. Fill packed jars with boiling syrup, leaving 1/2-inch head space. Adjust lids and process.	20	25

Rhubarb			Pints	Quarts
	Hot pack	Wash and cut tender unpeeled stalks into ½- to 1-inch lengths. Add ½ to 1 cup sugar to each quart fruit. Let stand in a cool place to draw out juice. Bring slowly to a boil. Pack hot into hot jars, leaving ½-inch head space. Adjust lids and process.	10	10
	Raw pack	Wash and prepare rhubarb. Cut into ½ to 1-inch lengths. Pack into hot jars, leaving ½-inch head space. Cover with boiling-hot medium or heavy sugar syrup. Adjust lids and process.	15	15

Canning Vegetables

METHOD OF PROCESSING

All vegetables except most tomatoes, pickled vegetables, and sauerkraut must be processed in a steam-pressure canner because a temperature of 240°F (10 pounds pressure at less than 2,000 feet above sea level) for a sustained time is required to destroy spoilage micro-organisms that can exist in low-acid foods.*

*The University of Minnesota Agricultural Extension Service has recently completed a three-year study concerning the use of 15-pound pressure for processing foods for canning in a pressure canner. According to the findings there are some advantages to using 15 pound pressure rather than the usual 10 pound pressure including reducing the time required to safely process certain foods.

Since the information and recipes are not available in time for publication in this book, the home canner who is interested can obtain the information through local home economics extension agents or directly from the University of Minnesota. Address requests to:

Bulletin Room
Agricultural Extension Service
Coffy Hall
University of Minnesota
St. Paul, Minn. 55108

Request bulletin No. 413 entitled "Home Canning—Fruits, Vegetables, Meat." Single copies are free.

For detailed instructions for preparing the canning equipment and using the pressure canner, see pages 16–43.

METHODS OF PACKING VEGETABLES FOR HOME CANNING

Vegetables may be packed for canning by the hot-pack method or the raw-pack method. All vegetables may be packed after pre-cooking or blanching, or by the hot-pack method. Only asparagus, beans, carrots, corn, peas, tomatoes, summer squash can be packed by the RAW PACK method, but these vegetables may also be packed hot. The home canner has the option of choosing the method preferred for only a few of the low-acid vegetables.

Sweet potatoes and yams may be packed by the dry-pack method. The precooked hot vegetable is packed into a hot jar and canned with *no added liquid*. The procedure is explained in the recipe given in the instructions for preparing and processing specific vegetables.

RAW-PACKING VEGETABLES

The raw-pack method may be used only for asparagus, beans, carrots, corn, peas, tomatoes, and summer squash. Pack the raw prepared vegetables firmly into the jars, leaving proper amount of headspace as noted in the directions, *except* corn, lima beans, shelled beans, and peas. Because starchy vegetables expand during processing, pack these *loosely* in the jar and leave the recommended head space. Add ½ teaspoon salt to each pint of vegetables and 1 teaspoon salt to each quart. Pour boiling water into each jar, keeping the head space as required.

Remove the air bubbles as directed on page 32, adding more liquid if needed, and proceed with the closure of the jar.

HOT-PACKING VEGETABLES

All vegetables may be packed hot, after precooking or brief

blanching, according to the directions for each vegetable. Pack the hot vegetables and their liquid, boiling hot, into the jars rather *loosely*, leaving headspace as recommended. If the vegetables were not salted in the pre-cooking process, add ½ teaspoon salt to pints and 1 teaspoon salt to quarts. Cover the vegetables with boiling cooking liquid or water, as directed, leaving head space as noted on the chart.

Remove the air bubbles as directed on page 32, add more liquid as required, and close the jar.

PROCESSING LOW-ACID VEGETABLES IN A STEAM-PRESSURE CANNER

Though detailed information on processing in a steam-pressure canner is given earlier in the book, for the reader's convenience, these step-by-step instructions, which pertain to vegetables only, are gathered here. Wherever these instructions conflict with the directions that came with the pressure canner you are using, however, follow the manufacturer's directions.

1. When ready to begin packing the prepared vegetables into the hot canning jars, place the rack in the bottom of the pressure canner and pour 2 to 3 inches of warm water into the canner.
2. Pack the jars one at a time, using a canning funnel and following specific directions for each vegetable.
3. Leave the proper head space, remove the air bubbles, and clean the rim and top of each jar before closing the jars (see pages 31–40).
4. Place the filled and closed jars on the rack in the canner, leaving space between the jars so that steam can flow around each one. If two layers of jars are put in, use a rack between them and stagger the second layer.
5. Fasten the canner cover securely so that no steam escapes except through the vent (which is either the petcock or the weighted-gauge opening, depending on the type canner that you have). Turn on the heat and watch until

steam pours steadily from the vent. Let it escape for a full 10 minutes, to drive out all the air in the canner.

6. After allowing steam to rise from the vent for 10 minutes, close the petcock or place the weighted pressure gauge on the canner. Pressure will now begin to build up in the canner.

7. As soon as the pressure reaches 10 pounds (240°F), begin timing the processing. (The pressure gauge will read 10 pounds or the weighted gauge will jiggle vigorously.) Keep the pressure *constant* by regulating the heat under the canner. *Do not try to lower the pressure by any other means.* Do not allow the pressure to fluctuate once the proper level is reached.

8. When the processing time is up, turn off the heat. Let the pressure canner stand undisturbed until the pressure is decompressed (the dial gauge will read zero, or no sound of steam will escape when the weighted gauge is touched). Then slowly open the petcock or remove the weighted gauge.

9. Let the pressure canner stand until steam no longer spews from the opening. Do not try to rush the procedure by pouring cold water on the canner or by any other method. When the canner is unquestionably decompressed, open it carefully, lifting the lid away from you so that the lid shields you from any rising heat.

10. Using a jar lifter, remove the jars from the canner. Place them upright, on a folded cloth or cooling rack, away from drafts. Complete seals if the jars are not self-sealing, (see pages 31–42).

11. Let jars cool undisturbed for 12 to 24 hours, then test the seal (see page 40).

12. Remove screw bands from sealed jars with two-piece closures with screw bands and self-sealing lids. Do not force the screw band off if it will not come off easily. Try to loosen it by covering it with a hot, damp cloth. If it still cannot be easily removed, simply store the jar with the screw band in place.

13. Wipe the jars with a damp cloth. Label them and store the canned vegetables in a cool, dry, dark place.

INSTRUCTIONS FOR PREPARING AND PROCESSING SPECIFIC VEGETABLES

Vegetable	Preparation and Packing	Minutes at 10 Pounds in a Pressure Canner	
		Pints	Quarts
Asparagus	*Preparation:* Wash stalks, trim off woody ends and tough scales, and wash again. Drain. Cut into 1-inch pieces or leave small stalks whole.		
	Raw pack: Pack tightly, without crushing, into hot jars, leaving 1/4-inch head space. Pack whole spears with tips up. Add 1 teaspoon salt per quart. Cover with boiling water. Adjust lids. Process in pressure canner.	25	30
	Hot pack: Blanch in boiling water for 2 to 3 minutes. Pack loosely into hot jars, leaving 1/2-inch head space. Pack spears with tips up. Add 1 teaspoon salt per quart. Cover with hot cooking liquid or fresh boiling water. Adjust lids. Process in pressure canner.	25	30
Beans, green wax	*Preparation:* Wash beans and remove ends and strings, if any. Cut into 1/2- to 1-inch pieces, or leave tender young beans whole. Beans can be French cut, if desired.		

Raw pack: Pack prepared beans tightly into hot jars. Leave ½-inch head space. Add 1 teaspoon salt per quart. Cover with boiling water. Adjust lids. Process in pressure canner.

20 25

Hot pack: Cover prepared beans with boiling water and precook 5 minutes. Pack hot beans loosely into hot jars, leaving ½-inch head space. Add 1 teaspoon salt per quart. Cover with boiling cooking liquid or fresh boiling water. Adjust lids. Process in pressure canner.

20 25

Beans, lima

Preparation: Shell, wash, and sort the beans according to size, if necessary.

Raw pack: Pack small beans *loosely* into hot jars, leaving a 1-inch head space for pints and 1½ inches for quarts. For large beans, leave a ¾-inch head space for pints and 1¼-inches for quarts. Do not pack down, since the beans will expand. Add 1 teaspoon salt per quart. Fill the jar with boiling water to within ½ inch of the top. Adjust lids. Process in pressure canner.

40 50

Hot pack: Cover prepared lima beans with boiling water and bring again to a boil. Pack the hot beans loosely into hot jars, leaving a 1-inch head space. Add 1 teaspoon salt per quart. Fill the jars to within 1 inch of the top with cooking liquid or boiling water. Adjust lids. Process in pressure canner.

40 50

Vegetable	Preparation and Packing	Minutes at 10 Pounds in a Pressure Canner	
		Pints	Quarts
Beets	*Preparation:* Cut off beet tops, except for 1 inch of the stems. Also leave root. Wash beets, scrubbing with vegetable brush, if necessary, but taking care not to break skins. Cover washed beets with boiling water and cook until the skins slip easily, 15 to 25 minutes. Remove skins and trim off stems and roots. Sort beets for size. Leave small beets whole; halve, quarter, slice, or cube larger beets.		
	Hot pack: Pack hot precooked beets into hot jars, leaving 1/2-inch head space. Add 1 teaspoon salt per quart. Cover with boiling water. Adjust lids. Process in pressure canner.	30	35
Carrots	*Preparation:* Wash and scrape carrots. Wash again. Slice or dice, or leave small carrots whole.		
	Raw pack: Pack prepared carrots tightly into hot jars, leaving 1-inch head space. Add 1 teaspoon salt per quart. Cover with boiling water. Adjust lids. Process in pressure canner.	25	30

		Pints	Quarts

Hot pack: Cover prepared carrots with boiling water. Bring to a boil. Pack hot carrots into hot jars, leaving ½-inch head space. Add 1 teaspoon salt per quart. Cover with boiling water or cooking liquid to ½-inch of top. Adjust lids. Process in pressure canner. — 25 — 30

Celery

Preparation: Wash and drain. Cut off tough ends and tops. Remove strings from stalks and cut into strips or 1-inch pieces.

Hot pack: Cover prepared celery with boiling water and boil 3 minutes. Drain. Pack hot celery into hot jars, leaving ½-inch head space. Add 1 teaspoon salt per quart. Cover with boiling water. Adjust lids. Process in pressure canner. — 30 — 35

Corn

Preparation: Use freshly gathered corn with milky kernels. Husk and remove silks. Wash and drain. To prevent loss of freshness, prepare quickly.

Cream Style
Cut corn kernels from cob at about the center of the kernels. Scrape cob.

Raw pack: Pack corn loosely into hot pint jars *only*. Leave 1½-inch head space. Do not pack down. Add ½ teaspoon salt per pint. Cover with boiling water to ½-inch of top. Adjust lids. Process in pressure canner. — 95 — NR*

*Not recommended.

Vegetable	Preparation and Packing	Minutes at 10 Pounds in a Pressure Canner	
		Pints	Quarts
	Hot pack: Measure cut corn and add ½ teaspoon salt and 1 pint boiling water to each quart of cut corn. Bring to a boil. Pack boiling-hot corn into hot pint jars *only,* leaving 1-inch head space. Adjust lids. Process in pressure canner.	85	NR
	Whole Kernel Corn		
	Cut corn from cob at almost the full depth of the kernel, but do not scrape cob.		
	Raw pack: Pack prepared corn loosely into hot jars, leaving 1½-inch head space. Add 1 teaspoon salt per quart. Cover with boiling water to ½-inch of top. Adjust lids. Process in pressure canner.	55	85
	Hot pack: Measure cut corn and add 1 pint boiling water and 1 teaspoon salt to each quart of measured corn. Heat to boiling. Pack the hot mixture into hot jars, leaving 1-inch head space. Adjust lids. Process in pressure canner.	55	85

Greens, all kinds	*Preparation:* Wash greens thoroughly in several waters, lifting the greens out of the water each time to drain. Cut out tough stems and midribs. *Hot pack:* Steam-blanch greens until well wilted, about 10 minutes, turning once and cutting through greens if leaves are large. Pack hot greens loosely into hot jars, leaving 1/2-inch head space. Add 1 teaspoon salt per quart. Cover greens with hot cooking liquid or boiling water. Adjust lids. Process in pressure canner.	70	90
Mushrooms	*Preparation:* Trim stems and discolored parts of mushrooms. Soak in solution of 2 cups water and 1 teaspoon lemon juice for 10 minutes. Wash in fresh water until clean. Drain. Leave small mushrooms whole, cut larger ones into halves, quarters, or profiles. Or separate stems and caps. *Hot pack:* Steam-blanch (see page 197) mushrooms for 4 minutes. Pack hot mushrooms into hot pint jars, leaving 1/2-inch head space. Add 1/2 teaspoon salt per pint and 1/8 teaspoon ascorbic acid per pint. Cover mushrooms with boiling water to 1/2-inch of top. Adjust lids. Process in pressure canner. If desired, mushrooms may be packed in 1/2-pint-size jars and processed in pressure canner for 30 minutes at 10 pounds pressure.	30	NR*

*NR = not recommended.

Vegetable	Preparation and Packing	Minutes at 10 Pounds in a Pressure Canner	
		Pints	Quarts
Okra (See also Tomatoes and okra)	*Preparation:* Use only young, tender pods. Wash and drain. Trim off stem ends without cutting into pods.		
	Hot pack: Cover prepared okra with boiling water and boil for 1 minute. Drain. Cut pods into 1-inch lengths or leave whole. Pack hot okra into hot glass jars, leaving 1/2-inch head space. Add 1 teaspoon salt per quart. Cover with boiling water. Adjust lids. Process in pressure canner.	25	40
Onions	*Preparation:* Use small white onions of uniform size, preferably 1-inch diameter. Cut off tops and roots. Peel onions under running water. Drain.		
	Hot pack: Cover prepared onions with boiling water and boil 5 minutes. Pack hot onions into hot jars, leaving 1-inch head space. Add 1/2 teaspoon salt per pint. Cover onions with hot cooking liquid or boiling water, leaving 1/2-inch head space. Adjust lids. Process in pressure canner.	40	40

Peas		40	40
Fresh green or "English"		
Fresh black-eyed (or Cowpeas) and all other fresh shelled varieties	40	40

Peas
Fresh green or
"English"
Fresh black-eyed
(or Cowpeas)
and all other
fresh shelled varieties

Preparation: Use just-picked tender peas, slightly immature. Shell, wash, and drain.

Raw pack: Pack prepared peas *loosely* into hot jars, leaving 1½-inch head space. Do not shake down. Add 1 teaspoon salt per quart. Cover peas with boiling water leaving 1-inch head space. Adjust lids. Process in pressure canner.

Hot pack: Cover prepared peas with boiling water. Bring small, tender peas to a boil only; boil larger peas 3 minutes. Pack hot peas into hot jars, leaving 1-inch head space. Add 1 teaspoon salt per quart. Cover with boiling cooking liquid or boiling water. Adjust lids. Process in pressure canner.

Option
One to two teaspoons sugar may be added to each quart of "English" or green peas when packing into jars.

Potatoes, new
white

Preparation: Wash, pare, and wash again. If preparing large amount, hold in salt water (1 teaspoon salt per quart of cold water) to prevent discoloration. Drain. Cut potatoes into pieces or, if no larger than 1 to 1½ inches in diameter, leave whole. Precook in boiling water, 10 minutes for whole potatoes, 2 minutes for cubes. Drain.

Vegetable	Preparation and Packing	Minutes at 10 Pounds in a Pressure Canner	
		Pints	Quarts
	Hot pack: Pack hot, precooked potatoes into hot jars, leaving ½-inch head space. Add 1 teaspoon salt per quart. Cover with boiling water. Adjust lids. Process in pressure canner. Note: Hot pack only because of the difficulty of preventing white potatoes from darkening.	Whole —30 Cubes —35	Whole —40 cubes —40
Potatoes, sweet, and yams	*Preparation:* Wash freshly dug potatoes, scrubbing with a vegetable brush. Boil or steam until barely tender, 20 to 30 minutes, until skins slip. Do not stick potatoes with fork. Drain. Remove skins and cut into pieces.		
	Hot pack (dry): Pack hot potatoes into hot jars, leaving 1-inch head space. Add no liquid or salt. Adjust lids. Process in pressure canner.	65	95
	Hot pack (wet): Pack hot potatoes into hot jars, leaving 1-inch head space. Add 1 teaspoon salt per quart. Cover with boiling water. Adjust lids. Process in pressure canner.	55	90

				55	90

Hot pack (syrup): Pack hot potatoes into hot jars, leaving 1-inch head space. Cover with boiling-hot medium-sugar syrup, leaving 1-inch head space. Adjust lids. Process in pressure canner.

Pumpkin and winter squash

Preparation: Wash, halve, and seed fully ripe pumpkin or winter squash.

Cubed Pumpkin or Squash

Hot pack: Pare vegetable and cut into 1-inch cubes. Add enough boiling water to barely cover. Bring again to a boil. Pack hot cubes into hot jars, leaving 1/2-inch head space. Add 1 teaspoon salt per quart. Cover with hot cooking liquid. Adjust lids. Process in pressure canner.

55   90

Pumpkin or Squash Puree

Hot pack: Cube pumpkin or squash as above and simmer or steam until fork tender, about 25 minutes. Put through food mill or strainer or blender. Reheat puree to simmering, stirring to prevent scorching. Pack hot puree into hot glass jars, leaving 1/2-inch head space. Adjust lids. Process in pressure canner.

Soybeans (fresh green) edible)

65   80

Preparation: Harvest edible soybeans when the pods are green and the soybeans bright green and firm. Wash and drain. To shell: Blanch green soybeans in boiling water for 5 minutes. Start counting the time when the beans are put into the boiling water. Drain, and cool the beans thoroughly

Vegetable	Preparation and Packing	Minutes at 10 Pounds in a Pressure Canner	
		Pints	Quarts
	in cold, running water. Drain again. Break the pods and shell out the soybeans.		
	Packing: Follow the packing directions for lima beans, raw pack or hot pack.	60	70
Squash, summer	*Preparation:* Wash and drain. Trim ends but do not pare. Cut into 1/2-inch slices. Halve or quarter slices if necessary.		
	Raw pack: Pack prepared squash tightly into jars, leaving 1-inch head space. Add 1 teaspoon salt per quart. Cover with boiling water, leaving 1/2-inch head space. Adjust lids. Process in pressure canner.	25	30
	Hot pack: Barely cover prepared squash with boiling water and bring to a boil. Pack hot squash loosely into hot jars, leaving 1/2-inch head space. Cover with hot cooking liquid. Adjust lids. Process in pressure canner.	30	40
Squash, winter, see *Pumpkin*			

		25	40

Tomatoes and okra

Preparation: Choose and prepare the okra as directed earlier in the chart; the tomatoes, as on page 92. Leave small okra pods whole or cut into 1-inch lengths. Quarter peeled tomatoes.

Hot pack: Place tomatoes and okra together—half tomatoes and half okra, or other proportion desired—in a large, heavy kettle over low heat. Stir and heat until juice flows and mixture boils. Simmer for 3 minutes. Pack hot mixture into hot jars, leaving 1/2-inch head space. Add 1 teaspoon salt per quart. Add boiling water if there is not enough cooking liquid to cover vegetables. Adjust lids. Process in pressure canner.

Vegetables, mixed

Preparation: Prepare each vegetable as directed in individual instructions, then combine according to preference: diced carrots and peas, peas and tiny onions, corn and lima beans, corn and fresh shelled beans, or other combination.

Hot pack: Cover the vegetable combination with boiling water and boil together for 3 minutes. Pack hot vegetables into hot jars, leaving 1-inch head space. Add 1 teaspoon salt per quart. Cover with hot cooking liquid or boiling water, leaving 1/2-inch head space, except for starchy vegetables; for them, leave 1-inch head space to allow for expansion. Adjust lids. Process in pressure canner for the longest time required for any of the vegetables in the combination.

89

Canning Tomatoes

SPECIAL CONSIDERATIONS

Properly prepared and selected tomatoes—even orange, yellow, and small tomatoes—have been proved by USDA tests* to be high enough in acid to be safely processed in a boiling-water bath.

Since there are a few new low-acid varieties of tomatoes on the market that are intended for fresh use, and because soil, environmental, and unusual conditions can affect acidity of tomatoes, it is a good safeguard to add acid to all tomatoes being canned.

Normal, traditional tomatoes contain enough acid to prevent the growth of spoilage organisms when properly canned. Botulism spores will not grow in properly processed high-acid foods. Acidifying tomatoes being canned ensures that the acid level will be adequate if the tomatoes are processed in the boiling-water bath. The USDA Bulletin #1677-77 states that "although there seems to be no need to artificially acidify tomatoes, some home canners may wish to acidify as additional insurance."

Warning: If low-acid vegetables such as celery, green peppers, onions, or carrots are added to tomatoes or to-

*The two year study conducted by the United States Department of Agriculture to assess the safety of home-canned tomatoes is entitled "Tomato Acidity and the Safety of Home Canned Tomatoes." It was conducted by G. M. Sapers, A. K. Stoner, and J. G. Phillips.

mato juice before canning, the acidity of the tomato mixture is lowered significantly. Such tomato mixtures must be processed in the pressure canner at 240°F (10 pounds pressure) for the longest time required for processing any of the low-acid vegetables added to the recipe.

See pages 89 and 96–98 for recipes for canning tomatoes with added ingredients and in combination with other vegetables.

SELECTING THE TOMATOES

The ideal red tomato for canning is

- Vine ripened, but firm and not *overripe*
- Without blemishes, free from soft spots and decay
- Of typical size, not over- or undersized
- Of characteristic tomato-red color

Vine-ripened tomatoes have the best flavor but they should not be allowed to become *overripe* if they are to be canned. Overripe tomatoes lose acidity.

Tomatoes with soft spots or decay should not be canned because they, too, lose acidity. One bad spot, overlooked, will cause the entire batch to spoil.

The size of tomatoes has no effect upon their acidity but the baseball-size we commonly associate with typical tomatoes fits into the mouth of the canning jar and makes an attractive product. When tomatoes have to be cut, they tend to lose their shape.

Red tomatoes that are tomato red will have better flavor and appearance than those that have ripened with green shoulders, or that have yellow blistered cheeks indicating they have withstood too-hot sunshine. Try to obtain the very best quality tomatoes for canning.

Do not pick tomatoes from dead vines for canning. Tests have shown some tomatoes to have lowered acidity when picked from dead vines.

YELLOW AND ORANGE TOMATOES

Yellow and orange tomatoes are suitable for home canning.

The light colored varieties were suspected, for a time, of not being acid enough to can safely. Pear tomatoes and small tomatoes were also suspect. In its recent study (see footnote, page 90) that assessed the safety of home-canned tomatoes, the United States Department of Agriculture determined that color and size of tomatoes is not a factor in their acidity.

AN OUNCE OF PREVENTION . . .

If you grow your own tomatoes, stake them and mulch the plants during their growing season so that the fruits do not lie on the ground. Not only do tomatoes ripen more evenly if staked, but the bacterial load of the tomatoes being canned will be reduced if they are not in contact with the soil. Soil contains bacteria that are difficult to kill during processing, so it makes sense to avoid contamination of the tomatoes if possible.

PREPARING THE TOMATOES

Wash and sort tomatoes, discarding for canning purposes any that are overripe or decayed. Cut off stem ends of tomatoes and peel.

To peel tomatoes, place a few at a time in a wire or blanching basket and dip in boiling water for half a minute to loosen the skins, then dip in cold water. Drain. Cut out the core and all green spots. Slip off the skins.

Or, rotate tomatoes held on a long-handled fork over a flame until their skins split. Then core and skin.

The peeled tomatoes may then be packed into canning jars by either the raw-pack or the hot-pack method.

ACIDIFYING TOMATOES FOR HOME CANNING

Tomatoes may be safely processed in a boiling-water bath since the acid in properly selected tomatoes is high enough to prevent the growth of the organism that causes botulism.

Proper selection means choosing fresh, firm tomatoes

that are not overripe or decayed. Overripe or decayed tomatoes may be exceptionally low in acidity. Never use such fruits for canning.

New tomato varieties developed "for table use" or advertised as "low-acid" may not actually be less acid than older traditional varieties. However, three varieties on the market—Ace, Ace 55F, and Cal Ace—are low in acid compared to other varieties that were tested during a recently completed two-year study conducted by the United States Department of Agriculture. These varieties were developed for fresh use and should not be canned.

Since the acidity of tomatoes can be affected by various factors—the stage of ripeness, the variety of tomato, and the environment in which the tomatoes are grown—there is no simple way that the home canner can determine the exact level of acidity of the tomatoes to be canned. As a safeguard, *it is recommended that extra acid be added to all tomatoes before processing to guarantee that the canned tomatoes will be sufficiently acid* to prevent spoilage and development of botulism toxin.

To properly acidify any tomatoes or tomato mixture being canned, the United States Department of Agriculture recommends adding either 1 tablespoon of bottled lemon juice or ¼ teaspoon crystalline citric acid per pint of tomatoes.

Bottled lemon juice is recommended because fresh lemons, too, vary in acidity while bottled lemon juice is standardized. In the USDA tests it was shown that 1 tablespoon bottled lemon juice provides about 0.75 grams citric acid and ¼ teaspoon citric acid contains almost one gram (1.00 gram) citric acid. These are the amounts recommended to be added to 1 pint of tomatoes to acidify them.

Vinegar added to tomatoes will also increase acidity but it is not as effective as citric acid or bottled lemon juice and produces an off-flavor that might be objectionable if used to acidify plain tomatoes. In pickled products, or in catsups and sauces, vinegar used as one of the ingredients will contribute to the acidity and flavor of the recipe.

There are commercial tablets available on the market for acidifying tomatoes and these, too, can be used according to the directions on the tin or package.

PROCESSING TOMATOES IN A BOILING-WATER BATH

THE HOT-PACK METHOD

1. Wash jars and lids; rinse thoroughly. Keep jars in hot water. Follow manufacturer's directions for preparing lids.
2. Pour 6 inches of hot water in water-bath canner and place on stove to heat. Let water heat to near boiling.

Place another container on the stove and heat enough water in it to finish filling the water bath canner with boiling water after the rack of filled jars is set into the canner.

Place a third kettle of water on the stove to boil, to prepare water for scalding the tomatoes.
3. Wash and sort enough firm, ripe tomatoes for one canner load, allowing about 2½ pounds of tomatoes per quart. Place tomatoes in a wire basket, a few at a time, and plunge into boiling water. Leave for a few seconds, until the skins loosen, then plunge the basket of tomatoes into cold water. Drain. Peel tomatoes and cut out stems, cores, blossom ends, and any green spots.
4. Quarter the peeled tomatoes into a kettle. Heat and stir the tomatoes until they boil.
5. Ladle the hot tomatoes into the hot jars, using a wide-mouth canning funnel. Cover the tomatoes with their own juice, leaving ½-inch head space.
6. If desired, add salt to each jar of tomatoes, ½ teaspoon per pint, 1 teaspoon per quart.
7. Add acidifying agent to each jar, 1 tablespoon bottled lemon juice or ¼ teaspoon crystalline citric acid per pint (double the amount for quart jars), or a commercial tablet. Follow the manufacturer's directions for use of the tablet.
8. Release air bubbles by running a nonmetal spatula down the sides of the jar.
9. Wipe rim and neck of the jar carefully with a clean, damp cloth.
10. Close each jar as soon as it is packed.

For the self-sealing lid and screw band closure, remove lid from hot water and place it on clean rim of the hot jar with the sealing composition next to the glass. Hold lid in place and screw on band by hand until tight.

For the zinc cap and rubber ring closure, place wet rubber ring on jar before packing. After the jar has been packed and the rim cleaned, partially seal the jar by screwing the cap down firmly, then turn back ¼ inch.

For the glass cap–rubber ring–wire bail closure, place wet rubber ring on jar before packing. After the jar has been packed and the rim cleaned, place the glass cap on top of the jar and the longer wire on top of the glass cap, but do not fasten down the shorter wire bail at this time.

11. Place packed jars in the canner rack and lower it carefully into the canner containing the near-boiling water. The jars should not touch each other and their bottoms should be ½ inch above the bottom of the canner. Add boiling water to cover the jars by 1 to 2 inches. Do not pour the boiling water directly on the jars. Cover the canner and bring to a rolling boil on high heat.

12. Start counting processing time as soon as a full, active boil is reached. That will indicate the water temperature is 212°F. Keep the heat adjusted so that the water boils steadily throughout the processing time. If necessary, add boiling water during the processing to keep the jars covered at all times by at least 1 inch of boiling water.

Process pints and quarts for 10 minutes at sea level.

13. As soon as the processing time is up, turn off the heat and remove the jars from the canner. Complete the seal, if necessary.

Do not tighten screw bands of self-sealing lid closures.

Screw zinc caps down tight, using a jar wrench.

Fasten down the shorter wire of the glass-cap closures.

14. Place jars upright on several layers of folded cloth or on a cooling rack, with a 1-inch space between jars and in a place where there are no drafts. Do not cover the jars while cooling.

15. Let jars cool for 12 to 24 hours.

16. Test to make sure jars are sealed (see instructions on page 40). Remove screw bands, if used.

17. Wipe jars clean. Store in a cool, dark, dry place until used.

THE RAW-PACK METHOD

Follow Steps 1, 2, and 3 for hot-packing tomatoes. Then—

4. Leave tomatoes whole after peeling, or if they are too large to fit into the jars, cut into halves or quarters.

5. Pack tomatoes, as soon as they are peeled, into hot jars, until all the jars are filled. Press the tomatoes down gently to fill spaces but do not mash and do not add water. Leave ½-inch head space.

Continue with Steps 6 through 11 for hot-packing the tomatoes. Then—

12. Start counting processing time when water boils (212°F).

Process pints for 35 minutes, quarts for 45 minutes, at sea level.

Complete the processing according to Steps 13 through 17 in the instructions for hot-packing.

MAKING AND CANNING SOME OTHER TOMATO PRODUCTS

Tomato Juice

Wash tomatoes, cut out stem ends, and core. Quarter, but do not peel. Simmer tomatoes in large saucepan until softened, stirring often. Put through a strainer. Add 1 teaspoon salt to each quart of tomato juice. Acidify juice as you would tomatoes for canning, adding either 2 tablespoons bottled lemon juice or ½ teaspoon crystalline citric acid per quart of juice (see Step 7 of instructions on hot-packing tomatoes, page 94).

Heat strained juice to boiling and fill hot jars, leaving ½-inch head space. Adjust lids and process pints and quarts in a boiling-water bath for 10 minutes. Remove jars from canner as soon as processing is finished. Complete seal, if necessary.

About 18 pounds of tomatoes are required for 6 quarts of juice.

Tomato Sauce

Prepare two quarts of fresh tomato juice according to the

recipe above. Clean and prepare 2 carrots, 1 medium onion, 2 cloves garlic, 1 medium-sized green pepper, 2 stalks of celery along with the celery leaves, and ½ cup fresh parsley. Using an electric blender, chop all of the vegetables, preparing each vegetable separately and using a little of the tomato juice in the blender to provide the necessary liquid. Combine the chopped vegetables and the remainder of the tomato juice in a large heavy saucepan. Add the seasonings: 1 teaspoon salt, ½ teaspoon freshly-ground black pepper, ½ teaspoon dried basil leaves; 1 teaspoon crushed dried rosemary leaves, and 1 teaspoon dried oregano leaves. If fresh herbs are available, use about three times more of the freshly minced herbs than of the dried herb leaves.

Bring the mixture to a boil and cook on medium heat in an uncovered pan for about 1 hour, stirring often, until the liquid is reduced about one half and the sauce is thick. Watch carefully and stir more frequently after the sauce begins to thicken.

Pour the hot sauce into hot pint jars, leaving ¼-inch head space. Adjust lids and process in the pressure canner for 30 minutes at 10 pounds pressure. Makes 2 pints.

Use this sauce in making stuffed green peppers, cabbage rolls, meat loaf or meat balls, eggplant parmesan, or in other recipes requiring seasoned tomato sauce.

Bloody Mary Cocktail Mix

Wash, core, and cut 2 dozen perfect ripe tomatoes into chunks. In a large heavy kettle combine tomatoes with 1½ cups chopped onions, 1 cup chopped sweet bell peppers, 1 cup chopped celery, 2 cloves minced garlic, ¼ cup horseradish, 1 to 2 teaspoons Tabasco sauce, ½ cup lemon juice, 1 tablespoon salt, and ¼ cup sugar. Simmer, covered, for 30 minutes or until the tomatoes are soft, stirring often. Put the mixture through a food mill or a fine sieve. Reheat the juice mixture to a boil and pour into hot jars, leaving ½-inch head space. Adjust caps and process for 30 minutes in the pressure canner at 10 pounds pressure. Makes about 4 quarts.

Best Bloody Mary

Combine 1½ ounces vodka, ½ cup Bloody Mary cocktail mix, salt and freshly ground black pepper to taste, the juice of half a lime, and additional Tabasco sauce, if desired. Pour into an ice-filled cocktail shaker. Shake quickly 9 times. Pour through a strainer into a glass and drop in 1 lime wedge. Garnish with a celery stalk. Makes 1 cocktail.

Herbed Tomatoes

Wash, peel, and core 7 pounds vine-ripened unblemished tomatoes and pack tightly into three hot sterilized quart jars, filling them half full. Add to each jar ¼ teaspoon basil, ¼ teaspoon celery seed, and 1 teaspoon salt. Fill jars with more tomatoes to within 1 inch of the top and add an additional ¼ teaspoon basil and ¼ teaspoon celery seed to each jar. Simmer the remaining tomatoes in a large heavy kettle until they are soft, about 30 minutes, and cooked down to juice. Press the tomatoes through a sieve or put through a food mill to extract the juice. Add the tomato juice to the tomatoes in the jar, leaving 1-inch head space. Adjust caps and process for 10 minutes in a boiling-water bath.

Tomato Paste

In a large, very heavy enamelware or stainless steel kettle, combine 8 quarts peeled, cored, and chopped vine-ripened tomatoes, 1½ cups chopped sweet red peppers, 2 bay leaves, ½ teaspoon oregano, ½ teaspoon basil, 2 cloves minced garlic, 3 tablespoons lemon juice, and 1 tablespoon salt. Cook slowly, uncovered, for 1 hour. Press mixture through a fine sieve or puree in a food mill. Return mixture to low heat and cook uncovered for 2 to 2½ hours, or until the mixture is reduced to a paste thick enough to round up on a spoon. Stir carefully during cooking to prevent sticking. Be especially watchful when the paste begins to thicken. Place kettle on a stove burner coil during the last part of the cooking period, if necessary. Pour into hot half-pint jars, leaving ¼-inch head space. Adjust caps and process for 35 minutes at 10 pounds pressure in a pressure canner. Makes about 9 half-pints.

PART II

Making the Sweets
and Sours

MAKING THE SWEET SPREADS

—•—

As a child, my after-school snack might be a piece of fresh fruit, a cookie, or a leftover dessert, but usually it was a slice of buttered bread spread with a sweet spread. Besides the jellies, jams, preserves, marmalades, and fruit butters that Mother made in summertime with our bounty of orchard fruits and wild fruits, we always had honey from Grandmother's beehives and gallons of sorghum made from cane that Dad grew on the farm. We did not make maple syrup, although Grandpa's yard was shaded by tall maples, because the southern tradition leans toward sorghum syrup rather than toward maple syrup. Besides, Dad said it was easier to grow sorghum cane than to gather maple sap.

With such an abundance of fruits on the farm, we made great use of sweet spreads made from strawberries, cherries, raspberries, wild blackberries, wild plums, peaches, and apples. As each fruit ripened in turn, its juices dripped from the jelly bag, then frothed and foamed in the jelly kettle in a rolling, tumbling boil that could not be stirred down. How familiar was the sight of my mother standing over the jelly kettle, her head enveloped in rising steam, alternately stirring the jelly and holding the spoon aloft to watch for the two drops that would slide off the spoon as one, the signal that the jellying point had been reached. By suppertime there would be another row of jars cooling on the counter and a sample bowl of the new jelly. A choice of sweet spreads was placed on the table at every mealtime, as surely as the hot quick breads and homemade yeast bread, which we called light bread. One required the other.

It might seem that our diet was overly sweet because bread-and-jelly were a daily twosome. But in those days of home-grown, home-canned foods, there were no "junk foods," and no sugar-loaded beverages or cereals. Dessert was often fresh or lightly sweetened fruits. And, although we sometimes made fudge or sorghum molasses taffy, we seldom had "bought" candy from Allen's General Store.

But at Christmas, when my father came home for the holidays from the school where he taught, he always brought treats we did not usually have—orange candy slices, chocolate drops, coconut bonbons, dates, Brazil nuts, cashews, English walnuts, almonds, and a bushel basket of tangerines, grapefruit, and oranges.

Bought fruits were as unusual to us as bought candy. We enjoyed the Christmas fruits long after the holidays. We packed oranges or tangerines in our lunch boxes and ate grapefruit for breakfast—a nice change from apples and canned fruit, which we usually ate. And Mother was never one to waste anything. As soon as the citrus rinds accumulated, she made something delicious out of them. She candied fruit peels to add to quick breads, cakes, and cookies, or to eat as confections. And she always made jars of orange marmalade that tasted bitter and sweet at the same time and seemed by far the most exotic of the homemade sweets we spread on slices of whole wheat bread at breakfast time.

This is our family recipe for candying the peel of the Christmas fruits.

Candied Fruit Peel

Use the fresh bright peelings of 6 oranges or 3 grapefruit. Wash, then remove the thick white membrane from inside the peels and cut them into thin strips. Cover with cold water and bring to a boil. Drain. Repeat this process twice more, then drain well. Next cook the peel in a syrup made of 1 cup sugar and ½ cup water. Simmer over low heat until all of the syrup is absorbed by the peel. Roll each piece on a plate spread with granulated sugar and spread out to dry. After the sugared peel is dry, store it in a tin.

Making marmalade was a kitchen chore that called for the long-bladed, all-purpose knife that we called the butcher knife. This knife was not actually a butcher's knife, according to today's classifications, but we called any sharp cutting knife with a long blade a butcher knife and any short bladed knife a peeling knife. And before every ambitious cooking project involving peeling and chopping, my father sharpened the knives.

At breakfast on the morning the marmalade was to be begun, my mother brought the knives to my father at the table and laid them beside his plate. When Dad finished his breakfast, he pushed away his cup and saucer and cleared a place on the table to lay out the knives. Then he picked them up, one by one, and ran a cautious finger along the edge of each knife blade.

"Dull as a froe," he would pronounce. "Sis, run and get my whetstones."

I welcomed the chance to gently rummage in the top drawer of his dresser—which was forbidden at other times because the shells for Dad's hunting gun were kept there. The satiny, dark rectangular whetstone, the smoothing hone, and its companion, the cutting hone, a light gray gritty whetstone, were found easily enough among the interesting accumulation of special objects in the drawer. And when I had found them, there was just a moment to spare to finger the gold watch kept there, and the World War I ribbons, and the old photographs. The seldom seen contents of that small drawer always piqued my curiosity.

But the sharpening of the knives was an often-seen, familiar ritual. My father pushed his chair away from the table and placed the rough cutting whetstone on his knee. To provide the moisture necessary to soften the stone, he simply spat on it. Then he cut down the knife blade on the rough whetstone with a series of slow, deliberate motions. At first he would hone toward the front edge of the whetstone with regular, rhythmic movements; then he would whet the blade away from himself, toward the back edge of the stone, drawing first one side of the blade, then the other, over the gritty surface. When he thought the blade should be sharp enough, he wiped both sides of it across the knee of his denim trousers, then raised the knife and passed his thumb along its keen edge. If it was not sharp enough to suit him, he spit on the whetstone again and repeated the honing. When he had cut the blade down to a sharp edge on the surface of the cutting stone, he smoothed it down by the same method on the finer-grained dark whetstone, using a circular motion.

Finally he laid the smoothing whetstone on the table.

"There." He was satisfied with what he had done. "Now that blade is sharp enough to cut my whiskers."

When Dad felt in a playful mood, he would take the knife to the small mirror hung above the washstand on the back porch and demonstrate its sharpness by cutting away a tiny patch of his bristly beard.

He never handed the sharpened knives to my mother without a word of caution—"Careful, now. They're sharp as razors!"—and they were.

Of the Christmas oranges, Mother chose a dozen and washed them at the sink. Then the oranges were cut into halves. It was my task to pry out the pips with the nut pick, gather them together, and tie them up in a muslin square. The pips were to be boiled with the marmalade in the kettle, to give it flavor. As the oranges were seeded, Mother juiced each half on the ribs of the glass juice reamer and put the juice into the preserving kettle. Then, with the mound of rinds in front of her on the cutting board, she sat down at the kitchen table to carefully cut the orange rinds into slices as thin as the blade of the sharp butcher knife. If there were some orange rinds left from breakfast, she used those, too, along with several sliced lemons. Then the slivered rinds were placed in the kettle along with the juice, the pips in their muslin bag, and a small amount of water, and the kettle was put onto the stove just long enough for the citrus juices to come to a gentle boil.

But that was only the first cooking. This was the beginning of a three-day process that made the kitchen as fragrant as a king's *orangerie*, with pungent fruity aromas arising from the kettle or escaping from the covered crock where the cooked orange rinds were put aside to stand in their juices until morning and the second cooking.

On the third morning, the rinds and the juice were measured and returned to the preserving kettle with an equal amount of sugar. All morning Mother attended the cooking mixture watchfully as it simmered on the kitchen range. With her long-handled wooden spoon, she stirred and tested, stirred and tested, until finally the tangy sweet syrup began to thicken and the slivers of rind became translucent. When the mixture looked "about right," she quickly took a clean metal spoon, dipped it into the boiling marmalade, and held it up to see how the drops of amber jelly fell off the side of the spoon. When the twin drops at the edge of the spoon merged and dropped off the spoon as one, Mother pushed the kettle to the back of the stove.

"It's jelled," she stated.

On the kitchen table, rows of squat, sparkling jelly jars were waiting for their bittersweet contents. Mother ladled the marmalade—a thickened, pale orange, shimmering jelly with slivers of translucent rind suspended in the clear jell—into the jars. Then, from a discarded coffee percolator saved expressly for this purpose, she poured melted paraffin over the top of the marmalade in each jelly jar.

Later, when the thin layer of paraffin had hardened and the marmalade had set, we tied waxed paper over the tops of the jars—and the winter's supply of marmalade was made.

This is the recipe for our orange marmalade:

Orange Marmalade

Juice 1 dozen thin-skinned oranges. Save seeds and tie in muslin bag. Cut the orange rinds as thin as possible. Also, slice 3 lemons, discarding the seeds. Measure the orange juice and add enough water to make 3 quarts. Combine juice, lemons, orange rind and the bag of orange seeds in a large kettle and bring to a boil.

Remove from stove and let stand overnight in a covered crock. On the second day, bring the mixture to a boil again. Discard the seed bag and let stand overnight as before. On the third day, measure the fruit and juice and add an equal amount of sugar. Cook slowly, stirring often, until the rinds become translucent and the mixture reaches the jelly stage (220°F). Pour into jelly glasses and seal while hot with melted paraffin. Cover tops with lids or waxed paper.

Making apple butter in the old cast iron kettle in the backyard was one of the all-day events that came around once during canning season and united the efforts of my grandparents and our family. First, Grandpa and my brothers gathered up dry firewood and piled it in the yard near the soot-blackened kettle that hung from its own tripod over a bed of gray ashes. This was our all-purpose kettle for outdoor cooking—it was used for heating water for butchering, for heating water for washing, for cooking apple butter, for rendering lard, for any large scale cooking project—so it had to be carefully scoured before the apple butter was cooked in it.

Some families used a polished copper kettle for cooking apple butter but we had only the trusty old black iron one. When it was clean, sweet apple cider was poured in— about ten gallons, at first—and a fire was laid and lit beneath the kettle's fat belly. While the cider boiled down, everyone who could be rounded up—my father, the hired girl, Grandpa—set about peeling the russet heap of apples. The smaller children were not permitted to use the sharp knives for peeling, but we made a great mound of peeled apples using the wobbly old apple peeler. Grandmother whisked off the bits of peel we left behind and made sure not one speck or bruise remained on the apples that went into the apple butter kettle.

When the apple cider had boiled down to about half its original volume, the peeled, cored, and quartered apples were stirred in, a few at a time, so that the slow boiling never stopped. All afternoon the apple butter bubbled and sputtered over a slow, even fire carefully tended by Grandpa. The apple butter had to be stirred constantly with a long-handled, hoelike wooden paddle, with holes in the end of it, so that the thickening mixture would not stick to the kettle and scorch.

Stirring was a chore that fell to my brothers and me, with an adult wisely keeping a watchful eye, but the long vigil at the apple butter kettle did not become tiresome because we took turns at the paddle, stirring, stirring, stirring. And there were distractions to keep our interest from lagging—Grandpa told stories and made whistles for us out of elderberry stems; there were new hickory nuts to crack on a certain flat rock in the walk; and Mother helped us carve features into peeled apples to make heads for apple dolls, which would gradually shrivel and become grotesque as they slowly dried.

There was much besides the chill of the first cold snap of autumn to keep us within the cozy circle of warmth around the apple butter kettle. The winey fragrance from the bubbling apple butter alone was enough to hold us close, and it was all mixed up with the faint odor of the wood smoke which sometimes swirled back over us with the vagaries of the wind. Even our hair and clothes smelled of smoke and spice!

Finally the glistening apple butter began to thicken, and Mother brought out the sugar and spices to stir in. Judging how much sugar and how much spice to add was a matter calling for much discussion and tasting and conferring.

"It won't take much sugar," Dad predicted. "We used a lot of sweet apples, along with the Winesaps."

After the first cautious addition of sugar and spices—usually cinnamon, nutmeg, cloves, allspice, and ginger—the apple butter was stirred well and cooked for a few minutes to dissolve the sugar and give the spicy flavors time to develop. Then a dishful of the reddish-brown apple butter was dipped out of the kettle and spoonfuls were offered to everyone who wanted to taste.

Wasn't it rich and spicy! One taste unleashed appetites

that had been held at bay all afternoon. Grandma brought out soda crackers and we dipped into the bowl for sweet spoonfuls to spread on the crisp squares—an unforgettable treat!

"No more ginger!" Grandpa was decisive. He was not fond of ginger.

"I told you it wouldn't need much sugar," Dad commented.

Mother stirred in a little more cinnamon, for this was the spice she favored in apple butter. Sometimes, when she made smaller batches of apple butter inside in the kitchen, she flavored a panful with a package of cinnamon Imperials, those tiny tongue-burning cinnamon candy pellets that we called "red hots." And, when she had stick cinnamon she used it to flavor the cooking apple butter because it darkened the mixture less than ground cinnamon.

"Don't you think it is about done?" Mother would direct Grandma's attention to the round, flat bubbles bursting on the surface of the apple butter with a soft—"llp! llp!"

"Let's see." Grandmother dipped a spoon into the spicy dark butter and placed a mound of it on a saucer. No liquid separated from the russet blend to run out on the saucer.

"Yes," Grandmother nodded. "It's had enough."

Grandpa raked the coals out from under the kettle so that the fire would die and my mother and grandmother dipped the apple butter out of the iron kettle and transferred it to the largest cooking pots we had. The boiling hot apple butter was hurried to the kitchen and placed on the back of the kitchen range to keep it hot while Mother and Grandmother jarred up the pints and quarts and sealed them. By dusk, the kitchen table was crowded with dozens of cooling jars of russet apple butter. Our families would use it all winter long, without stinting, as a sweet spread on hot biscuits, between the layers of spicy fresh apple cake, in pies, and simply spread on buttered bread for an after-school snack.

This recipe was followed, more or less, to make 25

quarts of apple butter in the old iron kettle over an open fire:

Open-Kettle Apple Butter

Bring 10 gallons of sweet apple cider to a boil in a large kettle hung over an open fire. Cook the cider down to about half its original volume. Gradually add 4 bushels of Winesap apples, Turley or Stayman, which have been peeled, cored, and quartered. Stir and cook for about 3 hours before adding sugar and spices. Sweeten with about 5 pounds sugar per bushel of apples. Add spices to taste using about ½ cup spices, all together. Use mostly cinnamon, with less of nutmeg, cloves, ginger, and allspice. Cinnamon sticks can be used (6 to 10) to keep the apple butter lighter in color. Cook for about 1 hour after adding the sugar and spices, or until no liquid separates from a spoonful of the butter when it is placed on a saucer. Makes about 25 quarts.

Mother made apple butter all during the autumn on her kitchen stove. No mere dozen jars, or so—our share of the apple butter cooked in the black kettle over the open fire— would last the Marshalls through the winter. Mother baked smaller batches in the oven and to this apple butter she sometimes added red hots. This is how she made it.

Apple Butter with Red Hots

Make 16 cups applesauce. Stir in 8 cups sugar, ½ cup apple cider vinegar, and 1 package "red hots" (about ½ cup). Bring to a boil on top of the stove, then bake in oven (350°F) for about 2 hours. Stir often. Makes 6 jars.

The sweet cider that added a special tang to our open-kettle apple butter was one of the plentiful commodities on our farm. We had apples by the wagon load from my father's fine orchard.

Early in the autumn, when the spreading apple trees were heavy with fruit, Dad and Grandpa moved the huge cider mill out of the storage shed and placed it near the house so that it could be readied for cider making. It was a heavy, old-style cider mill that stood as tall as my father, and the two men strained to move it about. But, after the cogs and wheels were greased so that they turned easily without binding and squeaking, one man could operate it by himself to make cider.

Then, on the first Indian-summer day late in September—usually on a Sunday afternoon, for making cider was a break in the urgent daily routine of picking and harvesting the hundreds of bushels of apples—Dad would hoist a basketful of apples high above his head, dump them into the hopper of the cider mill, and begin to grind apples to make the pomace from which the apple juice was pressed.

Dad operated the grinder that produced the pomace by turning a handle on the outside of the cider mill. If the hopper was not too full of apples, I could turn it myself, but filled, it was a job for a strong man. Every so often the big apples in the hopper had to be pushed into the grinders with the end of a stick, and the finer the apples were ground, the harder the handle turned.

When the slatted basket beneath the hopper was filled with ground apples, it was removed from the mill and placed under the cider press. To press the apple juice from the pomace, Dad turned the handle of a large jack screw which pressed a wooden disc down on the ground apples with enough pressure to make their juice run out between the slats of the basket into a trough, and out a spout into the tub below the cider press.

Nothing quenches thirst like a hearty draft of fresh cider caught at the spout of the cider press. And when the nectar is drunk while standing under apple trees bearing the very fruit from which the cider was made, with the aroma of sweet crushed fruit in the air all about, the flavor of the cider is truly the essence of apple.

Dad was not modest in acknowledging compliments on his cider.

"Of course it's good!" he would say. "We have plenty of apples so I use the best I have for cider. There are no scrub apples in *my* cider!"

Dad considered cider made of windfalls, imperfect, or rotting apples unfit to drink. Unlike some purists, however, he did not take time to cut and core the apples, to keep crushed seeds from possibly adding a trace of bitterness to the cider, but he did make sure the apples were all perfect, and washed clean.

My brothers and I sorted the apples before they went into the hopper of the cider mill.

"Look those apples over," Dad directed. "I don't want any wormy apples in *my* cider."

Dad did not swear by any particular variety of apple for cider-making, but he usually used a combination of apples. He might send my brothers to the apple shed to haul in the apples.

"Bring in several bushels—Romes, Winesaps, Golden Delicious—whatever comes handy."

Soon after the cider was made and before it began to ferment, both Mother and Grandmother cooked down kettles of the sweet cider until it became a dark, sweet-tart, syrupy liquid. For days the large kettles boiled gently on the back of the kitchen range. It took hours to reduce the cider to the right consistency and the apple-scented steam rising from the kettles carried promises of richly-flavored mincemeat, moist fruitcakes, and Mother's delicious boiled-cider pies.

This was Mother's way of making boiled cider:

Boiled Cider

Boil 5 quarts of sweet cider over a low fire until 1 quart is left. Use granite kettle and watch or it will burn. Seal in glass jars while hot, the same as canned fruit. Will keep until used.

Later, in the winter, when the fresh fruits were gone, we might have boiled cider pie:

Boiled Cider Pie

Mix well 1 cup boiled cider, the beaten yolks of 3 eggs, 1 cup sugar, 1 rounded tablespoonful flour, 1 cup fresh milk. Melt butter, the size of a walnut, and stir in. Last, fold in 3 stiffly-beaten egg whites. Pour into unbaked pie crust. Bake in a hot oven (450°F) for 10 minutes to set the rim, then finish baking in a moderate oven (325°F) for half-hour.

The making of the cider was, in my father's words, "a very simple operation," but the keeping of it presented some problems. We kept as much as we could, for drinking fresh, in the ice box and even suspended a jugful in the well, to keep it cool. But, without refrigeration, especially in the heat of Indian summer, fresh cider could only be held a few days, before fermentation began.

The point of Dad's cider making was not to make hard cider, since very little use was made of alcoholic beverages in our home. But we often ended up with more cider than my mother and grandmother could preserve by canning, or use up in making applebutter and boiled cider. So the extra kegful of cider would be put aside and eventually it would go to vinegar by itself.

One year, after we had made use of all the cider we needed, a left-over barrel of cider was left standing near the house under an apple tree—and all but forgotten. Sometime later, on a day when I stayed home from school alone because of an early-winter cold, I went to the window to see why our dogs were barking so wildly at the north side of the house. And there, visiting the barrel of hard cider, was a well-known tippler from town. I watched, covertly, as he siphoned out a jugful. Then he walked down the road toward town, with a decided spring in his step. When Dad came home from his school that weekend and investigated, he discovered that "Old Tadpole" had been there before—the cider barrel was half empty!

The Sweets

Jellies, jams, preserves, conserves, marmalades, and fruit butters are all fruits preserved with sugar. Most of them are jellied and some contain other ingredients in addition to fruit, juices, and sugar.

Jellies are made of jellied fruit juice and sugar. The ideal jelly has the full flavor of the fruit, a bright, sparkling, clear color, and is jellied enough to hold its shape, yet still be tender. Jelly cuts easily with a spoon but is firm enough to hold the angle of the cut or the shape of the jelly glass when turned out on a plate.

Jams are made of crushed or ground sweetened fruit and their juices, which have been cooked to a thick mass that is firm and jellied but less solid than jelly. Jams are not as sweet as preserves.

Preserves are made from whole fruits or large pieces of fruit cooked in a thick rich syrup of juices and sugar, which becomes slightly jellied. Preserves are sweeter than jams or jellies.

Conserves are jams made of several fruits, sometimes including citrus fruits, raisins, and nuts. They are as sweet as jams.

Marmalades are tender jellied jams made from slices or strips of fruits, often citrus fruits, and sugar. Marmalades are a variation of preserves and they are sweeter than jams.

Fruit butters are made from fruit puree and sugar cooked slowly together, sometimes with spices, to the consistency of a thick paste that can be spread. Butters are less sweet than jams or marmalades. One-half to two-thirds as much sugar as fruit puree is used for making fruit butters.

EQUIPMENT FOR MAKING JELLY

Most of the equipment needed for making jellies, jams, preserves, and other jellied products can be found among everyday kitchen utensils. A few pieces of special equipment that one might not already have on hand are essential.

A large, heavy kettle, 8- to 10-quart capacity, with a broad flat bottom and high sides, is necessary so that a jelly mixture can come to a full rolling boil without boiling over the sides. The kettle should have a lid to use for other preserving cookery. It should be of heavyweight metal because many sweet fruit mixtures stick easily and require long, slow cooking. When cooking down preserves or relishes, remember that the contents in a wide mouth kettle will be reduced more in a specified time than those cooked in a narrow mouthed kettle. If your jelly-making kettle is not heavy, you may need to use an asbestos pad or a metal coil between the stove burner and the bottom of the kettle. A good kettle is made of enameled cast iron. Heavy aluminum or stainless steel may be used, as well. Enamelware or graniteware kettles are easy to find in the right size and are inexpensive, but they are rather lightweight and thick substances cooked in them stick easily.

A jelly bag or an arrangement made of a colander lined with cotton flannelette, loosely woven muslin, or several layers of cheesecloth is needed to strain the fruit juice. The jelly bag or cloth should be dipped into hot water and squeezed out before straining juice through it.

A supply of paraffin and a melting pot are necessary. A double boiler delegated to that purpose is ideal, but a tin cup set in a pan of water will do as well. Paraffin is flammable and must not be heated on or exposed to direct flame.

114

A thermometer, either jelly, candy, or deep fat, is helpful in taking away the guesswork when cooking jelly without added pectin.

A clock with a second hand is necessary for accurate timing.

Jelly glasses, of course, are essential. However, jellies can be stored in glass containers other than regular jelly glasses, if wanted, because jelly does not have to be processed any further after cooking. The only requirement is that the glass be heavy enough to withstand the boiling-hot temperature of the jelly when it is poured in; fragile decorative glasses might break. It is also desirable that the jar have straight sides and no shoulder so that the paraffin used to seal the jar can be easily removed and the jelly turned out for serving. Canning jars with self-sealing lids are best if the jelly is to be stored where the temperature fluctuates from hot to cold because paraffin seals tend to loosen under such conditions.

The rest of the essential jelly-making equipment will probably be found in any well-equipped kitchen. Such equipment includes paring knives, a swivel-bladed parer, a coring knife, a food chopper, a potato masher, a long-handled spoon or skimmer, a ladle, a large bowl, an extra saucepan, measuring spoons and cups including a quart measure, a household scale, and a kettle and rack for sterilizing glasses.

Helpful but not absolutely essential are a cherry pitter, strawberry huller, juice reamer, fruit press, jelmeter, and grater.

MAKING SURE THE JELLY WILL JELL

Any fruit can be jellied if fruit acid, sugar, and pectin are present in the correct proportions.

Countless successful recipes using the standard proportions have been worked out for every fruit. Any imaginable jellied combination is possible, it seems. If one is using commercial pectin, there are more recipes in the folders that accompany the product than one could possibly use. Dozens of good recipes are included in every general cookbook. Every family has its own favorites as well as heirloom recipes that are used year after year.

Still, the jelly maker sometimes comes up with a combination of ingredients or an amount of juice that seems not to fit any recipe on hand. Or there is a recipe that somehow does not sound reliable as it is read. Or there is a substitution one wishes to make, if possible. For these times, it is good to understand what makes jelly "jell" so that a recipe can be made to fit the ingredients that are available, or so that an unfamiliar recipe can be analyzed and judged as to its probable success before the expensive ingredients are risked.

Here are some pointers and useful facts:

- A rule of thumb is that the proportion for acid and pectin in a jelly is usually 1 tablespoon of commercial powdered pectin and 1 tablespoon lemon juice for every cup of extracted fruit juice.
- When no extra pectin is being added, the amount of natural pectin in a fruit mixture determines the amount of sugar needed in a jelly. The more natural pectin there is in the mixture, the less sugar is needed. The usual ratio is ¾ cup sugar to 1 cup extracted juice with high pectin content, or 1 cup sugar to 1 cup extracted juice with average pectin content.
- Four cups of juice and 3 cups of sugar will make approximately 1½ pints of jelly.
- Powdered pectin does not dissolve readily in sweetened juices, so add the sugar after the fruit juice–pectin mixture has been brought to a boil and the pectin is dissolved.

WHY IS ACID NEEDED IN JELLY MAKING?

Acid is needed for gel formation and for adding flavor to insipid juices. It is the acid in the fruit juice that gives it the tartness of flavor. Fruit is usually acid enough for jelly making if it tastes as tart as sour apples, or compares with the flavor of a mixture of 1 teaspoon lemon juice, ½ teaspoon sugar, and 3 tablespoons water.

Fruits that are high in pectin are usually high in acid.

The amount of acid in fruit varies with the fruit. Underripe fruits usually are more acid than overripe fruits.

When fruits do not contain enough acid to make a good tasting jelly, or to jell well, lemon juice is usually added to the recipe. One tablespoon of lemon juice per cup of fruit is usually enough. One-eighth teaspoon of crystalline citric acid may be successfully substituted for each tablespoon of lemon juice called for in a recipe.

Another way of adding more acid to the fruit juice for making jelly is to combine a low-acid fruit with an acid fruit.

There is also some acid in commercial fruit pectins, which may be added to fruit for jelling. Pectin-poor fruits are usually low in acid as well.

THE ROLE OF SUGAR IN JELLY MAKING

Sugar gives flavor to jellied products and helps to preserve them. It also aids in gel formation by acting as the agent for precipitating the pectin in the liquid and it gives firmness to the jellied fruit.

Either cane or beet sugar may be used in jelly making. Jelly can be made with sugar concentrations of 40 to 70 percent of the finished product but the best texture and keeping qualities are obtained when 60 to 65 percent of sugar is used. Jelly made with a low concentration of sugar will be tough and high-sugar jelly will crystallize more readily.

Light corn syrup and light, mild-flavored honey can be used to replace part of the sugar in certain jelly recipes. If you are interested in substituting, here are the guidelines:

In jelly recipes with no added pectin, light corn syrup can replace up to one-fourth of the sugar, or honey can replace up to one-half of the sugar.

117

In jelly recipes using powdered pectin, light corn syrup can replace up to one-half of the sugar, or honey can replace up to 2 cups of the sugar.

In jelly recipes using liquid pectin, light corn syrup can replace up to 2 cups of the sugar, or honey can replace up to 2 cups of the sugar.

JELLIES MADE WITH HONEY

Honey can be substituted for up to one-half of the sugar in regular jelly recipes without the flavor of the honey becoming more pronounced than the fruit flavor.

In recipes where only honey is used for sweetening, it is possible for the jelly to be a honey-jelly with wine or herbs or flavorings added to compliment the honey flavor.

PECTIN

Pectin is a natural substance found in all fruits in varying amounts. When the proportion of pectin in a fruit juice is in the right balance with the sugar and acid in the recipe, the mixture can be jellied without the addition of other ingredients.

The juices of these fruits usually contain enough pectin and acid to make good jelly: tart apples, tart blackberries, crab apples, cranberries, currants, gooseberries, sour plums, quince, Concord grapes, and underripe raspberries.

The juices of these fruits usually lack either the amount or quality of pectin and/or acid: sweet apples, apricots, cherries, strawberries, pears, peaches, figs, elderberries, huckleberries, and blueberries.

To make up for the pectin deficiency in fruit juices so that jelly can be made, additional pectin should be added. Additional acid is usually needed when pectin is lacking, as well.

Commercial pectin, in liquid or powder form, is often added to pectin-poor fruit juices to ensure jelling. Homemade pectin can be easily extracted from other fruits, usually apple pomace or citrus albedo, and added to the juice. Or, the pectin-poor fruit may be combined with a pectin-rich fruit to obtain a good gel.

TESTING FRUIT JUICES FOR PECTIN CONTENT

The handiest way to test juice for pectin content is with a jelmeter, a calibrated glass tube which can be bought through mail order catalogues from companies handling canning equipment or from well-stocked hardware and housewares stores. The jelmeter is filled with extracted cooked fruit juice at room temperature; the juice is allowed to strain through the tube for 1 minute. The speed with which the juice flows indicates the pectin content. The amount of sugar to be added per cup of juice is figured according to the pectin content.

If you do not have a jelmeter, you can cook ¼ cup of juice with 2½ tablespoons sugar to see how well it jells.

Another way is to add 1 teaspoon of cooked fruit juice to 1 tablespoon of rubbing alcohol with 70 percent alcoholic content (poisonous isopropyl alcohol). If there is plenty of pectin in the juice to make jelly, within a minute the mixture forms a gelatinous mass that can be picked up with a fork. If the pectin content is low, the mixture will thicken only slightly. *Discard the mixture. Do not taste.*

If the test indicates a low pectin content in the juice, you may add commercial pectin to the fruit juice and test it again to see if you have added enough to make jelly.

To Retest: Add 1 tablespoon of liquid commercial pectin to each cup of extracted cooked juice to be used to make jelly. *In a separate bowl*, test the juice again, as before. Use 1 teaspoon of the juice with the additional pectin added and 1 tablespoon of rubbing alcohol. Mix together and let the mixture stand for 1 minute. *Do not taste. Discard this mixture* after testing, also.

Continue to add liquid pectin to the fruit juice and repeat to test in a separate bowl until the juice forms a gelatinous mass if you want a high-pectin content, or a mixture with large broken flakes of gelatin if you want a mixture of average pectin content. Each can be jellied when cooked with the proper amount of sugar. See page 117.

Add ¾ cup sugar to 1 cup extracted juice with high pectin; add 1 cup sugar to 1 cup extracted juice with average pectin.

When you have determined how much commercial liquid pectin must be added to a cup of the fruit juice to make it jell, you can calculate how much you need to add to the whole recipe. For example, if you added 2 tablespoons of commercial liquid pectin to 1 cup of cooked extracted juice before the sample would jell, you will need to add 2 tablespoons of the pectin to each cup of juice called for in the recipe. If the recipe calls for 4 cups of extracted juice, you will need to add 8 tablespoons of commercial liquid pectin.

If the test indicated that the extracted fruit juice was low in pectin and you do not wish to add commercial liquid pectin, you can combine the pectin-poor fruit with a pectin-rich fruit and test the juices for jelling.

Or, you may make your own pectin extract from underripe apples or from the white membrane inside the skin of oranges, and add it to the pectin-poor fruit juice. The recipe for apple stock is on page 130.

MAKING JELLY WITHOUT ADDED PECTIN

Less sugar per cup of prepared fruit juice is used when only the natural pectin in the fruit is used to make jelly than when commercial pectin is added. There is less volume of jelly when natural pectin is used than is yielded by recipes using commercial pectin. The cooking time required for natural jelling is longer than when commercial pectin is added.

Underripe fruit in the ratio of 1 part underripe fruit to 3 parts fully ripe fruit should be used when making jelly without added pectin.

If the fruit is not acid, add 1 tablespoon lemon juice per cup of extracted juice.

Juices with low pectin content require less sugar than fruit with high pectin content. (See page 116.)

If you are depending on the natural pectin for gel formation, you should test the extracted juice according to the test given in the preceding section, to determine the pectin content. Not only the ripeness of the fruit affects the pectin content, but also the climatic conditions, so juice that jelled with success one year may not be as successful for you at another time.

MAKING JELLY WITH ADDED PECTIN

When commercial pectin, powdered or liquid, is added to extracted fruit juice to make jelly, the cooking time required is shorter than that of jelly made with only the natural pectin in the fruit, and because of a high sugar content, the yield of jelly is much higher. The directions that accompany the commercial pectin should be followed exactly.

Do not substitute powdered pectin for liquid pectin called for in any of the recipes in this book, or vice versa. The difference lies in the order in which the ingredients are combined. Powdered pectin is added at the beginning of the procedure, before the juice is heated and before the sugar is added. Liquid pectin is added to the boiling juice and sugar mixture.

If you wish to use powdered pectin where liquid is called for, you may convert your powdered pectin to liquid pectin by mixing 1 package of powdered pectin with ½ cup water and boiling for 1 minute. Pour into a measuring cup and add enough water to make 1 cup. Use as you would use liquid pectin.

If you are inventing a jelly recipe, you usually need about 1 tablespoon powdered pectin per cup of prepared fruit.

A 1¾-ounce box of powdered fruit pectin contains 6 tablespoons plus 1 teaspoon (level measurements) of fruit pectin.

EXTRACTING JUICE FROM FRUITS

It is usually necessary to heat fruit to extract the juice and the pectin from it. Juice from raw fruit will seldom produce jelly. Heating the fruit converts the substance protopectin, which is found in raw fruits, to pectin. If the juice is extracted from raw fruit, the protopectin stays in the fruit pulp because it is not soluble in the juice unless heated. The exception to this rule is juicy berries, which may be crushed and the juice pressed out without heating.

A minimum of water is used with most fruits so that the pectin will not be unnecessarily dilute in the juice. Long boiling of fruits to extract juices must be avoided, too, because jellying power will be decreased by prolonged heating at high temperatures. The best results are obtained when the fruits are heated at 175° to 190°F and simmered for as short a time as possible depending upon the fruit used.

Hard fruits, such as crab apples, quinces, and apples, should be ground up or cut into small pieces so that the juices will be readily available and cooking time for juice extraction will be reduced. Soft fruits should be crushed.

Skins and cores contain a large amount of pectin so fruits being simmered to extract juice are usually not peeled or cored. In fact, the peelings and cores of apples alone can be used to make a pectin extract.

PROCEDURE FOR EXTRACTING THE JUICE FROM FRUITS FOR JELLY

Choose fruits that are firm and just ripe. Do not use moldy or overripe fruit. Include some underripe fruits, in the ratio of 1 part underripe fruit to 3 parts ripe fruit.

Wash fruits thoroughly and drain. Remove stems and cut out blemishes. Do not peel. Cut hard fruits into small pieces or grind, using the coarse blade of the food grinder. Crush soft fruits. Place prepared fruit in a pan with the correct amount of water (see chart page 123). Place pan on medium heat, cover, and bring the fruits to boiling, stirring often then simmer until the fruit is soft and the juices flowing. Do not boil hard and do not cook any longer than is necessary.

Place the simmered fruit in a dampened jelly bag and allow the juices to drip—without pressing, for the clearest jelly—for several hours or overnight.

EXTRACTING JUICE FOR JELLY

Kind of Fruit	Amount of Water to Add to Each Pound of Prepared Fruit	Bring to Boiling, Then Simmer in Covered Kettle to Extract Juice for
Apples		
Crab Apples	1 cup	20 to 25 minutes
Blackberries		
Firm	¼ cup	
Soft	None	0 to 5 minutes
Cranberries	3 cups	5 to 10 minutes
Currants	¼ cup or none	5 to 10 minutes
Gooseberries	¼ cup	5 to 10 minutes
Grapes		
Concord	¼ cup or none	5 to 10 minutes
Wild (before frost)	1 cup	5 to 10 minutes
Plums, wild goose	½ cup	15 to 20 minutes
Quinces	2 cups	20 to 25 minutes
Raspberries, red and black	none	0 to 5 minutes

MORE POINTERS

A colander lined with dampened cheesecloth, or cotton flannelette, may be placed over a deep bowl if a jelly bag is not available. Flannelette, cheesecloth, and loose-woven cotton muslin are all suitable fabrics for straining juices. The jelly bag or straining cloth should be dipped in hot water and wrung out before straining juice through it.

A greater amount of juice, but cloudy jelly, is obtained by twisting the bag of fruit tightly and squeezing it until no more juice can be extracted. A good compromise is to save the clear juice that dripped without squeezing the jelly bag for one batch of jelly, and use the additional juice squeezed from the pulp after the clear juice was extracted for the second batch of jelly.

If the juice is pressed out of the fruit, either by hand, with a fruit press, or through a colander, it should be clarified by re-straining through a clean jelly bag, a clean cloth, paper filters (coffee filters will do), or paper toweling. Wet the cloth or filters before using them for straining.

Measure the juice needed for one batch of jelly and proceed promptly with the jelly making, or can or freeze the juice to make jelly later. Do not double jelly recipes. You may cut down a jelly recipe with success, but increasing it may give poor results. For best results, never make jelly with more than 4 cups of juice at a time.

WHEN DOES JELLY JELL?

The jelly stage is reached at 8°F above the temperature at which water boils at your altitude on that day as registered on a jelly, candy, or deep-fat thermometer, or when two drops of jelly that run off the edge of a metal spoon slide together and sheet off the spoon in one drop.

Sheeting test to indicate jellying point

The easiest way to tell when you have cooked the jelly long enough is to use an accurate thermometer. The jelly stage may be marked on a sugar thermometer at 220°F, but your altitude and atmospheric conditions can raise or lower the temperature at which the jelly stage is reached. To cancel the chance of unusual conditions interfering with the success of your jelly, test the temperature at which water boils, where you are, before cooking the jelly, and add 8°F to that figure. That temperature is the one to which you should cook your jelly, that day, to achieve a satisfactory jell.

If you trust your eye, you can depend on the sheeting test. Dip a clean, cool, dry metal spoon into the boiling jelly and hold it above the pan. Tilt the spoon and watch the jelly run off the side. If it falls off in two separate drops, the jelly stage has not been reached. Let the jelly cook a bit more, then dip another clean, dry spoon into the jelly. When the two drops of jelly merge and sheet off the side of the tilted spoon as one drop, the jellying point is reached.

If you are a bit unsure at this point as to whether you have the jellying point, you can do a quick "make sure" test. Remove the jelly from the heat. Place a spoonful of the jelly that you think has reached the jellying point on a chilled saucer. Slip the saucer into the freezing compartment of the refrigerator for a minute. You will be able to tell, almost at once, if the jellying stage has been reached.

IF YOUR JELLY DOES NOT JELL

Jelly that does not jell can be recooked with additional pectin added. The quality of recooked jelly will be slightly inferior to that of jelly that is successful the first time around, but you *may* salvage expensive ingredients and come out with a product closer to the ideal. (If it doesn't work, use it for syrup or ham glaze.)

RECOOKING UNJELLIED JELLY

For every quart of jelly, measure ¼ cup sugar, ¼ cup water, and 4 teaspoons powdered pectin. Combine the pectin and water and bring to a boil, stirring constantly. Stir in the sugar and unjellied jelly. Stir well and bring to a full rolling boil over high heat, stirring constantly. Boil mixture hard for ½ minute. Test for jelling stage. Remove from heat, skim, and pour into hot sterilized glasses, and seal.

The addition of lemon juice along with the above ingredients may be necessary if the unjellied jelly was made of fruit that contained too little acid. Then add 2 tablespoons lemon juice for every quart of jelly.

CAUSES OF JELLY FAILURES

Soft Jelly
- Using more sugar than the pectin content of the fruit juice required.
- Not boiling the jelly long enough after adding the sugar.

Tough Jelly
- Using less sugar than the pectin content of the fruit required.
- Overcooking the jelly.

Crystals in Jelly
- Using too much sugar.
- Boiling too long before adding sugar to the juice so that the two were not boiled together long enough.
- In grape jelly—the tartaric acid present in all grape juice was not allowed to crystallize overnight in the refrigerator and removed before cooking the juice into jelly.

Cloudy Jelly
- Overcooking the fruit when extracting the juice.
- Not straining the extracted fruit juice carefully enough.
- In apple and crab apple jelly—because of the natural starch present, particularly in underripe apples.

SEALING JELLY

Jelly must have an airtight seal so that molds cannot form on it. It was formerly thought that a little mold on the top of jelly was not harmful but it is now recommended that the full glass of jelly be discarded if mold has begun to grow on top.

Paraffin makes a safe and satisfactory seal for jelly if it is stored for a few months in a cool, dry, dark place. If your climate is hot or if the temperature in the storage area goes from warm to cold, the paraffin may loosen and a syrupy juice will seep out around the edge of the paraffin. If this happens, mold may form under the paraffin and the jelly should be thrown away.

If you want to keep the jelly under less than favorable storage conditions, or for a period longer than a few months, put the jelly in regular canning jars and seal it with a self-sealing lid and screw band closure. If the jelly is boiling hot when it is poured into hot glasses, a vacuum seal will form.

Jelly glasses should be sterilized before pouring jelly into them.

SEALING JELLY IN JELLY GLASSES WITH A PARAFFIN SEAL

Skim jelly and pour it while boiling hot into hot sterilized jelly glasses to within ½ inch of the top of the jar. Cover the hot jelly quickly with a thin layer of hot paraffin, about ⅛ inch thick. Make sure the paraffin extends over the entire surface of the jelly and touches all sides of the jar. Rotate the jar slightly to make sure the wax touches the glass at the edges. Let the glasses stand, undisturbed, until the paraffin hardens and the jelly cools. Prick any bubbles that form on the surface. Place jelly caps on the cleaned jars and store the jelly in a cool, dark, dry place.

SEALING JELLY IN CANNING JARS WITH A VACUUM SEAL

Skim cooked jelly and ladle while boiling hot into a sterilized canning jar, leaving ⅛-inch head space. Wipe the rim of the jar with a clean, damp cloth. Put a hot sterilized self-sealing lid on the jar with the sealing compound next to the rim. Hold the lid in place and screw the band down tight by hand.

As an optional additional step, to sterilize the lid and reduce the chance for mold formation, hold the hot jar with a hot pad, turn it upside down for a few seconds so that the hot liquid jelly coats the inside of the self-sealing lid. Do this as soon as the lid and screw band are in place.

Place the jar upright on a folded cloth away from drafts to cool for 12 to 24 hours. Test for seal. Remove screw band, wipe jar clean, and store in a cool, dry, dark place.

SPECIAL POINTERS FOR MAKING GRAPE JELLY

Wash, stem, and crush the grapes. Put the grapes in a heavy kettle and crush them with a potato masher to start the flow of juice. Do not add water unless necessary, then add only a small amount, up to ¼ cup per pound of grapes except in the case of wild grapes (see page 123). Place on low heat and slowly bring almost to the boiling point (190°F), then reduce the heat and simmer the grapes for 10 minutes, or until grapes are soft. Heat for the shortest time possible for the best flavor and pectin content. Stir frequently.

Place the simmered fruit in a jelly bag and strain the juice. Place the strained juice in the refrigerator and let it stand overnight to allow the tartaric acid crystals to precipitate. If this is not done, white crystals will form in grape jelly.

The next morning, ladle the juice out of the container, leaving the sediment in the bottom. Measure the juice and proceed at once to make jelly according to the recipe you have chosen to follow.

Grapes usually require ¾ cup sugar to each cup of juice when making jelly without added pectin. You should have at least 4 cups of juice if you start with 3 pounds of grapes.

Do not throw away the pomace (pulp) that is left in the jelly bag after the juice has been extracted from the cooked grapes. It is quite sweet and flavorful and contains enough moisture and pulp to make a puree that can be used as the basis of catsup or grape butter, or in desserts, such as Grape Bavarian.

Grapes are very perishable and should be made into juice or used as soon as possible after picking, or refrigerated in the interim. The most popular American variety for jelly making is the Concord.

Spiced Grape Jelly with Cinnamon and Clove

Wash and stem about 3 pounds of ripe Concord grapes. Crush the grapes in a large heavy kettle. Add ½ cup cider vinegar, one 4-inch stick of cinnamon, and 1 teaspoon whole cloves. Bring the grapes to a boil on medium heat, then simmer 10 to 15 minutes until the grapes are tender.

Turn the spiced cooked grapes into a jelly bag and allow the juices to drip. Let juice stand in the refrigerator overnight. The next morning, measure out 4 cups of grape juice, being careful not to disturb the sediment in the bottom of the container.

In a large jelly kettle, combine the 4 cups of extracted grape juice with 7 cups of sugar. Place over high heat and bring to a boil, stirring to mix the sugar with the juice as the mixture is reaching the boiling point. As soon as the mixture boils, stir in ½ bottle liquid fruit pectin. Bring to a full rolling boil, stirring constantly, and boil hard one minute. Remove jelly from the heat, skim, and pour quickly into hot sterilized jelly glasses. Seal at once with ⅛ inch hot paraffin. Makes about 6 glasses of jelly.

Spiced Grape Jelly with Cardamon Seed

Options:1. Make as for Spiced Grape Jelly with Cinnamon and Clove, but omit the cinnamon and clove and substitute 6 crushed cardamon seeds.

2. If less sharpness of flavor is wanted, omit the vinegar when extracting the juice and use ½ cup water instead.
3. For a delicate flavor, make the extracted fruit juice of white Concord grapes and cardamon seeds. Omit vinegar and substitute ½ cup water instead.

Spiced Apple, Crab Apple, Currant, or Quince Jelly

Extract the juice from the fruit to be used and follow the directions for making Spiced Grape Jelly with Cardamon, or Spiced Grape Jelly With Cinnamon and Clove.

No-Cook Grape Jelly

To 2 gallons of Concord grapes removed from their stems, add 3 cups water. Mash the grapes and cook until soft, or about 15 minutes on low heat. Strain the grape juice and measure 6 cups of juice. Heat to boiling, but do not boil. Add 9 cups sugar and stir until dissolved while heating, but do not let the mixture boil. After the sugar has dissolved and the juice has heated, pour into hot sterilized jars. Let stand overnight. The jelly may not set immediately but should within 24 hours. The next day, seal with a layer of paraffin.

Mother's Blackberry–Red Plum Jelly

Extract the juice from the blackberries and red plums separately, following the directions on page 123.

In a preserving kettle, combine the blackberry juice and tart red plum juice in equal proportions, using no more than 3 or 4 cups of juice at a time. Test the combined fruit juices to determine the amount of sugar needed, usually 1 cup of sugar to each 1 cup of combined fruit juice. Bring to a boil over high heat and boil rapidly until the jelly stage is reached. Pour the boiling hot jelly into hot sterilized jelly glasses and seal with paraffin or self-sealing lids.

Apple Pectin (Jelly Stock)

Wash apples, trim carefully, and cut pieces into thin slices. Green apples and imperfect but sound fruit may be used, although green apples will not produce as clear jelly as mature fruit. Measure 1 pint of water for every 1 pound of trimmed fruit. Bring to a boil in a covered kettle and boil for 25 minutes on medium heat, stirring occasionally. Strain the juice through a colander lined with cheesecloth. Do not squeeze the pulp. Pour the hot (at least 190°F), free-running juice into hot sterilized jars. Adjust lids. Process in a simmering water bath for 10 minutes.

To freeze the jelly stock, let the juice cool and pour it into freezer containers, leaving 1-inch head space, and freeze at 0°F.

Apple Jelly

Test the apple pectin to determine the amount of sugar required (see pages 116 and 119). Combine 4 cups of strained apple pectin (jelly stock) with 3 to 4 cups sugar. Bring to a boil and boil rapidly until the jelly stage is reached, stirring constantly. Pour hot jelly into hot sterilized jelly glasses and seal.

Honey-Grape Jelly with Homemade Pectin

Combine 2½ cups unsweetened grape juice, ½ cup mild-flavored honey, 3½ cups sugar, and 2 cups homemade apple pectin (jelly stock). Bring the mixture to a boil, stirring constantly, and boil hard for about 10 minutes, or until the jelly stage is reached. Pour the boiling-hot jelly into hot sterilized jelly glasses and seal with paraffin or self-sealing lids.

Wild Chokecherry Jelly with Homemade Pectin

Cook bright red chokecherries with enough water to cover until the fruit is soft. Strain through a jelly bag. Combine 1 cup chokecherry juice, 3 cups homemade apple pectin (jelly stock), and 3¼ cups sugar. (Test for pectin to determine the amount of sugar to use—see pages 116 and 119.) Bring the mixture to a boil, stirring constantly, and boil hard until the jelly stage is reached. Pour the boiling-hot jelly into hot sterilized jelly glasses and seal with paraffin or self-sealing lids.

Spiced Crab Apple Jelly

Simmer 8 cups cut or ground crab apples with water to cover for 20 minutes. Strain the juice through a jelly bag or several layers of cheesecloth.

In a large kettle, combine 4 cups crab apple juice, ½ cup vinegar, and two 4-inch sticks of cinnamon. Add 2 cardamon seeds and 12 whole cloves, tied in a bag. Bring the mixture to a boil, then simmer for about 5 minutes to extract the flavor of the spices. Remove the spices. To the crab apple juice, add 5½ cups sugar and stir. Bring to a boil, stirring constantly. Add ½ bottle liquid fruit pectin while stirring, then bring the mixture to a full rolling boil and boil until the jelly stage is reached. Remove the kettle from the heat, skim, and pour jelly into hot, sterilized jelly glasses. Cover with a thin layer of paraffin or seal with self-sealing lids. Fills seven 8-ounce jelly glasses.

Crab Apple Jelly

To make plain, unspiced crab apple jelly, follow the recipe for Spiced Crab Apple Jelly, but leave out the spices.

Wild crab apples or crab apples from ornamental crab apple trees may be used for this recipe and the above recipe.

Herb Jelly

To prepare about 2 cups herb infusion, place ¼ cup dried herbs or 1½ cups fresh, bruised herb leaves (use sage, mint, thyme, tarragon, marjoram, or any combination). In an earthenware teapot pour 2¼ cups boiling water over the herbs, cover, and place over low heat (protect pot by placing an asbestos pad or a metal coil over burner). Steep for 30 minutes and strain.

Place 1¾ cups of the herb infusion in a large saucepan. Add ¼ cup vinegar, 1 tablespoon lemon juice, and 3½ cups sugar. Place over high heat and bring to a full rolling boil, stirring constantly. At once stir in ½ bottle liquid fruit pectin. Bring to a boil and boil hard for 1 minute more, or until the jelly stage is reached. Remove from heat, skim, and pour into hot sterilized glasses. Cover with a layer of hot paraffin or seal with self-sealing lids. Makes about five 8-ounce jars.

Sweet-Wine Jelly

In the top of a double boiler, combine 2 cups sweet wine, any flavor, and 3 cups sugar. Stir and heat until the wine and sugar are thoroughly heated. Mix ½ bottle liquid fruit pectin into the wine and sugar mixture, adding it all at once. Pour into sterilized jelly glasses and seal with a thin layer of paraffin. Fills about 5 small jelly glasses.

Golden Dandelion Jelly

Pick 1 quart of bright, fresh, dandelion blossoms. Rinse them quickly in cold water to remove any insects. Using the kitchen scissors, snip off the stem and green collar under each blossom.

In an enameled saucepan, boil the dandelion petals in 2 quarts of water for 3 minutes. Cool and strain, pressing the petals with the fingers to extract all the juice. Measure out 3 cups of the dandelion liquid. Add 2 tablespoons lemon juice and 1 package of powdered fruit pectin (1¾ ounces). Pour the mixture into a large jelly kettle and bring to a boil. Add 5½ cups of sugar, stirring to mix well. Continue stirring and boil the mixture for 2½ minutes. Pour into small glasses and cover with melted paraffin when the jelly is cool.

Elderflower-Gooseberry Jelly

Place 4 cups topped and tailed gooseberries in a heavy kettle with 4½ cups water. Cover and bring to a boil. Reduce heat and boil gently for 10 minutes, then mash berries and boil for another 5 minutes. Let the juice drain overnight through several layers of cheesecloth.

Combine 4 cups gooseberry juice, 1 box powdered fruit pectin (1¾ ounces), and a bag containing the blossoms of 1 large cluster of elderberry blossoms with no stems attached. Bring the mixture to a boil in a large kettle, stir in 5½ cups sugar, and bring back to a rolling boil while stirring constantly. Boil hard for one minute. Pour into 7 jelly glasses. Put elderflowers in the bottom of each jar, if desired, but do not include any stems. Cover the hot jelly with ⅛ inch hot paraffin. Makes 6 jelly glasses of jelly.

Mint-Honey Jelly

Pour 1¼ cups boiling water over ½ cup fresh chopped mint leaves. Cover tightly and let steep on an asbestos pad over the lowest heat for half an hour. Strain and discard the mint leaves.

In a jelly kettle, combine 1 cup of the mint extract, 3 tablespoons powdered fruit pectin, 2 tablespoons lemon juice, and a few drops of green food coloring. Bring to a boil over high heat, then stir in 2 cups of light-colored, mild-flavored honey. Bring to a full rolling boil, stirring constantly, and boil hard for 2½ minutes, or until the jelly stage is reached.

Remove jelly from the heat, skim, and pour at once into hot sterilized jelly glasses. Place a mint leaf in the bottom of each jelly glass, if desired. Seal at once with ⅛ inch of hot paraffin or self-sealing lids. Makes about 3 glasses of jelly.

Hot-Pepper Jelly

Prepare ¼ cup ground hot red peppers (dried) and 1½ cups ground sweet green bell peppers. Combine ground peppers with 6½ cups sugar and 1½ cups cider vinegar. Bring the mixture to a full boil and boil for 3 minutes. Remove from the heat and strain off the liquid, discarding the ground peppers. Return the liquid to the kettle and again bring to a boil. Stir in 1 bottle liquid fruit pectin and continue boiling, while stirring, for 1 minute or until the jelly stage is reached. Remove from the heat and add several drops of green food coloring if desired. Pour into hot sterilized jars and seal with paraffin or self-sealing lids. Makes 3 pints.

Green-Hot-Pepper Jelly

Follow the recipe for Hot-Pepper Jelly, substituting ground hot green peppers for the hot red peppers. Wear household gloves while preparing the peppers, and do not touch your eyes after touching the hot peppers.

Jalapeno Jelly

Follow the recipe for Hot-Pepper Jelly, using ¼ cup ground jalapeno peppers instead of hot red peppers. To remove the seeds from jalapenos, cut off stem ends, and hold under cold running water to wash away the seeds. Wear household gloves. If wanted, bits of jalapeno pepper can be left in the jelly instead of straining all the peppers out. Serve hot-pepper jellies with dark meats and wild game, or with omelets or English muffins.

Firm Red-Cherry Jam 1970

Wash and pit sour red cherries. In a large kettle, combine 4 cups pitted cherries and 1 box powdered fruit pectin (1¾ ounces) plus 3 tablespoons powdered fruit pectin in addition. Stir the mixture over high heat until it comes to a hard boil. Stir in 4½ cups sugar and bring again to a full rolling boil, stirring constantly, and boil for 2 minutes. Remove from the heat, and stir and skim for several minutes. Pour into hot sterilized half-pint jars. Adjust lids and process in a boiling-water bath for 10 minutes.

Blackberry Jam with Orange

Cook 6 cups blackberries with ½ cup water until well heated. Put half the berries through a sieve or a food mill to remove part of the seeds. Combine the blackberries with ¾ cup orange juice, 3 tablespoons lemon juice, 1 tablespoon grated orange peel, and 1 package (1¾ ounces) powdered fruit pectin. Stir over high heat until the mixture comes to a hard boil. Stir in 7 cups sugar and bring to a full rolling boil, stirring constantly, and boil hard for 1 minute. Remove from heat, and stir and skim for several minutes, and pour into hot sterilized half-pint jars. Adjust lids and process in a boiling-water bath for 10 minutes.

Black Raspberry Jam with Orange

Follow the recipe for Blackberry Jam with Orange substituting black raspberries for the blackberries, but put all the berries through a sieve if seeds are objectionable.

Good Strawberry Jam 1956

Clean and hull 2 quarts ripe strawberries. Crush most of the berries. Mix 4½ cups of the berries with 1 box (1¾ ounces) plus 2 tablespoons powdered fruit pectin. Bring to a hard boil, stirring constantly, then add 7 cups sugar. Stir and bring to a rolling boil, and boil hard for 2 minutes. Pour into hot sterilized jars and adjust lids. Process in a boiling-water bath for 10 minutes. Makes a rather firm jam.

Frozen-Fruit Strawberry Jam

Thaw two 12-ounce boxes of frozen sweetened strawberries. Add ⅓ cup water and 4 tablespoons powdered fruit pectin. Place over high heat and stir until mixture comes to a hard boil. Add 2½ cups sugar and stir. Bring the mixture to a full rolling boil, stirring constantly, and boil hard for 1 minute. Remove from the heat, stir and skim for 5 minutes. Pour into hot jars and adjust lids. Process in a boiling-water bath for 10 minutes.

Uncooked Strawberry Jam From Frozen Strawberries

Thaw 1 quart of frozen, sliced strawberries, which were frozen with 1 cup sugar, until they are icy. Mash the berries thoroughly. There should be about 2¾ cups of strawberry pulp. Add 5 cups of sugar to the mashed strawberries and stir gently. Let stand for 10 minutes. Combine 4 tablespoons lemon juice and 1 bottle of liquid fruit pectin (Certo, 6 fluid ounces) and add to the fruit mixture. Stir for 3 minutes. Ladle the jam into sterilized freeze-or-can jars. Let stand at room temperature for several hours, until set. Store the jam in the refrigerator until eaten, or freeze until needed. Makes 6 half-pint jars.

Uncooked Sour-Cherry Jam from Frozen Cherries

Partially thaw 1 quart of frozen, unsweetened sour red cherries. Put the cherries through a food grinder, using a coarse blade. Measure out 2 cups of pulp and juice and combine with 4 cups of sugar. Stir and let stand for 10 minutes. Combine 1 bottle of liquid fruit pectin (Certo, 6 fluid ounces) with 2 tablespoons lemon juice and add to the fruit mixture. Stir for 3 minutes to dissolve the sugar and blend. Ladle the jam into sterilized freeze-or-can jars. Let stand at room temperature for several hours, until set. Store the jam in the refrigerator until eaten, or freeze until needed. Makes 4 half-pint jars.

If an almond flavor is desired, add ¼ teaspoon almond extract to the cherry pulp.

Spiced Blueberry Jam

In a large pan, combine 2¼ cups blueberries that have been thoroughly crushed, 1 teaspoon grated lemon rind, 1 tablespoon lemon juice, ¼ teaspoon allspice, and 3½ cups sugar. Mix well and place over high heat. Bring to a full rolling boil, stirring constantly, and boil hard for 1 minute. Stir in ½ cup liquid fruit pectin, return the mixture to a boil, then remove from the heat. Stir and skim for several minutes to remove the foam and to prevent fruit from floating. Pour into hot sterilized half-pint jars, adjust lids, and process for 10 minutes in a boiling-water bath.

Banana Jam

Combine 3 cups sugar and 3 cups water in a saucepan and boil together for 10 minutes, stirring often. Add the grated rind and juice of 3 lemons, 8 ripe bananas, mashed, and 1 tablespoon whole cloves. Cook slowly for 45 minutes, stirring constantly. When the mixture is pale yellow and thickened, remove the cloves and pour jam into hot sterilized jars. Adjust lids. Process for 5 minutes in a boiling-water bath.

Apricot-Pineapple Jam

Wash, peel, pit, and chop enough fully ripe apricots to make 8 cups. Combine apricots with 1 cup fresh or canned pineapple chunks and 10 cups granulated sugar. Let the fruits stand overnight in the refrigerator.

The next morning, bring fruits to a boil and boil for 8 minutes. Add ½ cup lemon juice and boil for about 2 minutes longer, stirring constantly. When the mixture is thickened to the consistency of jam, remove from the heat, skim off the foam, and pour into hot sterilized jars. Leave ¼-inch head space. Adjust lids. Process 10 minutes in a boiling-water bath. Makes about 8 pints.

Apricot Jam

Follow the recipe for Apricot-Pineapple Jam, but omit the pineapple and use 9 cups of chopped apricots.

Gooseberry Jam

Wash 2 quarts gooseberries and drain. Remove stem and blossom ends. Put gooseberries through the food grinder, using a coarse blade. Measure 4 cups chopped gooseberries and combine in a large kettle with 6 cups sugar. Mix well. Bring to a full rolling boil over high heat, stirring constantly. Stir in ½ bottle liquid fruit pectin and boil hard for 1 minute, also stirring constantly. Remove from the heat, skim, and pour into hot half-pint jars. Adjust lids. Process in a boiling-water bath for 10 minutes. Makes 7 half-pints.

Cherry Tomato Preserves

Scald and peel enough ripe red cherry tomatoes to make 2½ cups. Combine tomatoes with 2½ cups sugar and let stand overnight in the refrigerator. The next morning add ½ teaspoon salt, 1 lemon, sliced thin, ¼ teaspoon each powdered cloves, allspice, and cinnamon. Stir in 1 package (1¾ ounces) of powdered fruit pectin and bring the mixture to a boil, stirring constantly. Boil gently until the mixture thickens, about 10 minutes. Pour into hot sterilized jars. Adjust lids. Process in boiling-water bath for 10 minutes.

Yellow-Tomato Preserves

Scald and peel 2 quarts of ripe yellow plum tomatoes. Place in a heavy kettle with 1 quart water and 2 cups sugar. Cook for 5 minutes, stirring to dissolve the sugar, then simmer for about two hours, stirring often. Then add 2 cups sugar, ½ teaspoon cinnamon, ½ teaspoon ginger, and 1 lemon, sliced thin. Cook for 20 to 30 minutes more, until the mixture thickens, or to 221°F. Pack in hot sterilized jars and adjust lids. Process in boiling-water bath for 10 minutes.

Pat's Pear Preserves

Wash 6 pounds of the firm variety of pears, which are nearly ripe but not soft. Remove cores and seeds and cut into very thin slices. In a kettle, combine the pears with 2 quarts of cold water and simmer until the pears are just tender. Add 4½ pounds of sugar and continue cooking slowly, stirring constantly, until the pears are glazed and the syrup thick. Pour into hot sterilized glasses, leaving ¼-inch head space. Adjust lids. Process for 10 minutes in a boiling-water bath.

Options: Thin slices of lemon and ginger may be added to this recipe to make Ginger-Pear Preserves. Use ½ lemon for each pound of fruit and 1 to 2 pieces of ginger root or a few pieces of candied ginger, minced fine.

Ginger-Pear Preserves

Follow the recipe for Pat's Pear Preserves, adding, for each pound of fruit, ½ thin-sliced lemon and 1 or 2 pieces of ginger root or candied ginger, minced fine.

Aunt Emma's Overnight Strawberry Preserves

Wash and hull 1 quart of strawberries. Cover with boiling water for 1 minute. Drain in colander. Place berries in a preserving kettle with 2 cups sugar and 1 tablespoon lemon juice. Bring to a boil, stirring carefully, and boil for 2 minutes. Remove from the heat. When the bubbling stops, stir in 2 cups additional sugar and return to the heat. Again bring to a boil and boil 4 minutes longer. Remove from the heat, skim, and pour berries into a large flat pan so they are about one inch deep. Let stand overnight. The next day, pour into hot sterilized cans and adjust lids. Process in a boiling-water bath for 10 minutes. The berries in these preserves will not come to the top of the jar.

Pumpkin-Chip Preserves

Cut a pumpkin into slices, remove the seeds and membranes, peel, and slice into thin chips. Spread 2 cups of the pumpkin chips on a flat pan and sprinkle with 2 cups sugar. Add 1 lemon, sliced thin, and let stand overnight. The next morning, place the pumpkin in a heavy pan, add 1 stick cinnamon, 1 teaspoon whole cloves, and 1 cup water. Boil all together gently until the chips are clear and crisp and the syrup thick, about 30 minutes. Pour into sterilized jars. Adjust lids. Process in a boiling-water bath for 10 minutes. Makes 2 half-pints.

Options: Substitute 1 ounce of finely chopped candied ginger for the cinnamon and cloves.

Ruth's Gooseberry Conserve

Wash gooseberries and remove stems and blossom ends. In a large kettle, combine 6 cups gooseberries, the grated rind and chopped pulp of 1 orange, 4 cups sugar, and 1 cup raisins. Bring to a boil and cook, while stirring, to the jelly stage, or about 20 minutes. Pour into hot sterilized jars and adjust lids. Process in a boiling-water bath for 10 minutes.

Damson Plum Conserve

In a heavy pan, combine 3 cups seeded, halved, unpeeled damson plums with 3 cups sugar, 1 cup seeded raisins, the juice of 1 lemon, and 2 seeded oranges with their rind cut fine, or chopped in the blender. Cook slowly until thick and clear, stirring constantly, about 30 minutes. Stir in 1 cup broken walnuts. Pour into half-pint jars, leaving ¼-inch head space. Adjust lids. Process in a boiling-water bath for 10 minutes. Makes about 6 half-pints.

140

Heavenly Grape Conserve

Separate the pulp from the skins of about 5 pounds of Concord grapes. Boil the pulp, with only enough water to prevent sticking, until soft. Press cooked pulp through a sieve or food mill to remove seeds. Put grape skins through the food chopper, along with the rind and pulp of 3 oranges and 3 or 4 apples, unpeeled. Measure the fruits; the grape skins, apples, oranges, and cooked grape pulp should amount to about 6 cups in all. Add an equal amount of sugar and cook the mixture until it thickens, stirring constantly, or about 15 minutes. When the conserve is almost finished, add 1 cup of chopped walnuts or other nuts and cook 5 minutes longer. Pour the boiling-hot mixture into hot jars, leaving ½-inch head space. Adjust lids and process 10 minutes in boiling-water bath.

Green-Tomato Marmalade

Wash and chop 6 pounds of unpeeled green tomatoes. In a large saucepan, boil 6 thin-sliced lemons in 1 cup of water for 15 minutes. Add the green tomatoes and 6 cups sugar (light corn syrup or honey may be substituted for half the sugar) and cook slowly, stirring constantly, until the mixture is thick and clear. Pour hot marmalade into hot jars, leaving ¼-inch head space, and adjust lids. Process in a boiling-water bath for 10 minutes.

Pear Marmalade

Wash, core, and grind 8 pounds of firm-variety ripe pears using the coarse blade of the food chopper. Wash, remove seeds and ends of, and grind 3 whole oranges and 3 whole lemons. Combine the fruits in a preserving kettle and add 6 pounds sugar. Stir well. Bring to a boil and cook slowly until the marmalade is clear and thickened. Pour into sterilized hot jars, leaving ¼-inch head space, and adjust lids. Process in a boiling-water bath for 10 minutes.

Quince Honey

Peel and core 6 quinces and 2 tart apples and put them through the food chopper, using a medium blade. Mix together and measure. In a large saucepan bring to a boil 8 cups of sugar and 2 cups of water, stirring constantly. Add 1 quart of the quince and apple mixture and let all boil for 15 minutes. Pack in sterilized jars, leaving ¼-inch head space. Adjust lids. Process in a boiling-water bath for 5 minutes.

Mary's Pear Honey

Grind firm peeled and cored pears. To each quart of ground pears, add 3½ cups sugar. Cook over medium heat until moderately thick, stirring often. Add one No. 2 can crushed pineapple and 1 lemon, sliced thin or ground. Cook the mixture until thick. Pour into hot sterilized jars. Apply self-sealing lid closure. Process 5 minutes in a boiling-water bath to ensure seal.

Option: Add 1 stick of cinnamon or 1 piece of crystallized ginger while cooking the honey. Remove before pouring cooked pear honey into jars.

POINTERS FOR COOKING FRUIT BUTTERS

Fruit butters are ready to can when only a tiny rim of liquid forms around a spoonful of hot cooked butter dropped onto a cold saucer.

Fruit butters cooked in a kettle on top of the stove require constant watching and stirring because they burn easily. If the butters are baked in a moderate (325°F) oven until thick, they need only be stirred 2 or 3 times an hour. Place the fruit puree and other ingredients in a large, flat pan, such as a turkey roaster, and leave uncovered for baking.

Cider Apple Butter

In a large kettle, cook 2 quarts peeled, cored, and fine-chopped apples and 2 quarts of sweet apple cider until the mixture is thick and mushy. Strain through a food mill or puree in a blender.

In a flat-bottomed roomy pan, such as a turkey roaster, combine the apple puree with 4 cups sugar, one 4-inch stick of cinnamon, and ¼ teaspoon each ground mace, allspice, cinnamon, and cloves. Bake in a 325°F oven, stirring 2 or 3 times an hour, until the apple butter is thick. Pour the butter into hot jars and process in a boiling-water bath for 10 minutes.

Spiced Apple Butter

In a kettle, combine 16 cups unsweetened applesauce, 2 tablespoons lemon or lime juice, ½ cup vinegar, 8 cups sugar, 1 tablespoon allspice, 2 tablespoons cinnamon, 1 tablespoon cloves, and 1 teaspoon nutmeg. Bring to a boil while stirring, and cook over low heat, stirring often, until the apple butter is thick and no liquid separates from it. Pour into hot sterilized jars and adjust lids. Process in a boiling-water bath for 10 minutes.

Peach Butter

Scald and peel very ripe peaches and remove the pits. Cook the peaches until tender, using only enough water to start the cooking. Press the pulp through a food mill or blend in the blender to puree.

To each cup of pulp, add ½ cup sugar. Add ground or stick cinnamon, if desired, in the proportion of ½ to 1 teaspoon (or one 4-inch stick) to each 4 cups of pulp. Cook the peach butter slowly on top of the stove, stirring frequently, or bake in a 325°F oven in an uncovered shallow pan until thick, stirring 2 or 3 times an hour.

Pack the boiling-hot butter into jars, leaving ¼-inch head space, and adjust lids. Process in a boiling-water bath for 10 minutes.

Option: Peach kernels impart an almond flavor to peaches. To flavor peach butter with kernels, crack 1 or 2 peach pits and remove the kernels. Scald them with boiling water and scrape off the brown skin. Add the kernels to the peach butter while it cooks and discard them before packing.

Pear Butter

Wash pears but do not peel. Cut out cores and cut into slices. Place in a kettle with a small amount of water to start the cooking. Boil gently until the pears are soft. Press fruit through a food mill or colander. To each cup of pulp, add ½ cup of sugar. Spices may be added to taste. Use ½ teaspoon to 1 teaspoon cinnamon to 4 cups pulp. Or use the same amount of ginger, or 2 tablespoons of candied ginger (or to taste), minced finely. Lemon juice may be added, if desired, using 2 tablespoons to 4 cups pulp.

In a kettle, cook the pear butter over medium or low heat until it is thick, stirring frequently to prevent burning. Or bake the pear butter uncovered in a flat, open pan in the oven at 325°F until it is thick.

Pack the boiling-hot pear butter into jars and adjust lids. Leave ¼-inch head space. Process in a boiling-water bath for 10 minutes.

Grape Butter

Use the pomace left in the jelly bag after extracting the juice for grape jelly, or cook Concord grapes in a small amount of water until soft. The pulp of wild grapes or other varieties of grapes may also be used. Make a puree by pressing the grapes or the pomace through a food mill or colander to remove the seeds.

For every cup of grape puree use ½ cup of sugar. Leave plain or use spices, as preferred. Cardamon or cinnamon and clove are compatible with grape flavor. Bake the grape butter in a flat, open pan in a 325°F oven for about 3½ hours, or until as thick as wanted. Pour the boiling-hot grape butter into hot sterilized jars and adjust lids. Process in a boiling water bath for 10 minutes.

Apple-Grape Butter

Follow the recipe for Grape Butter, adding one cup of unsweetened apple sauce for each cup of grape puree used.

144

Spiced Pumpkin Butter

Slice a pumpkin and remove the seeds and membranes. Peel and put pumpkin through a food chopper or chop fine. Prepare 6 pounds of pumpkin. Place the pumpkin in an enamelware container with 2 tablespoons ginger, 2 tablespoons cinnamon, 1 teaspoon powdered allspice, 5 pounds light brown sugar, and 5 lemons that have been seeded and put through the food chopper or chopped fine. Let stand overnight in a cool place.

The next day, add 1 pint of water to the pumpkin mixture and boil gently until the butter is clear and thick. Stir often. Pack into jars, leaving ¼-inch head space. Adjust lids. Process in a boiling-water bath for 10 minutes.

Option: For a lighter colored pumpkin butter, use white sugar, and whole spices tied in a bag.

Mother's Pumpkin Butter

To make pumpkin butter, Mother stewed a peeled, cubed pumpkin in water until the pieces were fork tender. The liquid was drained off and the cooked pumpkin mashed with the wooden potato masher. For every cup of pumpkin pulp, ½ cup sugar was added. The mixture was lightly spiced with cinnamon and nutmeg, about 1 teaspoon of the combined spices for every quart of pumpkin. The pumpkin butter was baked in the bottom of the turkey roaster in a slow (325°F) oven until thick and golden. Pumpkin butter was served with hot biscuits.

To can, fill hot sterilized jars with boiling hot pumpkin butter, leaving ¼-inch head space, Adjust lids. Process 10 minutes in a boiling-water bath to ensure seal.

MAKING THE SOURS

While the regular business of canning the abundances of fruits and vegetables was surely a source of housewifely satisfaction to her, it was in the making of the sweets and sours for our table that Mother was truly inspired. She was an indefatigable pickler. Our cellar shelves held sweet pickles, sour pickles, dill pickles, mixed pickles, lime pickles, mustard pickles, bread-and-butter pickles, and candied pickles. There were three-day, nine-day, and fourteen-day pickles. Anything might end up in a pickle: watermelon rind, zucchini, green tomatoes, quinces, green beans, okra, clingstone peaches, bell peppers, pumpkin, tiny ears of immature corn, green walnuts, and, of course, cucumbers. There was no end to the pickling. After the winter's butchering, there were even pickled pigs' feet.

And the labels! Penciled on the red-bordered rectangles affixed to each jar were the most fascinating names: end-of-the-garden pickles, ice-water dills, spiced Georgia Belles, turnip kraut, pepper hash, sweet gherkins, piccalilli, chow-chow, corn salad, chutney. These were not mundane preparations. There were rag pickles and rummage pickles, icicle pickles and Christmas pickles, sunshine pickles and California pickles, Thousand Island pickles and Indian pickles. Could such uncommon pickles ever be found in a grocery store? "Grandmother's Mustard Boona" and "Aunt Grace's Garlic Dills" simply could not be bought.

146

I doubt that my mother ever considered buying pickles beyond an occasional jar of olives from Allen's General Store or a sample jar of some friend's pickles donated to a community bazaar. I too walk quickly through the aisles of pickles and relishes at the supermarket, seldom glancing at the jars, because our cupboard shelves are stocked with an ample supply of the uncommon pickles that we put up.

Our specialties are served prudently—even hoarded—lest we run out of the favorites before another summer comes. All prefer the dilled green beans and the damson plum pickle made according to the family recipe, and any bought substitute that appears on the table is noisily protested. By now we are well established in the tradition of making our own pickles.

Making pickles is not difficult, no more trouble than preparing for a dinner party. But there are a number of basic concepts that must be understood and followed if one is to be successful.

Pickling

SELECTION OF FRUITS AND VEGETABLES FOR PICKLING

The freshness of the vegetables and fruits is one of the most essential considerations in pickling. My son gathers vegetables from our garden early in the morning before the heat of the sun warms them, and I begin to work up the pickles at once. Freshness is a fleeting quality, and vegetables that are not newly picked, that have lain around unrefrigerated, will have lost some of their crispness, flavor, vitamins, and moisture. No amount of alum or grape leaves or brining can substitute for the natural goodness that escapes through neglect or too-long storage between picking and pickling.

If we were not so fortunate as to have our own garden, I would hunt places to buy the freshest produce possible. Besides the farmers' markets, truck farms, and roadside stands, I would make the rounds of country places where garden stuff is offered to passersby on hand-lettered signs displayed on front lawns. Every appreciator of really fresh vegetables has found places where squash, green beans, cucumbers, sweet corn, and the like can be bought straight from the garden—and usually at less-than-market prices.

SELECTING OF CUCUMBERS FOR PICKLING

The fruits and vegetables to be preserved by pickling should be selected and prepared with the same attention to freshness, quality, and suitability for the recipe as those to be preserved by other methods. Specific pointers that apply to selecting and using cucumbers are:

- Pickle cucumbers as soon as possible after picking or store them in the refrigerator in the interim. Cucumbers lose their natural crispness quickly. Use them the same day they are picked.
- Do not use cucumbers for pickling whole if they have been waxed. Waxed cucumbers may be used in recipes calling for peeled cucumbers.
- Remove all traces of the blossoms from cucumbers because they contain an enzyme that causes softening of the cucumbers during fermentation. Some recipes direct that an ⅛-inch slice be trimmed from both ends of the cucumber.
- Cucumbers used for pickling should be varieties developed for pickling. See the seed packet or catalog for vartieties or contact your county extension home economist or agricultural agent for the names of varieties available in your area. Slicing cumcumbers are not suitable for pickling.
- Cucumbers for pickling should be picked when slightly immature.

KINDS OF PICKLES

Practically anything can be pickled. For most purposes, pickles are divided into four general classes according to the ingredients used and the methods of preparing them. They are: brined or fermented pickles, fresh pack pickles, relishes, and fruit pickles.

Brined or fermented pickles: Vegetables that are cured by brining are immersed in a salt solution where they are allowed to ferment usually from 3 to 6 weeks. After the

149

vegetables are cured, they may remain in the brine solution until used or they may be desalted and used in other pickle recipes.

Fresh pack pickles: Vegetables are brined for several hours or overnight in a weak brine, then drained and combined with a pickling solution of vinegar, spices, and other ingredients.

Relishes: Relishes are made from mixed vegetables or fruits that are chopped or ground before being combined and cooked with a spiced, sweet-sour solution. Relishes may be hot and spicy or mild and sweet-flavored. They are used to accent the flavor of other foods.

Fruit pickles: Fruits are pickled in spicy, sweet-sour vinegar syrup. They are left whole, as pickled peaches, or cut to size, as pickled watermelon rind.

PICKLING INGREDIENTS

Salt: Use only pure salt with no additives. Pickling salt, dairy salt, or kosher salt may be used. Do not use idodized salt or salt with an anti-moisture agent added because the pickles may darken or the brine become clouded. Granulated salt and flake salt have the same strength per pound but do not measure the same because flake salt has more volume. Increase the measure by one-half if using a flake salt. Do not use rock salt because it is not food quality.

Vinegar: Cider or distilled vinegar with a 40 to 60 percent grain strength (4 to 6 percent acidity) should be used in making pickles. The strength of commercial vinegar should be marked on the label; 5-percent acid strength is common. Cider vinegar is made from apple cider and is the general-purpose pickling vinegar. Its mellow flavor blends well with herbs, spices, and other ingredients used in pickle making. Distilled vinegar is made from dilute alcohol and is either white or cider flavored. The white distilled vinegar has no color and only its own characteristic sharp, acetic flavor so it is used with pale fruits and light-

150

colored vegetables that would be less attractive if combined with the amber-colored cider vinegar.

Vinegars can also be made of wine, homemade cider, beer, and various fruits, but for pickling, no vinegars of unknown strength or homemade vinegars should be used. It is important to have vinegars with the correct acidity because many vegetables that are pickled are low-acid and additional acid in the vinegar is needed to preserve the food safely. If the flavor of vinegar is too sharp, *do not dilute the vinegar with water, or cut down the amount called for in the recipe.* Instead, add more sugar to the recipe.

Water: Soft water is best for making pickling solutions. Minerals in hard water, especially iron, tend to darken pickles. Very hard water can interfere with fermentation. Other minerals may cause cloudy brine. If you do not have naturally soft water, use boiled, cooled rain water for pickling. Or, boil hard water for 15 minutes, let it stand 24 hours, remove the accumulated scum from the top of the water, and carefully ladle it out of the container so that sediment in the bottom is not disturbed. Add 1 tablespoon vinegar per gallon of boiled water before using it for pickling.

Herbs and spices: Use only spices and herbs that have been opened within the year. Spices and herbs that have been opened and on the shelf for more than a year may have lost their strength and pungency. Tie loose spices in a piece of muslin or cheesecloth and add the bag to the pickles while they cook; remove the bag before canning the product. Powdered and loose spices may cause the liquid and pickles to darken. You may leave loose spices in the pickling liquid if you like their appearance in the jar and do not mind the slight darkening that might occur.

Sugar: Brown or white sugar may be used in making pickles, as preferred. If used with light colored vegetables and fruits, brown sugar will darken the pickles slightly. Honey or syrup may be substituted for at least half the sugar.

Fresh dill: Fresh dill, which is superior in pickling to dried dill or dill seed, is not easy to find when it must be bought. But it grows easily, even in a flower bed, and often comes up as a volunteer plant after it is once planted. To ensure having fresh dill at pickling time, plant successive crops all summer. Extra dill can easily be frozen (see page 210) or dried (see page 287).

MAKING SPICED VINEGAR FOR PICKLES

Using the proportions and spice combinations given below, boil vinegar, sugar, and spices, tied in a bag, together for 15 minutes. Set the vinegar aside for about 3 weeks before removing the spice bag to achieve the best flavor. If more convenient however, the vinegar can be made just prior to use.

For sour pickles, use 1 gallon vinegar, 1 pound sugar, and your choice of spices (see below).

For medium pickles, use 1 gallon vinegar, 2 pounds sugar, and spices.

For sweet pickles, use 1 gallon vinegar, 5 to 6 pounds sugar, and spices.

These are some suggestions for spice combinations to use in making spiced vinegar. Tie the spices together in a bag before adding to the vinegar.

- One-half ounce allspice, ½ ounce cloves, 1 stick cinnamon, and 1 piece mace.
- One box mixed pickling spices and 2 tablespoons turmeric.
- Four sticks cinnamon, 4 tablespoons allspice, 4 tablespoons white mustard seed, and 1 tablespoon whole cloves.
- Two tablespoons allspice, 2 tablespoons mustard seed, 2 tablespoons celery seed, 2 tablespoons salt, 1 tablespoon turmeric, 1 teaspoon black peppercorns, 1 tablespoon mace, and 2 grated nutmegs.

CRISPING INGREDIENTS

Certain special pickling recipes call for the use of lime, alum, and grape leaves to give extra crispness to the products being pickled. However, these crisping ingredients are not needed in regular pickling recipes.

The United States Department of Agriculture states in Home and Garden Bulletin No. 92:

"Alum and lime are not needed to make pickles crisp and firm if good quality ingredients and up-to-date procedures are used."

Therefore, the following crisping ingredients should be considered as necessary ingredients only in the recipes that specifically call for their use.

Lime: The lime required in certain pickling recipes to ensure very crisp pickles is calcium hydroxide, sometimes called slaked lime or hydrated lime. *Do not use quicklime for making pickles.*

Hydrated lime can be bought at some hardware stores, drugstores, and at garden centers. It is often found in 10-pound sacks, unfortunately. A product called Mrs. Wages Pickling Lime is available in 1-pound quantities and is distributed throughout the country, but it is not a product that you find on grocery shelves everywhere. Eli Lilly & Co. of Indianapolis, Indiana, manufactures a product called Powder No. 40 Calcium Hydroxide, Lilly, which is available in 11.5-gram bottles from pharmacies throughout the country, and this amount makes 1 gallon of Calcium Hydroxide Solution, U.S.P.

The pickles are soaked in the lime water, which is thoroughly rinsed off before making the pickles. Such a small amount remains in the pickles that it cannot be considered a food additive.

The recipe should have enough acidity to offset the effects of the lime. Recipes for lime pickles are on pages 181–183.

Alum: Alum is an astringent chemical which gives crispness to pickles. A very small amount, usually less than

153

two-tenths of one percent, remains in the product. Alum is available at pharmacies and in the spice and herb shelves of groceries.

Grape Leaves: Some recipes call for the use of grape leaves to give crispness and flavor to pickles. Cherry leaves and horseradish leaves are also required in some recipies.

Some pickles should be stored for 6 weeks before using to allow their full flavor to develop. Chilling the pickles just prior to opening them will also enhance their flavor and add crispness.

METHOD OF PROCESSING PICKLES FOR STORAGE

Fresh pack pickles, brined pickles, relishes, fruit pickles and sauerkraut may be packed while hot into jars and processed for storage in a boiling water bath for the time indicated in the recipe or on the following chart.

Finished pickles should be heat-processed to destroy organisms that cause spoilage and to inactivate enzymes that cause deterioration of color, flavor, and texture. Pickles are high-acid products so processing at temperatures of 180° to 212°F is adequate to destroy the spoilage organisms that exist in acid foods.

Open kettle canning is not recommended for processing pickle products. Until recently, open kettle processing was widely used in preserving pickles, but it is no longer considered adequate to prevent spoilage. There are still many pickle recipes in circulation that do not specify processing in a boiling- or simmering-water bath. If the directions you are following do not give instructions for processing the pickles in a boiling-water bath, consult the following chart for the time recommended for processing the type of pickle you are canning, or find an up-to-date recipe.

PROCESSING TIMETABLE FOR PICKLES

Kind of Pickle	Minutes in Boiling-Water Bath	
	Pints	Quarts
Fermented pickles, whole		15
Fresh-pack dills, whole (unfermented)		20
Bread-and-butter slices	5	10
Chutney	5	
Cross-cut slices	5	
Dilled green beans, okra, green tomatoes:		
Hot-packed	5	
Cold-packed	10	
Gherkins, sweet	5	
Piccalilli	5	
Pepper-onion relish	5	
Corn relish	15	
Sauerkraut:		
Hot-packed	15	20
Cold-packed	20	30
Fruit pickles:		
Peaches or pears	15	20
Watermelon rind	5	10

To avoid overcooking, start counting the processing time as soon as the pickles are placed in actively boiling water. If the processing time is less than 15 minutes, pack pickles in sterilized jars.

BRINED OR FERMENTED PICKLES

Cucumbers, green tomatoes, and cabbage are the most commonly brine-cured vegetables. Green peppers, grape leaves, dandelion greens, turnips, and various other vegetables may be preserved this way, too. Salted cabbage and turnips are made into sauerkraut.

The brine for curing green tomatoes and cucumbers may be plain or it can have vinegar dill, garlic, or other herbs and spices added to it.

After the vegetables have been cured in salt brine for

155

several weeks and the fermentation process has stopped, there are several ways the pickles may be handled:

1. Cucumbers and green tomatoes that are cured in plain brine may be desalted and made into pickles with the addition of a plain or spiced vinegar solution.
2. Cured vegetables may be packed into canning jars, covered with their own salt brine, and processed in a boiling-water bath.
3. Cured vegetables may be kept in the fermenting crock in plain 10-percent salt brine until needed, even for months, then taken out and desalted for table use. During this time the top of the cucumbers should be covered to prevent undesirable film formation and spoilage. Pour a layer of melted paraffin, ¼-inch thick, on top of the cucumbers and liquid and cover with a close fitting lid. Store in a dark, dry, cool place.

MAKING BRINE FOR PICKLES

Brine is a solution of salt and water used for preserving foods. All vegetables that are to be made into pickles are placed in brine and processed for either a short or a long period of time.

Relishes and fresh-pack pickles are processed quickly by the short-brine method. Sauerkraut and brined pickles, as well as green tomatoes and some other vegetables, are processed by the long-brine method.

The strength of brine used for pickling is very important. It is measured by the percentage of salt to water, or by degrees registered on the scale of a salinometer.

A weak brine is used for quick-processing relishes and fresh-pack pickles. The recipes for fresh pack pickles and relishes may direct that the vegetables be covered with a weak brine of salt and water for only a few hours or overnight. There may be only a few tablespoons of salt used to a quart of water in relish recipes.

A strong brine of 10-percent strength (also called a 40 degree brine), is often used for brining cucumbers processed by the long-brine, or fermentation, method. A 10-percent brine is strong enough to "float an egg" and is made by combining pure granulated salt, dairy salt, or kosher salt with cold water.

Produce that has been properly cured in a 10-percent brine will keep almost indefinitely. The brine solution is strong enough to kill most of the bacteria that are present when the vegetables are put into the salt water. Those that survive salt are destroyed in due time by the lactic acid that is produced by the bacteria themselves when they decompose the sugar drawn out of the cucumbers by the salt, through the process of fermentation. The lactic acid formed is responsible for much of the desirable flavor of fermented pickles. The fermentation process can take from 3 to 6 weeks.

A 5 percent brine is used to allow quick fermentation and faster curing, but the pickles must be canned within a few weeks or they will spoil. A 5-percent brine is made by dissolving ½ pound salt in 9 pints of water.

The strength of the brine is somewhat depleted during the fermentation of pickles. Additional salt must be added to the brine that covers the pickles as the fermentation progresses to keep its salt concentration at the desired level or the pickles will spoil.

Only pure salt with no additives can be used or the pickles will darken. Do not use iodized salt or salt with anti-caking ingredients added (see page 150).

The volume of brine needed to cover the vegetables to be pickled should be about one half of their volume. Thus, if one gallon of pickles is to be packed, two quarts of brine will be needed.

Sometimes vinegar is added with the brine. Herbs, garlic, and spices may also be added to the brine.

Hot water should never be used in making brine since it will retard or stop the fermentation of acid necessary to begin fermentation.

Vegetables that have been properly cured in a 10-percent brine may be kept in the brine solution for months, and used as needed. Or, the cured vegetables may be taken out of the brine solution after curing is completed, desalted, and then made into pickles according to a specific recipe which usually includes heating in sweetened or spiced vinegar.

To desalt brine-cured pickles before making them into spiced or sweetened pickles, or before using them, soak them for a few hours in clear, cool water to take out the salt.

SUITABLE CONTAINERS FOR BRINING VEGETABLES

Crocks are well suited to brining vegetables but the best practice is to keep a pickling crock exclusively for making pickles. Other substances stored in porous crockery jars could be absorbed and leach out into the brine, causing pickles to spoil. For example, alkalis absorbed from milk by porous crockery may neutralize the brine when making pickles. Or grease absorbed by crockery could cause spoilage if pickles are brined in a crock used previously for lard storage. Cracked or chipped crocks should not be used, or foreign-made products that may have a high lead content in the glaze. Use only domestic food-quality stoneware for brining vegetables.

Glass jars are suitable if the contents are protected from the light to prevent fading of the brined pickles. The container may be placed in a paper bag, or a box, or covered loosely with a cloth. The opening of a glass container must be wide enough to accommodate the weight and the cover that keep the fermenting vegetables under the brine. Glass apothecary jars are often the right shape and size.

Plastic containers intended for food use, such as polyethelene, are suitable for fermenting vegetables. The shape of the container must allow for proper covering of the top of the vegetables with a plate and weight.

Stainless steel and unchipped enamel ware are fine for fermenting vegetables during brining if the right size and shape containers are available.

Do not use aluminum, copper, brass, iron, wooden, or galvanized containers to brine vegetables. In my grandmother's day, wooden barrels were used for salting down meat and vegetables, but they were made by local coopers expressly for the intended purpose and were not used for anything else. My grandmother used a wooden barrel for salting green tomatoes, and a stone jar for making fermented pickles.

GENERAL DIRECTIONS FOR MAKING
BRINED PICKLES

1. Carefully wash the vegetables. Remove all blossoms from cucumbers. Drain.

2. Weigh and measure the vegetables. Put them in a fermenting container of crockery, glass, or plastic suitable for food use. Cover the vegetables with a 10-percent brine solution made by dissolving 1 cup pure salt in 2 quarts of cold water. Use about 2 quarts of brine to each gallon of prepared vegetables.

3. To weigh the vegetables down so they remain under the brine, put a heavy plate or glass lid inside the container on top of the vegetables and place a weight on top of the plate or lid. A glass jug or canning jar filled with water will serve the purpose. Do not make the container airtight, but do cover the top with a clean cloth. If a glass container is being used, set it down inside a cardboard carton to keep the light from reaching the vegetables.

4. Keep the vegetables in a warm room during the brining process. The best temperature range for fermenting is about 80° or 85°F.

5. *Remove scum daily* when it forms on top of the brine. If scum is left on the pickles, the acidity of the brine will be

A weighted plate, using a stone for a weight, to hold pickles under the brine

destroyed and the pickles will spoil. Do not stir the vegetables but make sure they are completely submerged at all times. Make additional brine (1 cup pure salt to 2 quarts cold water), if needed.

6. On the second day, to maintain a 10-percent brine solution add 1 cup pure salt for each 5 pounds of vegetables in the container. Put the salt on top of the weighted plate or lid so that it does not sink to the bottom of the container, making the brine too strong there.

7. At the end of every week for 3 to 6 succeeding weeks, or until fermentation ceases (see Step 8), add ¼ cup pure salt for each 5 pounds of vegetables. Place the salt on top of the plate, as in Step 6.

8. When the fermentation is finished, which will occur in 3 to 6 weeks, the vegetables are cured. Bubbling will have ceased. Cucumbers will be olive green and their interiors will no longer be white, but uniformly translucent.

Options:

- Cured vegetables may be left in the brine until used. But add no more salt once the fermentation has stopped.
- Cucumbers may be packed in their own brine and processed for storage in a boiling-water bath (see page 154–159).
- Cucumbers may be desalted and made into pickles according to specific recipes (see below).

TO DESALT BRINED CUCUMBERS AND OTHER VEGETABLES Soak sliced or whole brined vegetables in cold water for several hours or overnight to remove the salt. Drain.

To shorten the time needed to remove the salt, use several times the volume of water as of vegetables and change the water often.

After the excess salt has been soaked out, the vegetables may be prepared for the table or used in other pickle recipes.

Brined Green-Tomato Slices

Follow the General Directions for Making Brined Pickles

above, using firm green tomatoes sliced ⅜ to ½ inch thick. When the tomatoes have fermented and cured, store them in a 10-percent brine until needed.

To use: Soak the slices in cold water until the salt is removed. Drain. Dip the slices in flour, or a mixture of flour and cornmeal, and fry until browned on both sides. Or use the desalted slices to make green-tomato pie.

Whole green tomatoes may also be brined, if preferred.

USDA Brined Dill Pickles

Select 20 pounds, or about ½ bushel, of cucumbers that are 3 to 6 inches in length. Cover the cucumbers with cold water. Wash thoroughly, scrubbing with a vegetable brush, but handle gently to avoid bruising the cucumbers. Take care to remove any blossoms. Drain on rack or wipe dry.

Measure out ¾ cup whole mixed pickling spices and place half the spices and a layer of fresh or dried dill in a 5-gallon crock or jar. Fill the crock with cucumbers to within 3 or 4 inches of the top. Place 2 or 3 bunches of fresh dill and the remaining pickling spices on top of the cucumbers.

If garlic is wanted, add a total of 10 to 20 peeled cloves for a 5-gallon crock of pickles and place them half below and half above the cucumbers along with the spices and herbs.

Make a solution of 2½ cups cider vinegar or white vinegar, 1¾ cups pure granulated salt, and 2½ gallons water. Mix well and pour the mixture over the cucumbers. Place a heavy china or glass lid inside the crock on top of the pickles. Place a weight on top of the lid or plate to keep the cucumbers under the brine. A glass jar filled with water makes a good weight. Cover the container with a clean cloth.

Keep the pickles at room temperature and remove scum daily when formed. Scum may start forming in 3 to 5 days. Do not stir the pickles, but be sure they are completely covered with brine at all times. If necessary, make additional brine, using the original proportions specified in recipe.

In about 3 weeks the cucumbers will have become olive green and should have a desirable flavor. Any white spots inside will disappear in processing.

To process the dills: After 3 weeks of fermentation, the

dills are ready for processing. The original brine, though it is usually cloudy because of yeast development during the fermentation period, is generally preferred for the flavor it adds. If used, however, it should be strained before heating to boiling. If the cloudiness is objectionable, make fresh brine, using ½ cup pure salt and 4 cups vinegar to 1 gallon of water, to cover the pickles when packing them into canning jars.

Pack the pickles firmly into clean, hot quart jars, but do not wedge tight. Add several pieces of dill to each jar, and garlic, if desired. Cover the pickles in the jars with boiling brine, leaving ½-inch head space. Adjust lids. Process jars in boiling-water bath for 15 minutes. To avoid overcooking the pickles, start counting the processing time as soon as the hot jars are placed into actively boiling water.

Remove the jars from the canner and complete seals, if necessary. Cool jars and store. Cloudiness of the brine is to be expected if the original fermentation brine is used as the covering liquid.

Brined Dill Green Tomatoes

Follow the directions for USDA Brined Dill Pickles, substituting whole green tomatoes for cucumbers. To process for long storage, use the same procedure as for the cucumbers.

Sweet Cucumber Pickles from Brined Cucumbers

Desalt enough brined cucumbers for the number of jars you wish to fill, and place them in a crock or suitable container. Make a sweet-sour spiced vinegar (see page 152), allowing about 1 pint of spiced vinegar for each quart of cucumbers to be canned. Pour the boiling-hot spiced vinegar over the cucumbers in the crock. Let stand overnight.

The next day, drain off the spiced vinegar, reserving the vinegar. Add sugar to the vinegar at the rate of ½ cup per pint of vinegar. Bring the mixture to a boil and pour back onto the cucumbers. Again, let stand overnight.

On the third day, drain off the vinegar again and add sugar in the same proportion as before. Bring the sugar-vinegar mixture to a boil.

Pack the drained cucumbers into hot sterilized canning

jars and cover with the boiling-hot vinegar, leaving ½-inch head space. Adjust lids. Process 10 minutes in a boiling-water bath at simmering temperature. Remove jars from canner, complete seal if necessary, and cool upright on a rack or folded cloth.

Sweet Mixed Pickles from Brined Pickles

Remove ½ gallon of brined cucumber slices or chunks from the salt brine and desalt by covering with boiling water and letting stand for 24 hours. Drain, add 2 tablespoons alum, and cover with fresh cold water. Let stand again for 24 hours. Drain and cover the pickles with hot water. Let stand until cool, then drain.

In a kettle, combine 1 quart vinegar and 12 cups sugar. Add a spice bag containing one 4-inch stick of cinnamon, 1 teaspoon mace, 1 teaspoon dill seed, and 1 tablespoon mixed pickling spices. Stir and bring the mixture to a boil. Pour the boiling syrup over the drained cucumbers and let stand for 24 hours in a cool place. Drain and repeat boiling the syrup and pouring it over the cucumbers once a day for the next 3 days.

On the fifth day, drain the syrup off the cucumbers and again bring it to a boil. To the boiling syrup, add 4 cups carrots, sliced; 2 cups green bell peppers, seeded and chopped; 4 cups small whole white pickling onions, peeled; and 1 small head of cauliflower, broken into pieces. Cook the vegetables in the syrup until they are just tender. Add the drained cucumbers and heat to the boiling point, but do not boil. Pack the boiling-hot pickles into hot jars, cover them with boiling syrup, leaving ¼-inch head space. Adjust lids. Process in a boiling-water bath for 15 minutes.

Sour Mixed Pickles

Follow the recipe for Sweet Mixed Pickles, but use only 3 cups of sugar.

FRESH PACK PICKLES

Fresh-pack, or quick-process, pickles are brined for several hours or overnight, then drained and combined with vinegar, spices, and other ingredients. Their tart, pungent flavor comes from the acid in the vinegar rather than that formed by fermentation, as in fermented or brined pickles. Whole-cucumber dills, dilled vegetables, sweet-cucumber pickles, cucumber slices, pickled onions, and the like are examples of fresh-pack pickles.

Kosher Dill Pickles

Wash thoroughly 4 pounds of 4-inch cucumbers and cut into halves lengthwise. In a saucepan, combine 3 cups white distilled vinegar, 14 cloves garlic, split in half, ¼ cup salt, and 3 cups water. Heat to boiling. Remove garlic from the mixture and put 4 of the halves into each jar. Pack the cucumbers in the clean hot jars with the garlic. Add to each jar 2 tablespoons dill seed or 2 sprigs fresh dill weed and 3 peppercorns or 1 small red pepper pod. Cover the cucumbers with boiling pickling solution, leaving ¼-inch head space. Adjust lids. Process in a boiling-water bath for 15 minutes. Makes about 7 pints.

Option: The garlic may be omitted to make plain dill pickles.

Fourteen-Day Sweet Pickles

On the first day, wash 2 gallons of pickling cucumbers. Leave them whole if the pickles are small enough, or cut them into chunks 1 to 1½ inches in length. Cover the cucumbers with "salt water strong enough to float an egg," or 2 cups salt to 1 gallon of cold water. Put the cucumbers in a stoneware jar and cover. Stir every day for seven days. On the eighth day, drain the saltwater off the pickles and cover them with fresh boiling water. On the ninth day, drain the boiled water off the pickles, and add fresh boiling water to cover and 3 tablespoons of alum.

On the tenth day, drain, and again add fresh boiling water to cover the pickles. Let the water cool and drain again. In a saucepan, combine 2 quarts of cider vinegar, 1 quart water, and 2 cups sugar. Mix well. Tie in a muslin spice bag 2 tablespoons whole mixed pickling spices, 1 tablespoon whole allspice, 1 tablespoon celery seed, and 4 broken sticks of cinnamon. Add spice bag to the vinegar mixture and bring the syrup to a boil. Pour the hot syrup with the spice bag over the drained pickles in the jar.

On the eleventh day, drain off the vinegar syrup, add 2 cups sugar, and bring the syrup to a boil with the spice bag. Again pour the vinegar syrup over the pickles in the jar. On the twelfth day, again drain off the vinegar syrup, add 2 cups sugar, and bring syrup to a boil with the spice bag. On the thirteenth day, repeat the procedure of the twelfth day. On the fourteenth day, drain the syrup from the pickles and bring it to a boil. Pack the pickles into hot sterilized jars, and cover them with the boiling syrup, leaving ¼-inch head space. Discard the spice bag. Adjust lids. Process in a boiling-water bath for 15 minutes.

I have let a day or two slip by during the second week without tending to these pickles, and no harm done—except that they were then sixteen-day sweet pickles.

Mustard Pickles

Make a brine of 2 quarts water and 1 cup pure salt. Pour over 2 quarts small cucumbers, 1 quart small white pickling onions, 3 green peppers, chopped, and 2 cauliflower heads, broken into pieces, and let stand overnight in a cool place. The next morning, bring the pickles to a boil in the same brine. Drain and discard the salt liquid.

In a saucepan, combine 1 tablespoon turmeric, 1 cup flour, 6 tablespoons dry mustard, 2 cups sugar, and 2 quarts vinegar. Bring to a boil and cook until thickened, stirring often. Add the cooked, drained vegetables and heat until mixture is simmering hot. Ladle the pickles into hot sterilized jars and leave ¼-inch head space. Adjust lids. Process in a boiling-water bath for 10 minutes.

Sweet Mustard Pickles

Follow the recipe for Mustard Pickles, but increase the sugar to 4 cups.

Mother's Bread-and-Butter Pickles

Select 25 to 30 crisp, fresh, medium-sized pickling cucumbers. Wash and cut a ⅛-inch slice off each end, but do not pare. Slice cucumbers crosswise as thin as possible, using a slicer to ensure uniform slices. Also slice thin 8 large onions and 2 large green bell peppers. Combine cucumbers and sliced vegetables with ½ cup pure salt. Let stand for 3 hours in a cool place. Drain thoroughly.

In a large pickling kettle, combine 5 cups sugar, 5 cups apple cider vinegar, 2 tablespoons mustard seed, 1 teaspoon turmeric, and ½ teaspoon ground cloves. Bring the mixture to a boil, then add the drained sliced vegetables. Carefully heat the vegetables to scalding, stirring frequently, but do not boil. Pack while hot into hot canning jars, leaving ¼-inch head space. Adjust lids. Process 5 minutes in a boiling-water bath. To avoid overcooking, start counting the processing time as soon as the water in the canner returns to boiling.

Mary's Bread-and-Butter Pickles

Wash and prepare enough unpeeled cucumbers to make 1½ gallons when sliced ⅛ inch thick. Also prepare 3 quarts thin-sliced white onions. Combine the vegetables with ½ cup pure salt and 4 trays of ice cubes. Let stand in a cool place for 24 hours. Drain thoroughly.

In a large kettle, combine 1 quart cider vinegar, 3½ cups sugar, 2 tablespoons mustard seed, 1 tablespoon celery seed, 1 teaspoon turmeric, ½ teaspoon white pepper, and 1½ teaspoons ground ginger. Heat the vinegar mixture and simmer for 10 minutes. Add the drained cucumbers and onions and bring to a boil. The cucumbers will change to a yellowish color. Pack the boiling-hot mixture into hot jars. Adjust lids. Process in a boiling-water bath for 5 minutes. Makes 8 pints. Serve cold.

End-of-the-Garden Pickles

Prepare 2 cups thin-sliced cucumbers, 2 cups chopped white cabbage, 2 cups chopped sweet red or green peppers, and 2 cups chopped green tomatoes. Put the vegetables in a large earthenware crock or bowl, add 8 cups water combined with ½ cup pickling salt, and chill the mixture, covered, overnight. Drain the vegetables in a colander.

Cut enough green beans into ½-inch lengths, chop

enough celery, and dice enough carrots to measure 2 cups each. In saucepans of boiling water, boil each vegetable separately until it is just tender but not soft. Drain the vegetables in a colander, refresh them under running cold water, and drain.

In a kettle combine 4 cups each of cider vinegar and sugar, ¼ cup mustard seed, and 2 tablespoons each of celery seed and turmeric. (Tie whole spices in a bag, if preferred.) Bring the liquid to a boil, stirring until the sugar is dissolved. Add both vegetable mixtures and 1 cup chopped onion. Return the liquid to a boil, and simmer for 10 minutes. Pack the pickles into jars and adjust the lids. Process in a boiling-water bath for 10 minutes. Makes about 8 pints.

Pickled Onions

Peel 10 pounds of small white pickling onions. (To peel pickling onions, cover the onions with boiling water and let stand for 2 minutes. Drain and dip onions into cold water. Drain and peel.)

Let stand overnight in salt water made in the proportion of 1 cup pure salt to 1 gallon of water. The next morning, drain the salt water off the onions and discard.

In a large kettle, combine 3 cups vinegar, 3 cups water, 3 cups sugar, 12 small hot red peppers, broken in pieces, and 4 tablespoons whole mustard seed. Bring the mixture to a boil and add the drained onions. Bring again to a boil. Pack the onions into jars and cover with the boiling vinegar solution, leaving ¼-inch head space. Adjust lids. Process pints and half-pints in a boiling-water bath for 10 minutes. Makes about 10 pints.

Sweet Pickled Carrots

Scrub and pare 18 medium carrots and cut into diagonal slices. (Or use 2 quarts baby carrots.) Cook the prepared carrots and 2 medium onions, cut into slices and separated into rings, in boiling salted water until almost tender, or about 5 minutes. Drain well and pack while hot into hot jars.

Meanwhile, combine 2 cups vinegar, 2 cups water, 1

cup sugar, 1 teaspoon salt, 1 teaspoon ground allspice, 1 teaspoon ground cloves, and 1 stick cinnamon in a kettle and bring to a boil over high heat. Boil for 5 minutes. Pour the hot syrup over the hot carrots in the jars. Adjust lids. Process in boiling-water bath for 30 minutes. Makes about 4 pints.

Pickled Hot Peppers

Thoroughly wash hot banana peppers and puncture each one in several places. Place peppers in a stoneware jar and cover with a brine made of 1 gallon of water and 2 cups of pure salt. Weigh the peppers down so that they stay under the brine (see directions page 159). Let stand overnight. The next day pack the peppers into hot sterilized jars. In each jar place half a clove of peeled garlic, 1 grape leaf, and 1 small sprig of dill.

Make a pickling solution of 1 gallon water, 1 cup pure salt, and 1 cup vinegar. Bring the mixture to the boiling point and pour over the peppers in the jars. Leave ¼-inch head space. Adjust lids and process in a boiling-water bath for 15 minutes. Let the pickles age for 6 weeks before using.

Pickled Sweet Peppers

Soak green bell peppers in salt water overnight, using water to cover and 1 teaspoon salt per pepper. The next morning, drain, remove the seeds from, slice, and pack the peppers into jars.

Combine 3 cups sugar, 3 cups vinegar, and 3 teaspoons mixed pickling spices and bring to a boil. Pour the boiling-hot pickling solution over the peppers in the jars, leaving ¼-inch head space, and adjust lids. Process in a boiling-water bath for 15 minutes.

Zucchini Bread-and-Butter Slices

Scrub and slice thin 3 pounds unpeeled zucchini. Place zucchini slices in a large glass bowl with 2 cups thin-sliced onions, separated into rings, and ¼ cup pure salt. Cover with water and let stand for two hours in a cool place. Drain.

In a large kettle combine 3 cups cider vinegar, 1½ cups sugar or honey or light corn syrup, 1 teaspoon mustard seed, 1 tablespoon celery seed, 1½ teaspoons turmeric, and 1 teaspoon dry mustard. Bring to a boil and pour the hot mixture over the zucchini and onions. Let stand for 1 hour, stirring occasionally.

Bring the zucchini mixture to a boil and simmer for 3 minutes. Pack the boiling-hot mixture into hot jars, leaving ¼-inch head space. Adjust lids and process in a boiling-water bath, 5 minutes for pints, 10 minutes for quarts. Makes about 5 pints.

Dilled Okra

Rinse 4 quarts firm young okra (use pods about 2 inches long), drain well, and trim the stems but not the caps. In a kettle, combine 8 cups cider vinegar, 4 cups water, and 1 cup pure salt. Bring the liquid to a boil and simmer the mixture for 15 minutes.

Pack the okra in 8 hot 1-pint canning jars. To each jar add 1 peeled garlic clove, 1 small red hot pepper, and a sprig of fresh dill. Fill the jars with the hot vinegar mixture, leaving ¼-inch head space. Adjust lids. Process in a boiling-water bath for 10 minutes. To avoid overcooking the pickles, start counting the processing time as soon as the jars are placed in actively boiling water.

Store the jars in a cool, dark, dry place for 6 weeks before using.

Dilled Green Beans or Unripe Cherry Tomatoes

Follow the recipe for Dilled Okra, using small whole green beans or green (unripe) cherry tomatoes instead of the okra.

Indiana Stuffed "Mangoes"*

Slice the tops from the stem ends of 12 large green or red bell peppers or some of both. Large, sweet, yellow "banana" peppers may also be used. Remove the seeds and membranes. Put the tops and the whole peppers into a

*In the Midwest bell peppers are commonly known as "mangoes."

large crock and cover with cold water. Sprinkle with 1 tablespoon salt and let stand overnight.

The next day, mix together well in a large bowl 4 cups shredded cabbage, 1 tablespoon salt, ½ to 1½ cups sugar, 2 tablespoons mustard seed, and 2 tablespoons celery seed. Drain the peppers well, then fill their cavities with the cabbage mixture. Replace the tops of the peppers and tie or sew them into place with white cotton string. Place the stuffed peppers in a large, deep crockery jar and cover with 1 quart of mild cider vinegar sweetened with ½ cup sugar, or more if needed. Put a weighted plate on top of the peppers to keep them under the vinegar. Cover the jar with aluminum foil or a lid and store in the refrigerator for 2 weeks before eating.

Green tomatoes may be used instead of bell peppers. Cut off the tops and scoop out their centers. Fill with the cabbage mixture, as above.

To can the stuffed mangoes, sterilize 3 or 4 wide-mouth quart jars. Lift the peppers out of the vinegar and sugar solution and into hot sterilized jars. Heat the solution to boiling and pour over the peppers. Leave ½-inch head space. Adjust the caps and process 15 minutes in a boiling-water bath.

Ripe Cucumber Pickles (Senfgurken)

Wash and peel 12 large, ripe cucumbers. Cut in halves lengthwise and remove the seeds. Let stand for 12 hours in a brine made of ½ cup coarse pickling salt and 4½ cups water, or to cover. Drain, rinse with fresh water, and drain again.

In a kettle, bring to a boil a mixture of 6 cups of sugar and 1 quart of vinegar. Boil with the mixture a spice bag containing 2 tablespoons yellow mustard seed, 1 tablespoon whole cloves, and 1 broken 3-inch stick of cinnamon. Add the cucumbers and cook slowly until the cucumbers begin to look transparent but are still crisp. Discard the spice bag. Fill hot sterilized jars with the cucumbers and cover with the hot syrup. Seal and process in a boiling-water bath for 5 minutes to ensure the seal. Makes about 3 quarts.

Pickled Beets

In water to cover, boil about 12 small beets with ½-inch stems until tender, about 30 minutes. Remove the skins.

In a saucepan, combine ½ cup cider vinegar, 1 cup sugar, 2 cups water, and 1 teaspoon pickling spices with red peppers removed. Stir and bring to a boil. Pour over the beets and store in the refrigerator until used, or pack beets into sterilized jars with the hot syrup leaving ½-inch head space. Adjust lids. Process in pressure canner for 30 minutes. Makes a small amount, about 2 pints.

Save the beet juice from the beet jar and use it to pour over peeled, hard-cooked eggs. Let the eggs stand in the beet liquid in the refrigerator for two days before eating.

Pickled Baby Corn Ears

When field corn or sweet corn is only 2 to 3 inches long, pick enough to fill 4 pint jars. Husk and clean the miniature ears and drop into a kettle of boiling water. Boil the corn for 4 minutes and drain.

At the same time, boil together in a separate pan for 5 minutes a solution of 1 cup water, 2 cups sugar, 2 cups white vinegar, 2 teaspoons salt, and 1 tablespoon pickling spices tied in a bag.

Pack the warm, drained, boiled corn ears in hot sterilized jars and cover with the hot vinegar solution. Leave ½-inch head space. Adjust lids. Process in a boiling-water bath for 10 minutes.

RELISHES

Relishes are made from mixed vegetables or fruits that are chopped or ground before being combined and cooked with a spiced, sweet-sour solution. Relishes may be hot and spicy or mild and sweet. They are used to accent the flavor of other foods. Chutneys, chowders, chowchows, piccalillis, and various "salads" and "hashes" are all relishes.

Zucchini Relish

Put enough zucchini (about 16), scrubbed and trimmed, through the coarse blade of a food grinder to measure 12 cups. Grind enough onion to measure 4 cups. In a large ceramic or glass bowl combine the zucchini, onion, and 5 tablespoons pickling salt, and chill the mixture, covered, overnight. Drain the zucchini mixture in a colander, rinse it under running cold water, and drain thoroughly.

In a kettle combine 4 to 6 cups sugar, 3 cups cider vinegar, 1 tablespoon dry mustard, 1½ teaspoons celery seed, 1 teaspoon pepper, and ¾ teaspoon turmeric and bring the liquid to a boil, stirring until the sugar is dissolved. Add the zucchini mixture and 2 sweet bell peppers (use 1 red and 1 green for color), both chopped fine, and simmer the mixture, stirring frequently, for 30 minutes. Pack into jars, leaving ¼-inch head space. Adjust lids and process in a boiling-water bath for 15 minutes. Makes about 5 pints.

Options: I have made this relish using 4, 5, and 6 cups of sugar in the recipe. All are good but my family liked the sweetest relish best.

Turnip or Summer Squash Relish

Follow the recipe for Zucchini Relish, substituting peeled turnips or unpeeled yellow summer squash for the zucchini. In the summer squash relish, you may substitute 1 cup of chopped sweet peppers, half red and half green, for 1 of the 4 cups of onion.

Chowchow

In a large earthenware crock or bowl, combine a 2½ pound head of white cabbage, shredded, 6 green and 6 red bell peppers, and 6 onions, all chopped, and 1½ pounds green tomatoes, cut into ¼-inch cubes. Toss the mixture with ¼ cup pickling salt and let stand overnight in a cool place. Drain the vegetables in a colander.

In a kettle combine 6 cups cider vinegar, 2½ cups sugar, 2 tablespoons each of mustard seed and prepared mustard, 1 tablespoon each of mixed pickling spice and celery salt, and 1½ teaspoons each of turmeric and ground ginger. Bring the liquid to a boil, then stir in the vegetables and simmer the mixture for 10 minutes. Pack the chowchow into jars leaving ¼-inch head space and adjust lids. Process for 10 minutes in a boiling-water bath. Makes about 8 pints.

Barbara's Green-Tomato Relish

Wash and core, but do not peel, 4 quarts firm green tomatoes. Put through the coarse blade of the food chopper. Also prepare and grind 10 medium onions and 6 sweet peppers, using red, green, and yellow peppers to add color. Combine the ground vegetables and mix with 6 tablespoons pure salt. Let stand for 10 minutes, then drain off any liquid that has formed.

Put the ground vegetables into a large kettle and add 6 cups sugar, 4 cups vinegar, and the following spices tied in a bag: 4 teaspoons celery seed, 2 teaspoons whole allspice, and 4 teaspoons mustard seed. Mix together and heat to boiling. Pack the boiling-hot relish into hot canning jars, leaving ¼-inch head space. Adjust lids. Process 15 minutes in a boiling-water bath. Makes 8 pints.

Jerusalem Artichoke Relish

Wash and scrub Jerusalem artichoke tubers with a brush. Trim, if necessary, but leave skins on. Using the coarse blade of a food chopper, prepare 2½ cups chopped Jerusalem artichokes. Also chop 1½ cups green bell peppers and ½ cup pimientos (or use 1 cup green bell peppers and 1 cup red bell peppers). Combine with the artichokes in a heavy kettle and add ½ to 1 cup chopped onions to taste, 1 clove garlic, minced, 2½ teaspoons salt, 1 cup cider or wine vinegar, and 3 tablespoons honey. (If a sweeter relish is wanted, use more honey or add sugar. If a dill flavor is wanted, add 1 teaspoon dill seeds.)

Bring the mixture to a full boil while stirring, then cook over lowered heat for about 5 minutes. Pour the relish into hot sterilized jars, leaving ¼-inch head space. Adjust lids. Process in a boiling-water bath for 10 minutes. Makes about 2 pints.

Grandma Marshall's Relish

Chop 1 quart green tomatoes and 1 quart ripe tomatoes into chunks about 1 inch square. Using the coarse blade of the food chopper, grind 1 average-sized head of cabbage, 4 red and 4 green bell peppers, and 1 dozen unpeeled red apples. Sprinkle the mixture with ½ cup pure salt and let stand overnight in a cool place.

The next morning, drain the mixture and place it in a large kettle with ½ gallon vinegar, 4 tablespoons ground mustard, 1 teaspoon horseradish, ½ teaspoon garlic powder (or 1 clove minced garlic), and 2½ teaspoons celery salt (optional). Bring to a boil while stirring and boil gently for 20 minutes, stirring often. Ladle into hot jars, leaving ¼-inch head space. Adjust lids. Process in a boiling-water bath for 10 minutes.

Pepper Hash

Peel 12 small onions and remove the seeds and membranes from 12 green and 12 red bell peppers. Put vegetables through the food chopper. Sprinkle the chopped vegetables with 2 tablespoons salt, then pour boiling water over them and let stand 15 minutes. Drain thoroughly.

In a large saucepan, combine 2 cups sugar and 2 cups vinegar. Bring to a boil, then add the drained vegetables. Cook slowly for 15 minutes. Pack into jars, leaving ¼-inch head space. Adjust lids and process 5 minutes in a boiling-water bath. Makes about 3 pints.

Options: This pepper hash can be made less sweet, with as little as ½ cup of sugar, as preferred. The addition of 1 hot red pepper will add zest.

Corn Salad

Cook 12 ears of sweet corn in boiling water for 3 to 5 minutes, drain, and cut the kernels from the cobs. Combine the corn with 2 onions, ground or chopped, 2 or 3 green and 2 or 3 red bell peppers, chopped fine, and 1 small head of chopped cabbage (about 1 quart).

In a large kettle combine ¾ cup prepared mustard, 1 tablespoon salt, 1½ to 2½ cups sugar, to taste, 4½ cups cider vinegar, and 1 cup water, and bring to a boil. Add the prepared vegetables and simmer for 30 minutes. Bring again to a boil and pack into jars, leaving ¼-inch head space. Adjust lids. Process 15 minutes in a boiling-water bath. Makes about 6 pints.

Option: Defrosted frozen corn or drained whole kernel canned corn may be substituted for fresh sweet corn. Use 2 quarts of corn.

Peach Chutney

Scald, peel, and pit 8 pounds fresh table-ripe peaches. Chop in small pieces and combine in a preserving kettle with 1 cup chopped raisins, 1 cup chopped onions, 1 large clove minced garlic, 3 pounds brown sugar, 2 quarts vinegar, 4 tablespoons chili powder, 4 tablespoons mustard seed, 2 tablespoons salt, and 1 cup crystallized ginger, minced fine. Bring to a boil while stirring, then cook slowly for about two hours, or until the chutney is brown and thick. Pour into sterilized half-pint jars. Leave ½-inch head space. Adjust lids, and process in a boiling-water bath for 10 minutes. Makes about 6 pints.

Tomato and Apple Chutney

In a preserving kettle combine 2 pounds green tomatoes, diced, 2 pounds apples, diced, 1 pound onions, diced, 2 carrots, grated, ½ pound raisins, 1 pound brown sugar, 1½ tablespoons salt, 2 cups vinegar, ½ teaspoon mace, ¼ teaspoon cayenne pepper, and 6 peppercorns, 6 whole cloves, and 2 bay leaves tied in a cloth bag. Place on high heat, bring to a boil while stirring, and simmer until all ingredients are soft, or about 2 hours. Pour into hot sterilized jars. Leave ½-inch head space. Adjust lids, and process in a boiling-water bath for 10 minutes.

Sally's Key Biscayne Mango Chutney

Peel and cut into cubes enough firm ripe mangoes to make 10½ pounds, about 35 medium-sized mangoes. Combine the prepared mangoes in a large heavy saucepan with 9 large sweet white onions, chopped; 9 cloves garlic, minced;

1½ pounds dark raisins; 9 ounces preserved ginger, chopped fine; 4½ pints cider vinegar; 1½ cups Key lime juice and the grated rind of 6 Key limes; 3 pounds white sugar; 3 pounds dark brown sugar; 6 tablespoons salt; 6 tablespoons chili pepper; 1½ tablespoons cinnamon; 1½ tablespoons celery seed; 1½ tablespoons mustard seed; 2¼ tablespoons whole cloves; and 1½ tablespoons allspice. (Tie the whole spices in a square of cheesecloth.) Cook the chutney over low heat, stirring often, until thickened, about 40 minutes. Pour the chutney into hot jars, leaving ½-inch head space. Adjust caps and process the chutney for 10 minutes in a boiling-water bath.

Elderberry Chutney

Put 6 cups of tart apples, which have been peeled and sliced, through the medium blade of a food grinder or chop them in an electric blender. Heat the apples with 2 cups of white vinegar, or elderflower vinegar, if you have it, stirring often, until the mixture boils. Then strain the vinegar off the apples into another pan and place the apple pulp in a crock. To the hot vinegar add 2 cups of stemmed ripe elderberries, 3 cups seedless raisins, 1 cup chopped dates, 1½ cups diced pineapple, 4 cups sugar, 2 tablespoons salt, ½ teaspoon cayenne pepper, 1 tablespoon ground ginger, and 1 stick cinnamon. Boil this mixture carefully for 10 minutes, stirring often. Pour the boiled mixture over the apples in the crock and let stand in the refrigerator for 24 hours. The next day, cook the chutney down, stirring frequently, until it is thickened, or about 30 minutes. Pour into hot, sterilized jars, leaving ½-inch head space. Adjust caps and process 10 minutes in a boiling-water bath. Makes 4 pints.

CATSUPS AND HOT SAUCES

"Catsup," "catchup," and "ketchup" are all names for a sauce consisting of the boiled, strained, and seasoned pulp of various fruits and vegetables. Tomatoes are most popularly used in making catsup, but it can also be made from cranberries, cucumbers, grapes, mushrooms, plums, and other fruits and vegetables. Catsups usually contain vinegar and spices, onions and green peppers, and other ingredients. Catsups are served with cold meats or added to sauces and stews to give flavor.

Hot-Pepper Sauce

In a large kettle, combine 3 quarts of chopped ripe tomatoes, 3 dozen hot red peppers, and 3 cups vinegar. Boil until the vegetables are soft. Strain the vegetables through a food mill and return to the kettle with 3 cups vinegar, 1 tablespoon salt, 1½ cups sugar, and a spice bag containing 2 tablespoons mixed pickling spices. Boil the mixture slowly until it reaches the desired thickness, stirring often. Discard the spice bag and pour the hot sauce into hot jars, leaving ¼-inch head space. Adjust lids and process in a boiling-water bath for 10 minutes.

Tomato Catsup

Wash and quarter, but do not peel, 8 quarts of ripe tomatoes. Place tomatoes in a large kettle with 1 small bunch of parsley, 2 cups fine-chopped onions, 1 clove garlic, minced, ½ cup sugar, 3 stalks celery and leaves, and 2 tablespoons salt. Mash the tomatoes to start the juice and simmer the mixture, stirring occasionally, until the vegetables are soft. Put the mixture through a food mill or strainer to remove the seeds and skins. Return the juice to the kettle and add the following spices tied in a bag: 1 tablespoon each celery seed, mustard seed, peppercorns, allspice, and 1 teaspoon cloves. Also add 1½ cups brown sugar and 2 cups vinegar. Bring the mixture to a boil, then reduce heat and simmer for several hours, until the mixture is thick with no water running from it when a little is placed on a saucer and the original volume is reduced one-third to one-half. Pour into jars, leaving ¼-inch head space. Adjust caps. Process in a boiling-water bath for 10 minutes.

Ruby's Mom's Chili Sauce

Pour boiling water over about 24 large ripe tomatoes, plunge into cold water, peel, and chop. In a large kettle combine 4 quarts chopped tomatoes, 2 green peppers, chopped, 2 sweet red peppers, chopped, 1½ cups celery, chopped, 1½ cups onion, chopped, 1½ cups sugar, 1 table-spoon hot sauce (Tabasco), 1 tablespoon salt, 2 cups cider vinegar, and the following spices tied in a cloth bag: 1 stick cinnamon, 1 tablespoon whole cloves, 1½ teaspoons mustard seed, and 1½ teaspoons celery seed. Bring the mixture to a boil, stirring often, then reduce heat and boil gently, stirring as needed, until the sauce is of the desired consistency, or about 3 to 5 hours. Pour into hot sterilized jars, leaving ¼-inch head space. Adjust lids. Process in a boiling-water bath for 15 minutes. Makes about 6 pints.

FRUIT PICKLES

Fruits are pickled in spicy, sweet-sour vinegar syrup. They are left whole, as pickled peaches, or cut to size, as pickled watermelon rind.

Damson Plum Pickles

Wash and remove the stems from about 1 quart of damson plums. You will need 2 cups of whole, unpitted damson plums and 2 cups of damson plums with the pits removed.

In a kettle combine 3 cups brown sugar and ½ cup cider vinegar. Tie ½ tablespoon whole cloves, 1 stick cinnamon, and ½ cup pits from the plums in a cheesecloth bag. Add to the sugar and vinegar and heat to boiling, stirring frequently. Boil 10 minutes. Remove the spice bag. Add the prepared plums and boil gently for 10 minutes, being careful not to break the fruit too much when stirring. Pack in hot sterilized jars leaving ½-inch head space. Adjust lids. Process in a boiling-water bath for 15 minutes. Makes 2 pints. Serve with meats.

Watermelon-Rind Pickles

Trim the green skin and red flesh from a thick watermelon rind and cut it into 1-inch cubes. Place 2½ quarts of the cubes in a large saucepan. Cover with boiling water and

178

boil the rind until tender but not soft, or about 10 minutes. Drain in a colander.

In a saucepan, combine 7 cups sugar, 2 cups cider vinegar, 1 teaspoon whole cloves, and 2 sticks cinnamon. Or tie the spices in a square of cheesecloth and then remove before canning, if preferred. Bring to a boil, stirring well to dissolve the sugar. Pour the hot syrup over the drained watermelon rind which has been placed in a crockery bowl, and let stand overnight at room temperature.

The next morning, drain the syrup from the watermelon rind and heat it in a saucepan to the boiling point. Again pour the hot syrup over the watermelon rind and let stand overnight.

On the third day, slice 2 small unpeeled oranges and 1 unpeeled lemon into small pieces, removing the seeds. Add the oranges and lemon to the watermelon rind and syrup and heat them together in a large saucepan until the boiling point is reached. Pack in hot sterilized jars and cover with boiling hot syrup. Leave ½-inch head space. Adjust lids and process in a boiling-water bath for 5 minutes. Makes about 5 pints.

Pickled Peaches

Plunge 6 pounds peaches into a kettle of boiling water for 1 minute, drain and peel, and insert 2 cloves in each peach. In an enamel kettle combine 6 cups sugar, 2 cups cider vinegar, and 3 cinnamon sticks. Bring the liquid to a boil over moderate heat, stirring and washing down any sugar crystals clinging to the sides of the pan with a brush dipped in cold water, and add the peaches. Simmer the peaches for 5 minutes, or until they are just tender, and transfer them with a slotted spoon to 3 sterilized 1-quart Mason-type jars, packing them tight. Put 1 cinnamon stick in each jar, pour the hot syrup over the peaches. Leave ½-inch head space. Adjust lids. Process in a boiling-water bath for 20 minutes. Makes 3 quarts.

Pickled Pears

Follow the recipe for Pickled Peaches, using any good firm

179

preserving pear. Peel the pears, cut into halves, and re-move cores, or pickle whole if Seckel pears are used. Tie the spices in a bag and cook the pears until they look clear and are tender. Pack and process as for Pickled Peaches.

Pickled Pears with Wine and Honey

Peel 12 firm ripe pears, all of uniform size. Combine 1 cup light-colored honey, ¾ cup distilled white vinegar, and 1 stick of cinnamon and bring to a boil, then simmer for 10 minutes. Add 1 cup sweet wine. Stick 3 cloves in each pear half and add pears to simmering syrup. Cook gently for about 5 minutes, or until pears are just tender. Turn the pears frequently during cooking. Pack in hot sterilized jars, leaving ¼-inch head space. If there is not enough syrup to fill the jars, additional wine may be used to cover the pears. Adjust lids. Process for 5 minutes in a boiling-water bath.

Old-Time Pickled Lemons

Scrub 16 small lemons with a brush and dry on a towel. In an enamelware kettle, combine ½ gallon vinegar and ½ cup pure salt. Bring to a boil and add the following spices tied in a cheesecloth bag: 1½ teaspoons each whole cloves, grated nutmeg, mace, and cayenne pepper; 4 tablespoons mustard seed; and 1 peeled clove of garlic. Add the lemons and simmer until they can be pierced with a skewer and are tender, or about 30 minutes. Discard the spice bag.

To seal in jars: Pack the boiling-hot lemons in hot steri-lized jars and cover them with the boiling-hot spiced vin-egar, leaving ¼-inch head space. Adjust lids. Process in a boiling-water bath for 10 minutes. Let the lemons ripen for several weeks before serving.

To keep in the refrigerator: Place the lemons and the spiced vinegar in a large stone jar, making sure the lemons are under the liquid. If necessary, weigh down the fruit to keep it under the liquid, using a china plate that will fit down in the jar and a canning jar filled with water on top of the plate. Cover the stone jar with aluminum foil. Stir the lemons daily for about 1 month before serving.

Pumpkin Pickle

Slice pumpkin, remove seeds and membranes, peel and cut into 1-inch cubes. Steam 6 cups pumpkin cubes, using a vegetable-steaming rack or a colander, until the cubes are just tender. Do not cook the pumpkin in the water. Drain.

Make a syrup of 2 cups vinegar, 2 cups sugar, two 4-inch sticks cinnamon, and 1 teaspoon whole allspice. Bring to a boil and simmer for 10 minutes, then add the pumpkin cubes and simmer for 5 minutes. Cool and let pumpkin cubes stand in the syrup in a cool place overnight. The next day, drain the syrup off the pumpkin cubes and heat it to boiling. Pour the boiling syrup over the pumpkin and again let the mixture stand overnight. The third day, bring the pumpkin cubes in the syrup to the boiling point. Pack the pumpkin into jars, cover with boiling syrup, and leave ¼-inch head space. Adjust lids. Process in a boiling-water bath, 5 minutes for pints, 10 minutes for quarts.

LIME PICKLES

Lime pickles deserve a special section of their own among pickling recipes. Anyone who has tasted lime pickles will be interested in trying more than one recipe.

Adding lime to pickles to make them crackling crisp is an old-fashioned practice that has long been in use. Some of these recipes are hand-me-downs, others have been developed by the manufacturers of the lime for pickling. (See the special information on lime, pages 153 and 353.)

Green-Tomato Lime Pickles

Cut 7 pounds green tomatoes in crosswise slices, ¼ inch thick. Put the slices in an enamelware pan and cover with a solution made of 2 gallons water and 2 cups hydrated lime. Soak the tomato slices in the lime-water solution for 24 hours, then drain. Cover the slices with clear water and soak for three hours, then drain and rinse several times in fresh water, until the water is clear.

Mix together 2 quarts cider vinegar, 5 to 7 pounds sugar, 1 tablespoon salt, 1 teaspoon celery seed, 1 teaspoon whole cloves, and 1 teaspoon mixed pickling spices from which the red peppers have been removed. Pour the vinegar solution over the tomato slices in the enamelware pan and let stand overnight. The next morning, bring the tomato slices and vinegar solution to a boil and boil for 30 minutes. Add 1 cup raisins and boil for 5 minutes more. Ladle the tomato slices and the pickling solution into hot, sterilized jars. Leave ¼-inch head space. Adjust lids and process in a boiling-water bath for 5 minutes.

Old South Cucumber Lime Pickles

Wash 7 pounds pickling cucumbers, slice off the blossom ends, and cut into crosswise slices, about ¼ inch thick. Cover with lime water made of 2 cups hydrated lime to 2 gallons cold water. Let stand for 24 hours in a crockery or enamelware container. The next day, remove the cucumbers from the lime water and rinse through three cold waters, or until the water is clear of lime. Let stand for 3 hours in ice and water. Remove cucumbers carefully from the ice water and drain.

Make a syrup of 2 quarts vinegar, 8 cups sugar, 1 tablespoon salt, and a few drops of green food coloring (optional). Stir until dissolved. Pour over the cucumbers. Add a spice bag containing either 1 tablespoon mixed pickling spices with the red pepper removed, 1 tablespoon whole allspice, and 1 tablespoon whole cloves; or 1 tablespoon each of celery seed, mustard seed, whole cloves, and mixed pickling spices, as preferred. Let the cucumbers stand overnight, or at least 5 or 6 hours, in the pickling solution. Place the container in the refrigerator during this time.

The next morning, bring the cucumbers and syrup to a boil and cook gently for 35 minutes, stirring often. Do not boil hard. Pack into clean hot jars. Cover with hot syrup and leave ¼-inch head space. Adjust lids. Process in a boiling-water bath, 5 minutes for pints, 10 minutes for quarts.

Watermelon-Rind Lime Pickles

Trim the green skin and red flesh from a thick watermelon rind and cut it into 1-inch cubes. Place 4 pounds of prepared cubes in an enamelware pan. Combine 2 quarts cold water and 1 tablespoon slaked lime (Eli Lilly & Co. Powder No. 40 Calcium Hydroxide). Pour the lime water over the watermelon rind and let stand for one hour. Drain the lime water off the rind and rinse with fresh cold water. When the water is clear, cover again with fresh cold water and simmer the rind until tender, or about 1 hour. Do not boil.

Combine 1 quart cider vinegar, 1 quart water, and 4 pounds sugar in a large kettle. Add a spice bag containing 2 tablespoons whole allspice, 2 tablespoons whole cloves, and ten 2-inch pieces of stick cinnamon. Heat the mixture until the sugar dissolves. Pour over the rind and simmer for 2 hours. Do not allow the pickles to heat above the simmering point. Remove spices and pack the rind in hot sterilized jars and cover with boiling syrup. Leave ¼-inch head space. Adjust lids and process in a boiling-water bath, 5 minutes for pints, 10 minutes for quarts.

Cantaloupe Lime Pickles

Cut cantaloupes into quarters, remove seeds, and pare. Cut into 1-inch cubes to make 3 quarts of cantaloupe cubes. Cover cantaloupe with a lime-water solution made of 1 cup hydrated lime to 1 gallon water. Let stand 24 hours. Drain, and wash thoroughly until the water is free of lime. Drain and place in a large kettle with fresh water to cover. Bring the cantaloupe and water to a boil, remove from heat, and drain again.

In a large kettle, combine 5 pounds of sugar with 2 quarts white vinegar and a spice bag containing 3 tablespoons whole cloves and 6 sticks cinnamon. Boil the vinegar mixture for about 15 minutes, then add the melon cubes and cook slowly in the syrup until tender and slightly transparent, or about 1 hour. Remove the spice bag. Slice 1 lemon and 1 lime as thin as possible. Add to the melon-syrup mixture and boil for about 1 minute more. Pack in clean hot jars and cover with hot syrup, leaving ¼-inch head space. Adjust lids. Process in a boiling-water bath, 10 minutes for quarts, 5 minutes for pints. Makes about 7 pints.

Crystallized Pumpkin*

Cut 1 large yellow pumpkin and remove the seeds, membranes, and rind. Cut the pumpkin pieces into 1-inch cubes. Place the pumpkin cubes in a large enamelware pan and cover with a well-mixed solution of 1 cup hydrated lime and 1 gallon water. Let stand overnight.

The next morning, rinse the pumpkin in clear water several times until the lime is removed and the water runs clear again. Drain.

In a large preserving kettle, combine 6 to 8 pounds of sugar, depending on the size of the pumpkin used, with enough water to make a thick syrup, and heat to simmering. Add the drained pumpkin and stir and baste, cooking slowly, until the sugar crystallizes. Add 2 tablespoons vanilla, remove from the fire, and cool while stirring.

Spread out on flat pans to dry. Store on the shelf in airtight tins until used.

REFRIGERATOR AND SHORTCUT PICKLES AND SWEETS

Refrigerator and shortcut pickles and sweets are not intended for long storage. They are made from fresh or canned fruits and vegetables, then stored in the refrigerator until used. No special equipment is needed since these pickles and sweets are not sealed or canned.

Martha's No-Canning Pickles

Wash and cut into thin slices enough cucumbers to measure 6 cups. Combine with 1 cup chopped white onions (must be white onions) and 1 cup chopped green or red bell peppers.

Mix together 1 cup white vinegar, 2 cups sugar, 1 teaspoon celery seed, and 1 teaspoon salt. Pour over the prepared vegetables and mix well. Store in a covered container in the refrigerator. Do not can. These pickles will keep in the refrigerator for several months.

*This recipe is included with the lime pickles because it is made with lime.

Uncooked Cabbage Relish

Prepare and grind 12 onions, 1 large head cabbage, 8 medium carrots, 4 green bell peppers, and 4 red bell peppers. Mix well with ½ cup pure salt. Let the vegetables stand for two hours, then press out all the juice and discard.

Combine 1 quart vinegar, 6 cups sugar, 2 teaspoons mustard seed, and 2 teaspoons celery seed. Stir the mixture until the sugar is dissolved, then add it to the ground vegetables. Store the relish in the refrigerator until used.

Uncooked Cucumber Catsup

Peel and seed twelve 8-inch-long cucumbers. Grate them on a kitchen grater. Peel and grate 2 small onions and combine with the cucumbers. Drain the mixed vegetables in a sieve for about 1 hour. Mix with 1 cup wine or herb vinegar, 2 teaspoons salt, and pepper to taste. The catsup will be the consistency of jam. Store in the refrigerator.

Ripe-Tomato Relish

Wash, scald, and peel 7 pounds of ripe tomatoes. Dice or mash them and combine them with 7 medium onions, peeled and chopped fine or ground. Add 1 cup of pure salt and let stand in a cool place for half a day. Then place mixture in a cheesecloth-lined colander or a bag and let drain overnight.

The next morning add 1 cup chopped celery, 2 diced green bell peppers, 2 diced red bell peppers, 2 cups sugar, 2 cups vinegar, ½ teaspoon cinnamon, and ½ teaspoon mustard seed or dry mustard. Mix well and let stand for 1 hour. Pack in jars and chill until used. This relish will keep all winter in the refrigerator. Makes 4 pints.

Stone-Jar Green-Tomato Pickle

Wash and core but do not peel 1 gallon firm green tomatoes. Slice into thin slices. Prepare 10 medium-sized onions and slice into thin rings. Place in a stoneware crock or jar in alternate layers. Sprinkle ¼ cup pure salt and 1 tablespoon mustard seed over the tomatoes and onion. Let stand overnight in a cool place.

The next morning, drain off liquid thoroughly and discard. Combine 1 cup sugar and 1 quart vinegar and stir to dissolve the sugar. Pour over the tomatoes and onions. Cover the stone jar with a plate and let stand in the refrigerator for 24 hours.

Dill Crock

Clean 2 to 2½ dozen small to medium-sized pickling cucumbers and prick them with a fork.

In a kettle, bring to a boil 3 cups cider vinegar, 9 cups water, 4 tablespoons salt, and 4 tablespoons sugar, stirring occasionally. Remove from the heat and cool.

In the bottom of a 1-gallon stoneware jar, put a layer of fresh dill, using the heads, leaves, and stalks of the upper part of the plants. Scatter on the dill ½ teaspoon mixed pickling spice and half a clove of garlic, chopped. Make sure there are several bay leaves and small red peppers in the pickling spices. Next arrange a layer of pickles on the dill. Continue making layers of dill spread with pickling spice and garlic and topped with cucumbers, until the jar is filled, making about 4 or 5 layers in all. Top the crock with sprays of fresh dill.

Pour the cooled vinegar mixture into the crock, filling it almost to the rim, cover with a plate, and weight down with a heavy object (not limestone). Let stand for 4 or 5 days at room temperature. A cloudy film will form on top of the liquid. When the pickles are well flavored, skim the film off the surface of the liquid and remove the pickles from the jar. Discard the dill and the spices. Put the pickles in a clean jar, cover them with some of the pickling liquid, add a spray of dill, cover the jar, and store the pickles in the refrigerator until well chilled, then serve.

Other vegetables, such as tender green beans, raw cauliflower, and carrot strips, may be included in the dill crock, if desired.

Refrigerator Rhubarb Jam

In a large, heavy preserving kettle, combine 4 cups cubed rhubarb and 4 cups sugar and stir over medium heat until the mixture boils. Cook and stir constantly for 12 minutes.

Then add 2 cups canned crushed pineapple. Stir and again bring the mixture to a boil and cook for 3 minutes more. Add 1 package of strawberry-flavored gelatin (3 ounces) and stir to dissolve. Pour into hot sterilized jars and cool. Cover and store in the refrigerator until used.

Lemon Curd

In the top of a double boiler or in a heavy saucepan, melt ½ cup butter. Stir in 2 teaspoons freshly grated lemon rind and ½ cup freshly squeezed lemon juice. Add 2 cups sugar and stir until well mixed.

Beat 3 whole eggs and 3 egg yolks in the small mixer bowl for 1 minute. Blend into the lemon mixture in the saucepan and cook, stirring constantly, over hot water or on low heat until the mixture is very thick, or about 8 or 10 minutes. Do not allow the lemon mixture to boil; keep just below simmering. Immediately pour into sterilized jars. Cover with sterilized lids and store in the refrigerator until used for tart filling, cake fillings, or as a spread. Keeps several weeks in the refrigerator. Makes four 8-ounce glasses.

Short-Cut Relish

Prepare 4 medium onions and put them and 2 large dill pickles through the coarse blade of a food chopper. Add 1 jar of prepared mustard of your choice and mix thoroughly. Store in the refrigerator until used.

Stone-Jar Beet Pickle

Place 1 gallon of canned or freshly cooked beets in a stone jar. If small, they may be left whole. Cut larger beets into slices or quarter. Mix together ⅓ cup prepared mustard, ¼ cup salt, 3 cups vinegar, 2½ cups brown sugar, and ½ cup cold water. Pour the mixture over the beets in the stone jar. Mixed pickling spices may be added, if wanted; use 1 tablespoon of the spices with the red pepper removed. Store in refrigerator. Let stand 24 hours before serving.

Vardine's Candied Dills

Buy 1 quart of dill pickles. Drain the pickles and discard the liquid. Cut in ¼-inch circles or slices. Mix ½ cup tarragon vinegar and 2¾ cup sugar together. Tie 2 table-spoons mixed pickling spices in a cheesecloth square and add to the vinegar mixture. Pour the vinegar over the pickles and let the mixture stand at room temperature until the sugar dissolves, or about 4 hours. Then put the pickles back in the jar, cover them with the vinegar syrup, and chill 4 days before using.

Shortcut Bread-and-Butter Slices

Drain the liquid from 2 quarts of dill pickles. Cut the pickles crosswise into ¼-inch thick slices. Put them back into the jars along with 1 clove of garlic, peeled and cut into quarters.

In a saucepan, combine 4 cups sugar, 2 cups vinegar, 1 stick cinnamon, broken, 1 tablespoon celery seed, 1 tea-spoon ground ginger, and 1 tablespoon dry mustard. Heat to boiling and pour over the sliced pickles in the jars. Keep pickles in the refrigerator for 1 week before eating. Do not reseal or process. Store in the refrigerator until used.

Shortcut Pickled Beets

Drain two 16-ounce cans of sliced beets, reserving 1 cup of the beet liquid. Combine beet liquid with 1 cup vinegar, ¾ cup sugar, 1 teaspoon mixed pickling spices with red pepper removed, and ¼ teaspoon salt. Bring mixture to a boil, add the sliced beets and 1 large onion, peeled and sliced thin, and again bring just to the boiling point. Remove from the heat, cool, and let stand 24 hours in a cold place before serving. Keep refrigerated; do not reseal.

Shortcut Pickled Pears

Drain the juice from one No. 2 can of pear halves into a small saucepan. Add 2 tablespoons honey, 2 tablespoons cider vinegar, and 1½ teaspoons pickling spice from which the red peppers have been removed. Stir the mixture and bring to the boiling point. Simmer, uncovered, for 5 minutes. Pour the vinegar mixture over the pears. Let stand in a cold place for 24 hours before serving. Do not reseal.

PART III

Freezing Vegetables
and Fruits

FREEZING SUMMER'S PLENTY FOR OUR WINTER TABLE

Thinking back, I cannot remember a single summer without a garden. Some were small pleasures, others burdensomely large. Some were weedless beauties testifying to hours of careful planting and tending, others overly ambitious projects that innundated us with lettuces and cabbages and beans or fell into neglect by season's end.

All of our gardens were pleasant places to work, to walk, and to escape into solitude. We have always grown bright summer flowers, zinnias, marigolds, sunflowers, and daisies, among the handsome rows of vegetables, and the fences are bordered with berry bushes, fruit trees, and fragrant summer herbs—dill, thyme, summer savory, and basil. Our gardens have been a perpetual delight and a satisfaction to us, a fascinating world where small boys explored leafy green aisles hung with cucumbers, squashes, and eggplants and where the inhabitants were bees, butterflies, toads, ladybugs, hummingbirds, and goldfinches.

The gardens I remember have enriched our larder as well as given us pleasure. We have known the constant luxury of fresh fruits and vegetables on our summer table. The small boys have grown tall and strong and healthy on sweet corn, sun-warmed berries, and vine-ripened tomatoes. And no matter what size our garden—from the tiny flower-bed variety we had when we were apartment dwellers years ago to the acre plots we grew later on as my husband developed into an avid, green-thumb, organic gardener—we have always had a surplus of fruits and vegetables to freeze for our winter table.

Though an abundance of produce grows within a few steps of our kitchen door, we cannot always provide ourselves with all we need or want. Sometimes we face seasonal shortages. When there are too few cucumbers to make pickles, or if there are only enough peas for table use with none left over for the freezer, I arrive early at the farmers' market to buy pecks of freshly picked vegetables. We pick strawberries in the ten-acre strawberry field a short distance from our house because my husband found maintaining a strawberry patch too much work to suit him and we never seemed to be able to beat the birds to the berries. When blueberries come into season, I ask my grocery produce manager to save a dozen boxes, and I claim the berries within half an hour of his call. I reserve a bushel of white-fleshed Georgia Belle peaches at a near-by orchard and put my name on the list for red raspberries, which are only available on an unpredictable basis. We also gather many wild foods from the fields and woods, and this produce from nature's own garden provides us with an extra freezerful of wholesome free fruits and vegetables. Sometimes our friends and family give us their surplus garden stuff, whether we need it or not. A gift of homegrown vegetables or fruits cannot be refused, even when one's own bushes are bending with harvest. We ourselves once picked, cleaned, and delivered to the doorstep of friends a surplus from our garden that we could not bear to waste and came home to find a bushel of tender kale on our own doorstep. Even without a garden, we could stock our freezers very well from these convenient sources.

Freezing goes hand in hand with other methods of food preservation that I use, but it is often preferred over canning because it is easier and quicker. Freezing is somewhat more expensive than canning because of the cost of buying and operating a freezer, but it is still more economical than buying frozen or tinned foods in a store. It is especially economical if all or part of the fruits and vegetables are grown in a home garden.

Almost all foods can be frozen successfully, and the flavor of some when frozen is better than the same variety canned. Frozen foods, prepared for the table, look and taste more like fresh produce than foods preserved in any way other than dry storage. Freezing is the best method for preserving nutritional value. If foods are handled properly during preparation, freezing, and storage, they will retain the ephemeral vitamins, flavor, and freshness that they had when they were put into the freezer.

General Instructions

SELECTING VEGETABLES AND FRUITS FOR FREEZING

Choose only the very best vegetables and fruits for freezing. The quality of food that comes out of the freezer can be no better than the quality of food put in. Freezing retains food quality but does not improve it.

Certain varieties are better for freezing than others. If you have your own garden and orchard, you will probably have selected seeds, bushes, and trees with food preservation in mind. But if you do not grow your own crops, inform yourself of the best varieties available in your area and look for them in the marketplace. Local utility companies, the agricultural agent or home extension agent, and garden stores and seed catalogues can be of great help in selecting these varieties. You can discover your own best choices through year-by-year experimentation, or by trading information with others who keep a freezer stocked.

Vegetables and fruits for freezing should be harvested at their peak of flavor and development. Vegetables, in particular, change rapidly on the vine: Monday's young, tender snap beans will be old and tough by Wednesday. Some berries, such as red raspberries, are extremely perishable, and ripe ones need to be picked every other day in

194

good weather. Often berries picked after a rain will not be of top quality. Taste the fruits to be sure their flavor is good.

Everything should be in readiness when a freezing project is planned so that there are no delays between harvesting or buying the produce and storing it. Ideally, vegetables and many fruits should be stored in the freezer within two or three hours after picking, but if vegetables cannot go directly from garden to freezer, they must spend the interim in the refrigerator or be held on ice or in ice water, as coolness retards the action of natural enzymes that rush vegetables to overripeness. Fruits should be stored in the refrigerator, not in ice water.

If you do not have your own garden, go early in the day to buy fresh produce from a truck farmer, farmers' market, or roadside stand. These fruits and vegetables probably will have been picked early in the morning before the sun has had time to warm or wilt them. If you suspect that the produce you are considering has been picked prior to the night before, look further. Or arrange to go directly to the truck farm or orchard to select your produce. Insist upon freshly picked produce for your freezer and you will be amply rewarded.

PREPARING VEGETABLES AND FRUITS FOR FREEZING

The preliminary preparation for freezing is the same as for table use. Vegetables and fruits that must be washed should be rinsed under cold running water or immersed in panfuls of cool water until clean. Vegetables in their own pods or husks do not need to be washed. Berries and other delicate fruits that may be damaged by water must be washed carefully and swiftly.

Produce, especially vegetables, should be sorted according to size because the blanching time varies according to size. Sorting also gives uniformity to the foods packaged. Imperfect, immature, or overripe vegetables and fruits should be discarded and any bruised parts of larger ones cut away.

After the preliminary washing, peeling, cutting, and sorting, fruits are ready to be packaged in one of three recommended ways: in sugar syrup, with sugar, or without either. Vegetables must be heated, usually by blanching, and cooled before packaging.

BLANCHING VEGETABLES BEFORE FREEZING

Practically all vegetables should be blanched, either in boiling water or in steam, before freezing. A few, such as pumpkins or yams, can be heated in the oven or in a pressure cooker. Blanching is partial cooking at high temperature, which helps to preserve flavor, vitamins, color, and tenderness. Nutritionally, it is one of the most important procedures in successful freezing. It is necessary to stop the action of the natural enzymes that bring on ripening and eventual decomposition. Blanched vegetables can be stored longer in the freezer than those that are not blanched and

Equipment needed for freezing, including vegetable blancher, ricer for puree, and colander

their nutritional value is higher. Approximately a pound to a pound and a half of prepared vegetables can be blanched at a time, with careful note given to the time recommended for each vegetable. If you live five thousand feet or more above sea level, one minute should be added to the time required. Vegetables should not be overcooked. Blanching in boiling water is preferable because it requires less time than steam-blanching. Blanching destroys almost all bacteria that may be present and helps ensure cleanliness of the frozen food.

Steam-blanching is recommended for a few vegetables, notably broccoli, sweet potato, squash, and pumpkin. It is not satisfactory for leafy greens, which tend to mat together unless they are blanched in a large amount of boiling water. Steam-blanching may be used in place of water blanching for any vegetable with a high content of the water-soluble vitamins or for cut and peeled vegetables, which retain a higher percentage of their natural juices and vitamins if they are not immersed in boiling water.

WATER-BLANCHING In a vegetable blancher with a perforated blanching basket and its own lid, or in a kettle with a 2-gallon capacity, bring to a boil over high heat at least 1 gallon of water for each 1 to 1½ pounds of vegetables. Lower the prepared vegetables into the boiling water in the blanching basket, or use a deep-frying basket or colander, or tie the vegetables in a cheesecloth bag. If the water is boiling hard and the correct amount of vegetables is added, the boil will stop for only a few seconds. Cover the blancher tightly and keep the heat high. Start timing at once and remove the vegetables from the water immediately at the end of the blanching time. The water in the blancher can be used several times, although it may be necessary to add fresh boiling water to make up for any loss.

STEAM BLANCHING In a large kettle bring 2 to 3 inches of water to a boil over high heat. Put the prepared vegetables on a rack with legs long enough to stand above the boiling water or in a vegetable-steaming basket with its own legs. Set the rack or basket in the kettle, cover the kettle, and begin timing when steam escapes freely around the lid. With a few exceptions, steam-blanching takes 1 minute longer than blanching the same vegetable in boiling water. Remove the blanched vegetables from the kettle immediately at the end of the steaming time.

COOLING VEGETABLES AFTER BLANCHING

Lower the blanched vegetables, still in their container, into another container holding ice water or water 60°F or cooler. Let them cool thoroughly in the water, allowing about the same length of time for cooling as for blanching, remove them from the water, and drain them well. To maintain the proper temperature, the cold-water bath must be changed frequently as more blanched vegetables are added. The vegetables can also be cooled under cold running water.

Vegetables must be cooled to their centers before packaging or excess ice crystals will form among them when they are frozen. To test, bite or cut into a cooled piece of vegetable. The vegetables may be packed for freezing as soon as they are cooled and drained well on towels or in a colander. If the vegetables are packaged before they are well drained, the individual pieces will freeze together in a block of ice. If the vegetables are not cooled promptly at the end of the blanching process, they will continue cooking in the heat they retain, resulting in an unnecessary loss of crispness.

PACKING FRUITS FOR FREEZING

If only every method of home food preservation were as simple and quick as freezing fruits! Most fruits freeze well and require little more preparation for the freezer than they do for the table. They are usually packed with sugar, in syrup, or unsweetened. Sweetened fruits hold their quality and nutritive value longer than unsweetened fruits, partly because the sugar helps retard enzyme action. The unsweetened dry pack is also recommended. It is easy and quick to put fruits directly into the freezer without sugar, and these unsweetened fruits can be used in recipes calling for fresh fruits. The recipes need not be adjusted for the prior addition of sugar as they must be when using frozen sweetened fruits.

THE SUGAR PACK

An antidarkening agent may be required in the freezing of certain fruits to prevent discoloration during freezing. If necessary, it should be added to the sugar, and the fruit should be turned gently in the mixture to distribute it evenly. The fruit and sugar should be mixed until the sugar is just dissolved and the juices begin to flow from the fruit.

Specific ratios of sugar to various fruits are recommended in the chart for freezing fruits (beginning on page 000), but these amounts may be altered to suit individual taste. Four parts fruit to 1 part sugar is the proportion that offers adequate protection of flavor, nutritive value, and color during freezing and storage, but it would not be too extreme to vary the proportion from 3 to 5 parts fruit to 1 part sugar, if desired.

Spoon the sugared fruit into rigid, leakproof containers, or put it into freezing boxes with plastic liners and wipe the edge of the containers to ensure good seal. Seal the containers, leaving head space between the packed fruit and the lid to allow for expansion during freezing. Freeze quickly at zero or sub-zero temperature, preferably −10°F.

THE SYRUP PACK

Make the freezing syrup in advance by dissolving sugar in cold water or in boiling water according to the following proportions:

Syrup	Cups Sugar to Cups Water
20% (very light)	1 to 4
30% (light)	2 to 4
40% (medium)	3 to 4
50% (heavy)	4 to 4
60% (very heavy)	5 to 4

Stir the syrup, let it stand until it is clear, and chill it. Add an antidarkening agent (see below), if necessary, just before using. The medium syrup is recommended for most fruits; the lighter and heavier ones should be used for very sweet and very sour fruits, respectively. Up to one fourth of the sugar may be replaced by corn syrup or honey without a noticeable change in flavor. If honey or corn syrup makes up more than twenty-five percent of the sweetener, its flavor becomes more dominant. Honey, too, seems sweeter than sugar and less of it than of other sweeteners can be used.

To pack, put the prepared fruit in rigid, leakproof containers and cover it with syrup, using about ⅔ cup or less for each pint package of fruit. Wipe the sealing edges of the container, leaving adequate headspace, and close the container. Freeze quickly at zero or sub-zero temperature, preferably −10°F.

THE UNSWEETENED PACK

Cranberries, blackberries, green grapes, blueberries, elderberries, rhubarb, gooseberries, and whole strawberries are some of the fruits that I freeze without sugar. Spread the loose prepared fruits on a baking sheet and freeze them quickly at zero or sub-zero temperature, preferably − 10°F. When the fruits are frozen, in 1 to 2 hours, package them in polyethylene bags and squeeze out all of the air before closing the bags with wire twist ties. (Purée of native American persimmons should also be frozen without sugar but should be packaged in a rigid, leakproof container.) In general, it seems that the unsweetened pack is best for solid, rather tart fruits that do not require peeling or pitting.

The unsweetened pack can be used for fruits that tend to darken easily, but an antidarkening agent must be dissolved in a little cold water, sprinkled over the fruit, and mixed in well before packing. Alternatively, the antidarkening agent can be dissolved in the juices of the fruit.

TO KEEP FRUITS FROM DARKENING

Certain fruits, especially light-colored tree fruits, must have an antidarkening agent, such as pure ascorbic acid (vitamin C), a citric acid–ascorbic acid mixture, citric acid, lemon juice, or rose-hip concentrate, combined with the syrup or sugar that is added to the fruit to prevent possible discoloration during freezing or later thawing.

Ascorbic acid for use in freezing fruits can be bought at a drugstore in crystalline or powder form or in tablets. I find that ½ teaspoon of pure ascorbic acid in fine crystalline or powder form for each quart of water used in making syrup, or to each 2 cups of dry sugar, or to each quart of fruit is a good proportion. There are commercial ascorbic acid mixtures sold under several brand names at grocery stores. Directions for their use is on the tin or package. Because the ascorbic acid is diluted in such commercial preparations by its mixture with sugar or citric acid, more of the mixture is required than of pure ascorbic acid. Pure ascorbic acid costs about nine dollars a pound, although it can be bought in smaller amounts, and is currently less expensive than the commercial mixtures.

Lemon juice and citric acid are also used to retard darkening. Pure lemon juice can be squeezed over the fruits or the fruits can be dipped in 1 gallon of water to which 3 tablespoons of lemon juice has been added. Or the fruits can be immersed for 1 minute in 1 gallon of cold water in which 1 teaspoon of citric acid (from the drugstore) has been dissolved.

Rose-hip concentrates containing natural ascorbic acid are available, usually in health food stores, in liquid or powdered form. It may be necessary to experiment to determine how much to use to deter darkening of fruits, but no harm can come from adding a bit more than is necessary. A good rule of thumb is about 1 teaspoon of rose-hip concentrate for each pint of prepared fruit.

The directions on the chart for freezing fruits suggest, in most cases, adding pure ascorbic acid to prevent darkening, but alternate methods may be substituted where preferred.

201

PACKAGING VEGETABLES AND FRUITS FOR THE FREEZER

When fruits and vegetables have been prepared for the freezer, they should be packaged in suitable containers or packaging material to preserve their original food value, moisture, flavor, color, and texture. To retain the highest quality in frozen food, packaging materials should be moistureproof and vaporproof, such as tempered glass, stainless steel, and rigid plastic containers, or at least moisture or vapor resistant, such as most bags, wrapping materials, and waxed cartons made especially for freezing.

The better the packaging, the longer the foods will remain at top quality when stored at 0°F. Cheaply made or unsuitable wrapping materials do not give adequate protection against the deterioration of foods. The dry air of the freezer can penetrate certain unsuitable materials and dry out the food, causing "freezer burn." Ordinary wax paper, lightweight aluminum foil, bread wrappers, cellophane, thin plastic wrap, butcher's paper, bakery boxes, ice-cream cartons, and thin plastic containers cannot protect fruits and vegetables for long-term freezing.

The best economy is to buy the proper materials and containers, since many can be reused year after year. There is a wide selection of freezer-packaging materials available, although it may be difficult to find everything in one place. Most grocery stores carry the basics: plastic containers in pint and quart sizes, freezer-weight aluminum foil and freezer-wrap paper, freezer tape, plastic freezing bags, and perhaps, wide-mouthed freezer jars. The housewares departments of many stores also carry freezing equipment, as do hardware stores, mail-order companies, and community frozen-foods locker plants. Specific directions for packaging often accompany the materials.

LABELING FROZEN FOODS

Label all frozen foods with special marking pencils or crayons, giving the freezing date. In addition it is helpful to note the variety of fruit or vegetable frozen so that preferred ones can be distinguished. A freezing diary might be useful for more detailed records.

If the fruit is to be used in jam or jelly, it is important that the amount of sugar used to sweeten it be recorded so that allowance can be made for it in recipes. Less than optimum results may be obtained if the proportions of fruit, sugar, acid, and pectin are not correct. Note any addition of lemon juice as well.

If you are interested in perfecting your freezing techniques, note might also be made of the method of blanching vegetables and the length of blanching time, the type of antidarkening agent used with fruits, and any special details that might be forgotten in a year's time.

HEAD SPACE

Care should be taken to exclude as much air as possible from plastic bags and containers when packing fruits and vegetables, but a small amount of head space must be allowed for expansion during freezing. Between the packed food and the closure of a rigid container, leave ½-inch of head space for all produce packed without added sugar or liquid. Squeeze as much air as possible from plastic bags but leave some space for the food to expand or the bag will split during freezing.

Vegetables that pack loosely, such as peas and broccoli, require no head space. Purees and juices need 1 to 1½ inches to expand. The more watery the produce, the more room is needed. Fruits packed in juice, sugar, syrup, or water should be given ½ inch of head space in wide-top pint containers and 1 inch in quart containers with wide-top openings. If the container has a narrow-top opening, the head space must be increased about a half inch. Too much head space permits drying inside the freezing container.

STORAGE IN THE FREEZER

Blanched vegetables, and fruits packed in sugar, will keep in the freezer for twelve months when stored at 0°F. Fluctuations in temperature below 0°F, as when the temperature of the new packages of food are added to the freezer, do not affect the quality of the frozen foods, but if the food is subjected to temperatures rising above 0°F, ice crystals may form inside the packages. If this happens repeatedly, the quality of the foods will be affected.

Freeze fruits and vegetables as soon as they are packed and sealed. Speed them into the freezer. Do not let filled containers stand at room temperature while others are being filled. Instead, keep the filled containers in the refrigerator until all the others are ready. Having unfrozen foods cold when they are put into the freezer helps them to freeze faster and conserves electricity.

When you plan a freezing project set the temperature control of the freezer at a lower temperature the night before. Check the freezer thermometer, which should be kept in the freezer at all times, to make sure that the temperature has fallen below 0°F (the temperature at which frozen foods should be stored) to sub-zero, if possible. A temperature of −10°F is best. The lower the temperature, the faster the fruits and vegetables will freeze. The faster the freezing, the smaller the ice crystals formed in the foods and the better the product.

A representative of an appliance company selling and servicing freezers has concluded from long experience and observation that maintaining a −10°F temperature in the freezer at all times, both for storage and for freezing new foods, is best. He has found that properly wrapped foods will keep at this temperature long beyond the usual periods of time stated in freezing manuals. However, many home freezers do well to maintain the 0°F temperature which is necessary for storing frozen foods. Keep a close check on the temperature inside your freezer and try to maintain a constant 0°F, at least.

When adding new foods to an upright freezer, spaces should be cleared on several shelves so that each new package will be in contact with a freezing surface. One shelf can be kept empty for freezing projects, but this is believed to be not as efficient as spreading the food out on several shelves partially filled with frozen foods. When the new packages are frozen solid in twenty-four hours they can be stacked elsewhere in the freezer.

The coldest shelf of a frostfree freezer is the one closest to the vent where the air enters—either at the bottom of the freezer or at the top—and foods will freeze fastest on this shelf. Since air is entering on the coldest shelf, there could be some danger of drying out the foods if they are not properly wrapped.

In a chest-type freezer, new packages should be placed with one surface resting on a freezing surface of the freezer—on the bottom of the freezer or against the side walls—and spread out with an inch or so of space between them.

No more than two or three pounds of food for each cubic foot of freezer capacity should be frozen at one time within a 24-hour period. If too much food is added at once, the freezing will take longer, larger ice crystals will form, the frozen packages of food in the freezer will warm up more than they should, and the freezer will have to run constantly and for a longer time. Foods will freeze more quickly in smaller packages than in large ones. Pints and quarts are the best size containers.

The most efficient and economical freezer is one that is kept as full as possible—not *overloaded*, but full to capacity. For example, a 15-cubic-foot freezer has the capacity to hold and keep frozen about 35 pounds of food per cubic foot. The frozen packages help to maintain the coldness of the freezer. An empty shelf holds cold air, which falls out when the freezer door is opened, and the freezer must again cool the air held by the empty shelf when the door is closed. A freezer must run more to keep an empty shelf cold than to maintain its temperature when the shelves are filled. If the freezer is less than three-fourths full, the empty portions can be filled with bags of ice cubes or milk cartons frozen full of ice. (Three gallon-size milk cartons of ice make more than enough crushed ice to fill my gallon churn-type ice-cream freezer. The ice can be crushed inside the milk carton by putting the ice in the carton on a concrete surface such as a side-walk or garage floor and pounding it with a hammer.)

FREEZING VEGETABLES

Vegetable	Preparation	How to Blanch*
Artichokes Globe or French	Remove outer leaves and trim stems to 1 inch. Cut off about 1 inch of tops. Trim tips of leaves and rub cut surfaces with lemon. Blanch a few at a time. Cool, drain inverted on towels, and wrap individually. (Better if used within 10 months.)	Boiling water with juice of 1 lemon per 2 quarts water: Small artichokes (2½ inches or less), 3 minutes. Medium artichokes (2½ to 4 inches), 4 minutes. Large artichokes (4 inches or more), 5 minutes.
Artichoke hearts	Use small artichokes. Prepare as for whole artichokes but trim to a cone.	Boiling water with juice of 1 lemon per 2 quarts water: 2 to 3 minutes.
Asparagus	Clean and wash well. Sort stalks according to thickness. Snap off woody ends where they break naturally or cut all stalks the same length. Leave whole or cut into 1-inch pieces. Blanch, cool, drain, and pack, arranging tips of whole stalks in opposite	Boiling water: Small stalks, 2 minutes. Medium stalks, 3 minutes. Large stalks, 4 minutes.

	directions if packing in flat box.	1-inch pieces, 3 minutes. Steam: With tips up.

Beans
  Green
  Snap
  Wax
	Select young, tender beans. Wash, snip off ends, and remove strings, if necessary. Leave whole, cut into 1½-inch pieces, or slice French style. Blanch, cool, drain, and pack.	Boiling water:
		Whole beans, 3 minutes.
		Cut beans, 2 minutes.
		French style, 1 minute.

Beans, green shelled ("shellie") Black-eyed peas	Select green beans that have matured beyond snap beans, when beans inside pods are fully formed but still moist and before pods yellow. Select black-eyed peas with well-filled flexible pods and tender peas. Shell the vegetables. Blanch, cool, drain, and pack. If green snap beans are available at same time, both snap beans and shellie beans, prepared separately, may be packed together.	Boiling water: 2 minutes.
Beans, lima	Shell beans and sort according to size. Blanch, cool, drain, and pack, discarding any beans that yellow during blanching.	Boiling water: Tiny limas, 1 minute. Medium limas, 2 minutes. Large limas, 3 minutes.
Beets	(Beets are most commonly prepared by methods other than freezing.) Select small, tender beets. Cut off all but ½ inch of stems and leave tails on. Scrub	—

* Steam-blanching may be substituted for water-blanching if preferred, unless directions indicate steaming is not satisfactory. If steam-blanching is used, increase water-blanching time by 1 minute unless otherwise noted.

FREEZING VEGETABLES

Vegetable	Preparation	How to Blanch*
	and cook in water to cover until tender: for small beets about 30 minutes, for large beets, 45 minutes or more. Drain, cool, slip off skins, and trim. Slice, quarter, cube, or leave whole. Pack.	
Black-eyed peas	See Beans, green shelled.	
Broccoli	Remove outer leaves and split stalks as desired. Remove insects by soaking 30 minutes in salted water (4 teaspoons salt to 1 gallon water). Rinse, blanch, cool, drain, and pack.	Steam: 5 minutes, with flowerets up.
Brussels sprouts	Soak as for Broccoli. Rinse, blanch, cool, drain, and pack.	Boiling water: 3 to 5 minutes, depending on size.
Cabbage Chinese Red	Select solid heads and remove coarse outer leaves. Wash and drain and cut into wedges, shred coarsely, or separate into leaves, according to intended use. Blanch, cool, drain, and pack. (Use in cooked dishes only.)	Boiling water: Wedges, 3 minutes. Shreds, 1½ minutes. Leaves, 2 minutes.
Carrots	Remove tops, scrub, and scrape or peel. Leave small carrots whole, cut larger ones into ¼-inch slices or dice. Blanch, cool, drain, and pack.	Boiling water: 2 to 5 minutes, depending on size.

208

	Preparation	Blanching
Cauliflower	Prepare as for Broccoli. Break into 1-inch flowerets.	Boiling water with 4 teaspoons salt to 1 gallon water or juice of 1 lemon to 1 gallon water: 3 minutes. Blanch purple cauliflower in plain water.
Chives	See Onions, Chives, Scallions.	
Corn On the cob	Select freshly picked corn with full kernels that spurt milk when punctured. Husk, remove silk, and cut away bad spots. Blanch, cool, drain, and pack whole.	Boiling water: Small ears, 6 minutes. Medium ears, 8 minutes. Large ears, 10 minutes.
Cream style	Prepare for blanching as for Corn on the cob. Blanch on the cob, cool, drain, and cut off cob with a razorsharp knife, cutting through middle of kernels. With the back of the knife gently scrape cob to extract milky juice and hearts of kernels. Pack.	Boiling water: 4 to 5 minutes, depending on size of ears.
Whole kernel	Prepare for blanching as for corn on the cob. Blanch on the cob, cool, drain, and cut off cob with a razor-sharp knife or corn cutter. Do not scrape cob. Pack.	Boiling water: 4 to 5 minutes, depending on size of ears.

FREEZING VEGETABLES

Vegetable	Preparation	How to Blanch*
Eggplant	Select firm, ripe eggplants with smooth skin. Do not freeze large, overmature eggplants. Wash, peel, and cut into slices 1/2 inch thick. To retard darkening drop into salted water (4 teaspoons salt to 1 gallon water). Blanch, cool, drain, and pack with sheets of freezer paper between slices.	Boiling water: 4 minutes.
Greens Beet Chard Collard Kale Mustard Spinach Wild	Wash well several times in deep panfuls of water. Discard thick stems, mid-ribs, and yellowed leaves. Blanch in larger quantities of water than for other vegetables. Cool, drain, and pack whole leaves or chop.	Boiling water: Most greens, 2 minutes. Collards, 3 minutes. Very tender greens, 1½ minutes. Steam blanching not recommended.
Herbs Basil Bouquet garni Dill Parsley Summer savory	Herbs for use in cooking may be frozen instead of dried. Harvest on a sunny morning before plants blossom. Tie in small bundles, blanch, and cool in ice water. Drain on towels. Pack in amounts according to intended use. Alternate Method: Omit blanching. Snip,	Boiling water (salt may be added, 1 teaspoon per quart water, if desired): Dip into water and swish around for a few

210

Thyme Others	package, and freeze.	seconds. Steam blanching not recommended.
Kohlrabi	Prepare as Turnips.	Boiling water: 1 minute.
Mushrooms	Select fresh, tender mushrooms. Wipe with damp cloth. Cut away tough portions of stems. Leave buttons whole, slice medium mushrooms into halves or profiles. To prevent darkening, soak 5 minutes in 2 quarts water acidulated with juice of 1 large lemon. Blanch, cool over cracked ice, drain, and pack. Mushrooms may be sautéed, then frozen: Sauté 1/2 pound prepared mushrooms in 1/4 cup butter 4 to 5 minutes, or until almost done. Large caps may be blanched, cooled, drained, and stuffed before freezing. (Use stuffed mushrooms within short time and bake without thawing.)	Steam blanch only: Buttons, 3 minutes. Slices, 4 minutes. Whole or 1-inch pieces, 5 minutes.
Okra	Select tender, young pods less than 4 inches long. Remove stems without cutting into seed sections if leaving whole or cut into 1-inch lengths after blanching. Cool, drain, and pack.	Boiling water: 2 minutes.
Onions	1. For use as cooked vegetable: Select small, mature onions and peel. Heat in small amount of water until onions are hot through to centers. Drain, cool, and pack.	Boiling water: 2 minutes.

FREEZING VEGETABLES

Vegetable	Preparation	How to Blanch*
Onions Chives Scallions	2. Chopped onions for use in cooking may be blanched in water or steam. Prepare as above. For use in cooking: Peel onions, rinse chives, and clean and trim scallions. Chop onions, snip chives, and slice scallions thin, including tops, if desired. Freeze without blanching on baking sheets, then pack. (Vegetables will not be crisp enough for use in salads.)	
Parsnips	Prepare as Carrots.	Boiling water: 2 to 5 minutes, depending on size.
Peas	Select young, sweet peas. Shell, blanch, cool, and drain. Freeze loose on baking sheet and pack.	Boiling water: 1 minute.
Pea pods, edible	Select young peas. Break off tips and remove strings, if necessary. Wash, blanch, cool, drain, and pack.	Boiling water: 3½ minutes.
Peppers Bell Green hot	Select firm but tender peppers. Wash, cut out stems, and remove seeds and ribs. Freeze without blanching in form for intended use: whole, in	

Vegetable	Preparation	Blanching
	strips, or diced. Whole peppers may be frozen on baking sheet and stacked inside one another, with sheet of freezer paper separating them. Pack in freezer bags.	
Pumpkin	See Squash, winter.	
Rutabagas	See Turnips.	
Sauerkraut	Pack cured sauerkraut and freeze.	
Scallions	See Onions, Chives, Scallions.	
Soybeans	Select soybeans with bright green pods and tender, fully formed beans. Wash, blanch in pods, cool, and drain. Squeeze beans out of pods and pack.	Boiling water: 5 minutes.
Squash Summer Zucchini	Select tender, young squash with small seeds and skin that can be punctured with a fingernail. Wash and cut into ½-inch slices or cubes. Blanch, cool, drain, and pack. May be simmered in small quantity of water as for table use, cooled, drained, and packed. If seasonings and butter are added, pack in freeze-and-cook bags.	Boiling water: 3 minutes.
Squash, winter Pumpkin	Wash, remove seeds, peel, and cube. Cook in water, in steam, in pressure cooker, or in 350° F oven until barely fork tender. May be baked without peeling and pulp may be scooped out of rind when vegetables are tender. Cool, drain, if necessary, and pack.	

FREEZING VEGETABLES

Vegetable	Preparation	How to Blanch*
Sweet potatoes Yams	Sweet potatoes should be cured 2 to 3 weeks after digging by storing in a cool, dry place. Sweet potatoes and yams may be boiled before peeling. Wash and leave whole or cut as desired. Cook in water, in steam, in pressure cooker, or in 350° F oven until barely fork tender. Cool, drain, if necessary, and pack.	
Tomato juice	Wash, core, and quarter fully ripe tomatoes. Mash slightly to make enough juice to cover bottom of enamel or stainless steel kettle. Cover and simmer, mashing often, until soft. Do not overcook. Put through medium disk of food mill. Add 1 teaspoon salt per quart juice. Pack in rigid containers, leaving ample head space, and cool in refrigerator. Additional seasonings may be added before juice is frozen or after it is thawed. (The juice may separate from solids during freezing, but that does not affect quality. Simply stir to blend after juice is thawed.)	
Tomato Puree	Wash, core, and quarter ripe tomatoes. In enamel or stainless steel saucepan simmer tomatoes in own juice, covered. Mash and stir often and cook over	

low heat 30 minutes, or until liquid is reduced to a puree of desired consistency. Put through medium disk of food mill into a bowl. Add 1 teaspoon salt per quart puree. Cool quickly by setting bowl containing puree in another container filled with ice or ice water. Pack in rigid containers, leaving ample head space.

Turnips
Rutabagas

Select tender, young small or medium vegetables. Scrub, peel, and cut into ½-inch cubes. Blanch, cool, drain, and pack. May be frozen mashed or pureed. Simmer cubes in small amount of water until just fork tender. Drain, mash, cool, and pack.

Boiling water: 2 minutes.

Yams

See Sweet potatoes.

FREEZING FRUITS

Fruit	Preparation	How to Pack
Apple sauce	Wash, core, and quarter apples good for making apple sauce (e.g., Early June Transparent, Turley Winesap, or Jonathan). Simmer until tender in heavy pan (not iron) with just enough water to be visible among apples. Mash and stir occasionally. Remove from heat when apples are mushy and put through medium disk of food mill. Sweeten to taste and add spice, if desired. Pack in rigid containers, leaving adequate head space.	Sugar: 1/4 to 1 cup per quart apple sauce. Honey or corn syrup may replace part of sugar but amount of cooking water should be reduced accordingly.
Apple slices	1. Peel and core and slice uniformly thick firm, crisp apples. To prevent darkening, drop quickly into cold salted water (2 tablespoons salt to 1 gallon water). Drain. Blanch in boiling water or steam 1½ to 2 minutes, depending on thickness. Cool, drain, and pack.	Sugar: 1/2 cup, with 1/2 teaspoon ascorbic acid, per quart sliced fruit. Syrup: 40% with 1/2 teaspoon ascorbic acid per quart syrup. Unsweetened dry pack:

	Preparation	Pack
		½ teaspoon ascorbic acid per quart sliced fruit.
	2. Peel and core firm, crisp apples. Slice into pint container with ½ cup syrup. Press slices down into container so that they are covered with syrup and put crumpled freezer paper in head space to keep slices under syrup.	Syrup: 40% with ½ teaspoon ascorbic acid per quart syrup.
	3. Peel, core, and slice firm, crisp apples. Sprinkle evenly with sugar and pack.	Sugar: ½ cup, or to taste, with ½ teaspoon ascorbic acid, per quart sliced fruit.
Apricots	See Peaches.	
Avocados	Peel, pit, and mash soft-ripe pulp. Blend in antidarkening agent and pack. Freeze with sugar if desired.	Unsweetened pack: ⅛ teaspoon ascorbic acid per quart pulp. Or 2 tablespoons lemon juice per avocado.
Berries Blackberries Boysenberries Dewberries Loganberries Mulberries	Wash, drain, sort, and pack.	Sugar: 1 cup, or to taste, per quart fruit. Unsweetened dry pack. Syrup: 30% to 50%.

FREEZING FRUITS

Fruit	Preparation	How to Pack
Blueberries Huckleberries	Wash, drain, sort, and stem, if necessary. Freeze loose on baking sheet at lowest possible temperature and pack.	Unsweetened dry pack. Syrup: 40%. Sugar: 1/2 cup per quart fruit.
Cherries, sour	Wash, drain, sort, stem, and chill 1 hour to firm before pitting. Pit, then pack in rigid, noncardboard containers.	Sugar: 3/4 to 1 cup, with 1/8 teaspoon ascorbic acid, per quart of fruit. Unsweetened dry pack: 1/8 teaspoon ascorbic acid dissolved in little water per quart fruit. Syrup: 50% to 60% with 1/8 teaspoon ascorbic acid per quart syrup.
Cherries, sweet	Wash, drain, sort, stem and chill 1 hour to firm before pitting. Pit, then pack. (Stems and pits need not be removed if frozen without sweetening.)	Sugar and unsweetened dry pack same as for sour cherries. Syrup: 30% to 40% with 1/8 teaspoon ascorbic acid per quart syrup.

Citrus fruits Grapefruits Oranges	Peel and section, removing seeds and membranes, or slice. Pack in tempered glass containers. Use within 6 months.	Unsweetened pack: Combine sections or slices in own juice with ½ teaspoon ascorbic acid per quart fruit. Sugar: 1 pound, or to taste, dissolved in citrus juice with 1 teaspoon ascorbic acid, per 5 pounds fruit. Syrup: 30% to 40% made with excess citrus juice extended with water, if necessary, with ½ teaspoon ascorbic acid per quart syrup.
Citrus fruit juices Grapefruit Orange	Do not use the juice of navel oranges. Use chilled ripe fruits. Halve, extract juice without pressing oils from rind, and seed. Straining optional. Sweeten to taste. Pack in tempered glass containers, leaving adequate head space. Use within 4 months.	Unsweetened pack: ¾ teaspoon ascorbic acid per gallon juice.

FREEZING FRUITS

Fruit	Preparation	How to Pack
Lemon Lime	Squeeze fruits and freeze juice in ice-cube trays. Remove and pack. Use in drinks or for flavoring.	
Cranberries	1. Select firm berries. Wash, drain, sort, stem, freeze loose on baking sheet, and pack. Or grind and pack. 2. Raw relish: Combine 4 cups ground berries, 2 seedless oranges unpeeled and ground, and 2 cups sugar. Pack. After thawing, ingredients such as raw apple, crushed pineapple, nuts, or flavored gelatin may be added. 3. Puree: Simmer 1 cup water with 1 pint berries until skins burst. Put through medium disk of food mill or puree in blender. Sweeten to taste. Pack.	Unsweetened dry pack. Syrup (whole berries): 50%.
Currants	Wash, drain, sort, stem, if necessary, and pack.	Sugar: 1 cup per quart fruit. Syrup: 50%. Unsweetened dry pack

Elderberries	Wash, drain, and sort. Stem by pulling through teeth of large comb. Freeze loose on baking sheet and pack.	Unsweetened dry pack.
Figs	Wash, drain, and stem soft-ripe fruit. Sort for sour fruit. Peel, if desired. Halve, slice, or leave whole. Handle gently. Pack. (Prepared figs may be crushed or coarsely ground in food chopper or blender and sweetened with 1/2 cup honey or 1 cup sugar per quart figs. Add 3/4 teaspoon ascorbic acid per quart crushed figs. Pack.)	Unsweetened pack: 3/4 teaspoon ascorbic acid dissolved in small amount water per quart fruit. Syrup: 30% to 40% with 3/4 teaspoon ascorbic acid per quart syrup or 1/2 cup lemon juice per quart syrup. Water pack: Cover with water with 3/4 teaspoon ascorbic acid per quart water.
Fruit purees, raw	Puree fully ripe soft fruits in blender, mash, or put through sieve or medium disk of food mill. Sweeten to taste and add antidarkening agent, if necessary. (See instructions for individual fruits.) Pack. Use as topping for ice cream or desserts, in recipes requiring fruit puree, or in uncooked jams.	

FREEZING FRUITS

Fruit	Preparation	How to Pack
Gooseberries	Wash, drain, sort, remove blossom ends and stems, and pack.	Unsweetened dry pack. Syrup: 40%.
Grapes, table	Wash, drain, sort, and stem. Leave seedless grapes whole; halve and seed others. Pack.	Unsweetened dry pack. Syrup: 40%.
Grapes, Concord	1. Wash, drain, sort, and stem fully ripe grapes. In enamel saucepan heat over low heat 8 to 10 minutes, or until skins burst. Drain excess juice and use separately. Put through medium disk of food mill. Sweeten to taste. Cool and pack. Use within 6 to 8 months. If gritty when thawed, heat slightly.	
	2. Wash and stem *unripe* Concord grapes. Freeze loose on baking sheet and pack. (Use unripe grapes for green grape pie.)	Unsweetened dry pack.
	3. For juice and jelly making: Wash, drain, sort, and stem fully ripe grapes. Freeze loose on baking sheet and pack in freezer bags.	Unsweetened dry pack.
Huckleberries	See Blueberries.	
Mangoes	See Peaches.	

Melons	Seed and peel. Slice, cube, or cut into balls. Several varieties may be packed together.	Unsweetened dry pack. Syrup: 30%.
Cantaloupes		
Cranshaws		
Honeydews		
Muskmelons		
Persians		
Watermelons		
Peaches	Select full-flavored, just-soft fruit. Freeze small quantities at a time. Wash, drain, peel, pit, and halve or section. Pack and freeze at once, minimizing exposure to air. If syrup is used, slice fruit into syrup with antidarkening agent added and put crumpled freezer paper in head space to keep fruit under syrup. Work quickly. Varieties resistant to darkening (e.g., Red Haven and Redskin) may be packed without antidarkening agent. Peaches sweetened with honey and treated with lemon juice are delicious in pies.	Sugar: ¾ to 1 cup, with ½ teaspoon ascorbic acid, per quart cut fruit. Syrup: 40% with ½ teaspoon ascorbic acid per quart syrup. Unsweetened dry pack: 1 teaspoon lemon juice per quart fruit, ½ teaspoon ascorbic acid per quart fruit, or other antidarkening agent, as preferred.
Apricots		
Mangoes		
Nectarines		
Pears	Select firm ripe pears that are not mealy. Wash, peel, core, and drop into an anti-darkening agent during preparation period. Use a solution of 1 teaspoon ascorbic acid and	Blanch in 40% syrup for 2 minutes (see directions for preparation).

FREEZING FRUITS

Fruit	Preparation	How to Pack
	1 tablespoon citric and 1 gallon of cold water. Leave pears in halves, cut into quarters, or slice. Drain and blanch in a 40% syrup for 2 minutes. Cool and pack pears in blanching syrup in rigid freezer containers and freeze.	
Persimmons Cultivated American varieties Native wild American	Select fully ripe, not puckery, persimmons. Remove dried calyx and rinse fruits, if necessary. Put through medium disk of food mill to extract pulp, a difficult process because of large seeds, or press through a colander. Pack. Keeps more than 1 year.	Unsweetened pack: $\frac{1}{8}$ teaspoon ascorbic acid per quart fruit.
Persimmons, Japanese	1. Select soft-ripe persimmons with no astringency. Wash in ice water, peel, and slice. Sprinkle with dissolved antidarkening agent, sweeten, if desired, and pack.	Sugar: $\frac{1}{2}$ cup per quart sliced fruit, sprinkle with $\frac{1}{2}$ teaspoon ascorbic acid, dissolved in small amount water.
	2. Puree in blender and sweeten, if desired. Add antidarkening agent. Pack.	Unsweetened pack: Add antidarkening agent, as above.

Fruit	Preparation	Syrup/Sugar
Pineapples	Select fragrant ripe pineapples free from decay. Leaves should pull out easily. Peel, remove core and eyes, and slice or cut as desired. Pack. May also be covered with pineapple juice or other compatible fruit juice and frozen.	Syrup: 30% to 40%. Sugar: 1 part to 4 parts fruit. Unsweetened pack.
Plums Prunes	Sort and wash freestone plums and prunes. Halve and pit. Pack. In enamel saucepan crush overripe or clingstone plums slightly. Add water to cover bottom of pan and bring to a boil. Simmer until soft. Puree, add lemon juice or antidarkening agent, and sweeten with sugar or honey to taste.	Syrup: 40% to 50% with ½ teaspoon ascorbic acid per quart syrup. Sugar: ¾ to 1 cup, with ½ teaspoon ascorbic acid, per quart fruit. Unsweetened dry pack: ½ teaspoon ascorbic acid per quart fruit.
Raspberries	Wash quickly, drain, and sort. Pack.	Sugar: 1 cup, or to taste, per 5 cups fruit. Unsweetened dry pack. Syrup: 30%.
Rhubarb	Wash, drain, and peel, if necessary. Cut into 1-inch slices. May be simmered in enamel saucepan in water to cover bottom of pan with sugar added to taste until just tender. Pack.	Unsweetened dry pack. Syrup: 40%.

FREEZING FRUITS

Fruit	Preparation	How to Pack
Strawberries	Wash quickly, drain, and hull. Best frozen sliced with sugar. Pack.	Sugar: 1 cup, or to taste, per quart sliced fruit. Syrup (whole berries): 40%. Unsweetened dry pack: whole berries.

Special Instructions for Freezing Certain Foods

Frozen Cream-Style Corn

Husk freshly picked corn and remove the silks with a vegetable brush. Wash the corn briefly under running water only if necessary. Cut the kernels off the cob, cutting through the middle of the kernels, then scrape the cob to obtain the rest of the milky juices and the heart of the corn kernels. Put the cut corn in a pan with 2 tablespoons of butter or margarine for each 2 cups of corn. Simmer the corn in its own juices and season it with salt and pepper as for table use. The corn needs only to simmer gently until it is hot throughout. Stir carefully as the corn is heating. When heated, remove the pan from the heat and place it in a pan of ice water to cool it quickly. When cooled, package the corn for the freezer in rigid plastic containers or in freeze-and-cook bags.

To thaw for serving, put the block of frozen corn in a covered saucepan on low heat. Add 1 to 2 tablespoons of water or milk and heat slowly, breaking the block apart with a fork as soon as possible. Additional cream and butter may be added to taste, if desired.

The frozen corn may also be heated in the top of a double boiler. If freeze-and-cook bags are used, follow the cooking timetable provided by the manufacturer.

Juanita's Frozen Cucumbers for Frying

Slice freshly picked cucumbers crosswise, to a thickness of about ½ inch. Spread out the slices on a cookie sheet, freeze them at once, then sack in plastic freezer bags in portions large enough to serve your family. Store in the freezer.

When ready to cook the cucumbers, take the package out of the freezer about 1½ hours before cooking and let the cucumbers thaw at room temperature. Lay the thawed pieces on a paper towel, salt and pepper them, dip them in flour, and fry them in bacon fat until browned on both sides.

Frozen Cabbage

Remove the outside leaves of the head of cabbage, rinse off the outside of the cabbage, and wipe dry. Cut the head into halves, then cut each half into triangular wedges about 2 inches wide at the outside. Cut off part of the core but leave enough to hold the leaves together. (Do not wash the cabbage now.) Put the wedges on a tray, freeze, then bag in family-size portions for the freezer.

To cook, remove the wedges from the freezer and drop them into a pan with a small amount of boiling, salted water, not more than ½ cup, and simmer, covered, until just tender. Do not overcook. Or steam the wedges in a vegetable steaming basket until tender. Serve with butter, salt, and pepper.

For longer storage, the cabbage wedges should be blanched in 1 gallon of boiling water for 2 to 3 minutes, chilled, drained, and frozen.

Freezer Cole Slaw

Shred 1 medium head of cabbage as for cole slaw, or chop it fine in an electric blender according to the directions accompanying the blender. Mix 1 teaspoon salt into the cabbage and let it stand 1 hour.

In a saucepan, combine 1 cup of vinegar, ¼ cup water, 1 teaspoon whole mustard seed, 1 teaspoon celery seed, and 2 cups sugar. Mix well and bring to a boil. Let the mixture boil 1 minute. Cool.

After the cabbage has been combined for 1 hour with the salt, squeeze out the excess moisture. Add 1 grated carrot and 1 green pepper, chopped fine. Pour the cooled vinegar solution over the cabbage and mix well. Package in 1-pint plastic containers and freeze.

One medium onion, chopped fine, can be added to the recipe, if desired.

For the best flavor, store in the freezer for a short time, preferably only a month or so.

To serve, thaw the cole slaw in the refrigerator and serve cold.

Frozen Green-Tomato Slices

Wash green tomatoes, remove the stems, and wipe dry. Cut in crosswise slices ⅜ inch thick, and spread in a single layer on a tray. Freeze, then package in freezer bags. For the best flavor and texture, store in the freezer for a short time, preferably less than 6 months.

To cook, remove the slices from the freezer and thaw only slightly. Dip each slice in white or yellow cornmeal or a mixture of cornmeal and flour. Season with salt and pepper and fry in a single layer in a skillet with 2 tablespoons or more of butter or bacon fat. Brown on both sides. Serve plain or with milk gravy to spoon over the tomatoes.

If wanted, the frozen tomato slices can be dipped into a beaten egg *before* coating with flour and/or cornmeal.

Crushed cracker crumbs can also be used for coating the egg-dipped frozen tomato slices.

Easy-Way Frozen Tomatoes

Wash ripe, perfect tomatoes, drain, and freeze whole without removing skins. To use, drop the frozen tomatoes into soup and later remove the curled-up peelings with a slotted spoon.

If preferred, the peelings can be removed before freezing by plunging the whole tomatoes into scalding-hot water, then into cold water. Freeze the whole peeled tomatoes on a cookie sheet, then package them in plastic freezer bags. Use the frozen tomatoes in cooking or whirl them in the blender to make puree.

FREEZING WILD FOODS

Hunting and gathering wild foods in meadows and woods is a worthwhile pastime that sooner or later captures the interest of many outdoors enthusiasts. Once captivated, few of us can limit ourselves to eating the berries on the spot, as the forest creatures do, or even to carrying back a conservative hatful of crab apples, or a few nuts tied up in a kerchief. Most of us tend to gather up sackfuls, and bucketfuls, and basketfuls of the delicious wild findings. Then, following our natural instincts to squirrel away the found foods, we haul home quantities of wild vegetables and fruits to preserve for later use.

And why not? The wild foods are flavorful and nutritious, a resource that should not be ignored by those who have access to the surplus of the wayside. The wild harvest is the only crop that does not cost us our time or money or effort in its cultivation. Wild foods are *free* and they are ours for the taking.

When brought into the kitchen, wild foods are prepared and preserved, for the most part, in the same ways their tame counterparts are prepared and preserved. As with cultivated varieties, some wild foods seem better suited to certain methods of preservation than others. If you prefer frozen asparagus to canned asparagus, you probably will prefer frozen fiddleheads to canned fiddleheads. Each person must select the methods that are most appealing and convenient for the curcumstances and the wild food being preserved.

Freezing tends to be my preferred method of preserving wild vegetables and fruits, partly because I like the ease of preparation and the flavor of the frozen wild foods, and partly because I have three home freezers and plenty of freezer space.

230

Then, too, the quantities of wild food to be stored away are sometimes too small to make canning or drying practical. There may be only enough wild blueberries to freeze in a small packet, in readiness for a winter batch of blueberry muffins. Or there are a few precious morels to tuck away in the corner of the freezer in the company of the other packages with intriguing contents. Pawpaws, persimmons, dandelion roots and greens, chokecherry juice, elderberries, sassafras—the wild foods in the freezer extend the realm of the frosty cache from everyday foods to gourmet fare.

A significant portion of the family's food can be provided by wild foods if one includes them in the harvest of summer's bounty that is to be preserved for winter's use.

Caution: Never gather and prepare for food any wild plant that you cannot positively identify as edible and safe.

To Freeze Morels

Wash the morels (*Morchella esculenta*) in lightly salted water, drain on toweling, cut into halves, and trim as necessary. Freeze the cleaned morels in a single layer on a baking sheet then pack them in quantities needed for one meal. Use plastic freezer bags or other suitable containers.

Do not thaw frozen morels before preparing them for the table. After taking them from the freezer, immediately dip them in batter and sauté them, still frozen, or put them into sauces or casseroles to be baked without thawing. Morels thaw quickly and tend to become limp and watery upon thawing.

Morels keep best from one spring to the next but I have kept them in the freezer for as long as two years.

Other Mushrooms

Chanterelles (*Cantharellus cibarius*) may be frozen in the same manner as morels. They are not as delicate as morels and hold their shape better when thawed, so chanterelles may be partially defrosted before preparing them for the table after freezing.

Chanterelles and other firm-variety mushrooms may be canned for storage. See directions page 83.

To Freeze Native American Persimmon Pulp

Use only fully ripe persimmons. One puckery persimmon will spoil the lot. Remove the stems and blossom ends of persimmons and rinse them quickly, a handful at a time, with the spray at the sink, if necessary. Do not attempt to wash the ripe persimmons in a pan of water because they are too soft and mushy. Press the persimmon pulp through a colander, using a wooden potato masher, or use the Foley food mill to process a few persimmons at a time. Empty out the seeds frequently.

The persimmon puree can be frozen just as it is because it has a very high vitamin C content and holds its color well. But I always add a bit of ascorbic acid or antidarkening agent, such as Fruit Fresh, just to guarantee good color.

Package the persimmon puree in the quantities you will be using for your favorite recipes, measuring out accurately ½ cup or 1 cup, as wanted. Use moisture vapor-proof containers, or put the persimmon pulp in yogurt or cottage cheese containers with an overwrap to prevent freezer burn.

Thaw the frozen persimmon puree in the refrigerator before using it in recipes. Persimmon pulp seems to keep forever in the freezer. After one year, frozen persimmon puree looks and tastes as fresh as yesterday's; after two years' storage at 0°F and lower, in good packaging, I have found it still top quality.

Native American Persimmon Pudding

In the bowl of an electric mixer, combine 2 cups sugar and 2 cups frozen persimmon pulp which has been thawed in the refrigerator. Add 2 eggs and beat well.

Pour 1½ cups buttermilk into a measuring cup and add to it 1 teaspoon baking soda. Stir until the foaming stops. Add the buttermilk mixture to the persimmon mixture.

Sift together 1½ cups flour, ⅛ teaspoon salt, 1 teaspoon baking powder, and 1 teaspoon cinnamon. Add the sifted dry ingredients to the persimmon mixture gradually, and beat well with the mixer on low speed. Stir in 1 teaspoon vanilla extract and ¼ cup light cream.

In a 9 × 13 × 2-inch baking pan, melt 2 tablespoons butter. Pour the melted butter into the persimmon pudding batter, leaving just enough in the pan to grease the bottom and sides. Stir the melted butter into the pudding batter, pour the batter into the baking pan, and bake in a 350°F oven for about 45 minutes. The pudding is done when it pulls away from the sides of the pan and the center is set. It will fall after being taken from the oven. Serve warm or chilled, with whipped cream.

To Freeze Pawpaw Pulp

Pawpaw puree can be frozen to be used in baking or to mix with fruit salads. Prepare the puree by forcing the peeled pawpaws through a sieve or use the Foley food mill, which is a rather bumpy procedure because of the seeds, but easier and faster than other methods.

Add at once ½ teaspoon pure ascorbic acid per pint of puree, or Fruit Fresh or other color keeper according to the directions on the can, or use fresh lemon juice generously, as much as 2 tablespoons to the pint. Pawpaws discolor quickly but will keep their color quite well after an antidarkening agent is added.

Pack the pawpaw puree into rigid freezer containers, leaving ½-inch head space, and freeze. To thaw, place the frozen pawpaw puree, still covered in the freezer container, in the refrigerator. Use as soon as it has thawed. If the top of the thawed pawpaw puree darkens, remove that portion and use the rest in the recipe.

Pawpaw Cake

Measure and sift together 1¾ cups flour, 1 teaspoon baking soda, 1 teaspoon baking powder, and ½ teaspoon salt. In a measuring cup combine ½ cup milk and 1 tablespoon lemon juice and set it aside to sour. In the bowl of the electric mixer, cream ½ cup shortening, add 1½ cups sugar gradually, and beat until fluffy. Beat in 2 eggs, one at a time, and add 1 teaspoon vanilla. Then add the sifted dry ingredients alternately with ½ cup pawpaw puree and the soured milk. Fold in 3 eggs whites, beaten stiff, and ½ cup chopped pecans or hickory nuts. Pour the batter into two lightly greased and floured 9-inch layer-cake pans. Bake in a moderate oven (350°F) 35 to 40 minutes. When cool, frost with Lemon Butter Frosting.

Lemon Butter Frosting

Cream ½ cup butter until fluffy, using an electric mixer. Blend in 1 tablespoon lemon juice and the grated rind of 1 lemon. Add 1 pound of sifted confectioners' sugar and enough cream (about 6 tablespoons) to make the frosting of the right spreading consistency. Run the beaters long enough to make the frosting very fluffy. Spread between the layers and on top of cake and garnish with a grating of lemon peel.

To Freeze Fiddleheads

Snap off the crisp, bright green coiled tops of ostrich ferns when they are in the crosier-shaped stage. The "fiddleheads" are covered with a dry brown casing, called "cat," which should be rubbed off, or winnowed* off, before washing the greens. Stubborn particles of "cat" that remain on the fiddleheads can be floated off during several consecutive washings before blanching the fiddleheads prior to freezing them.

To blanch fiddleheads, place them in the blanching basket and immerse them in boiling-hot water for 1 minute. Remove the fiddleheads from the vegetable blancher and transfer them to a container filled with ice water for quick cooling. Drain and package for the freezer in moisture vapor-proof boxes or bags. Freeze at 0°F, or lower, and store at 0°F. Fiddleheads retain top quality for more than a year in the freezer.

*To winnow the brown papery particles off the fiddleheads, place them in the salad basket and whirl it outdoors, or place an electric fan where it will blow away the loose casing as the greens are poured from one pan to another, or blow it out of the pan by holding a portable hair dryer with the setting on "cool" above the pan containing the fiddleheads.

234

Fiddleheads with Garlic

Melt ½ stick of butter in a heavy frying pan over low heat. Add 2 cloves of minced garlic (use a garlic press) to the butter. Add 1 package of frozen fiddleheads (about 2 cups) and squeeze the juice of 1 lemon over the fiddleheads. Simmer the fiddleheads in the garlic butter, breaking apart the block as soon as possible with a fork and tossing often, until they are tender but still crisp like asparagus. Season to taste with salt and freshly ground pepper. Serve hot.

Fiddleheads with Mushrooms

Prepare Fiddleheads with Garlic, as above. At the same time and in a separate pan, gently sauté 2 cups fresh sliced mushrooms in ¼ cup butter. When the mushrooms are cooked, drain the dark liquid off and combine them with the prepared fiddleheads. Season with salt and pepper.

To Freeze Wild Greens

Wash the wild greens in several cool waters and drain in the colander. Blanch in boiling water just until heated through and wilted, barely 1 minute. Drain and cool in cold or iced water. Drain, package in moisture/vapor-proof packages, and freeze.

Freeze each of the wild greens separately and label them clearly. All frozen greens look alike.

Wild greens may be cooked with seasonings and frozen, ready for the table. To thaw, place the frozen greens in a covered saucepan over low heat and heat slowly until thawed enough to bring to boiling before serving. If the excess pot liquor was saved and frozen separately, it can be thawed and used as cooking liquid. Drop the frozen greens into the boiling pot liquor and cook until well heated.

To Freeze Poke Sprouts

Cut the poke sprouts when they are about 6 inches tall and their top leaves are still unfurled. Do not break the shoots off below the ground. Wash them in cool water and drain. Blanch them in rapidly boiling water for barely a minute.

Change the blanching water when it discolors. Drain well. Place the blanched poke shoots in a single layer on a baking sheet and freeze.

To package, wrap two or three poke shoots separately in aluminum foil or clear plastic wrap, then place the wrapped bundles in a suitable freezer container. The frozen portions are then ready to use in preparing the recipe for Rolled Ham and Poke Sprouts.

If the poke sprouts are to be used in a recipe calling for steamed or stewed poke sprouts, steam the frozen poke sprouts in a vegetable steamer over boiling water until tender.

Rolled Ham and Poke Sprouts

In a saucepan, melt 4 tablespoons butter. Blend in 4 tablespoons flour. Stir continuously over low heat until the mixture bubbles, then gradually add 2 cups milk while stirring. Cook until the sauce thickens. Season with 1 teaspoon salt and ½ teaspoon lemon pepper. Remove from the heat and cool. Fold in ½ cup heavy cream, whipped, and 2 teaspoons grated lemon rind.

Spoon a small amount of the sauce into a shallow baking dish. Remove 6 portions, containing 3 shoots each, of poke sprouts from the freezer, and roll a thin slice of cooked ham around each bundle of frozen greens. Place the rolled ham and poke sprouts bundles in the baking dish with the open side down. Spoon the remaining sauce over the ham rolls. Sprinkle the rolls and sauce with grated Parmesan cheese, using at least ½ cup. Bake in a moderate oven (375°F) for 15 minutes, or until the sauce is bubbling. Finish under the broiler, about 4 inches from the heat, until the top is browned lightly, about 3 minutes.

Frozen, medium-sized asparagus spears may be substituted for the poke sprouts in this recipe.

PART IV

Home Drying
of Fruits and Vegetables

OLD-TIME FLAVORS:
Leather Breeches and Stack Cake

The low sloping tin roof of a shed attached to the chicken house was the hottest place to be found near the farmhouse in summertime. This was where Mother spread out the apricots, peaches, and apples that she dried for our winter use. The temperature on the roof must have reached 150° on the clear, hot, dry, sunny days that were ideal for drying fruits. My cousin, Annabelle, said the tin roof was hot enough to fry eggs at high noon and she swiped some from the nests and broke them on the roof to prove it. But the eggs slid off the slanting corrugated roof before we could see if she really knew what she was talking about.

The roof was a favorite playing place of ours, a hideaway that could be reached easily without a ladder by simply stepping up from a nearby tree limb. But when Mother was ready to carry the peeled, sliced fruits up to the roof for drying, she leaned a small ladder against the side of the building. The fruit slices were laid out in a single layer on a clean discarded window curtain, then covered with another sheer curtain to keep insects off while they were drying.

It took several days of hot sunshine to dry peach, apricot, and apple slices or halves until they were as pliable and leathery as Dad's belt. During this time Annabelle and I kept a close eye on the fruit slices that were spread out on

239

the roof to make sure that the curtain covering them did not blow out from under the bricks that weighted down the edges. Several times a day we were sent up to the roof to turn the pieces of drying fruit, and on the second day of drying, we pushed the center of each apricot half inward with our thumbs, to hurry up the drying.

And every afternoon when the sun went down, we were sent out to bring in the partially dried fruit slices to keep the evening dew from dampening the slices and to keep the fruit safe from the field mice who might steal it during the night if it were left out on the roof.

There were lots of little chores connected with the slow process of drying fruit in the sunshine. But we did not care to stay around when Mother burned flowers of sulfur under an overturned box that covered the fruit slices that were to be dried. The sulfur fumes made the fruit insect-proof and kept its colors bright, but they made a stink worse than rotten eggs which ran us out of the back yard until the smell went away.

Not all of the foods that we dried were sun-dried on the tin roof. Grandmother dried certain fruits and vegetables by hanging them above or behind the black kitchen range. There were garlands of apple slices and leather breeches beans strung on strings hanging from ceiling hooks. Bunches of herbs, tied together at the stems, dried upside down near the ceiling. Sometimes Grandmother cut cored apples and small pumpkins into doughnut shapes, instead of crescent slices, and ran them onto a round stick which was suspended from the ceiling by wires, one on each end. And there were always shallow pans, spread with fragrant leaves, crisping on the lowered door of the warming closet on top of the stove. In addition, Grandpa had made a metal corn dryer especially for drying sweet corn on top of the kitchen range.

The fruits and vegetables dried slowly and thoroughly within the circle of warmth shed by the kitchen stove and they were handy for Grandmother to tend to them while she worked in the kitchen. When they were finally dry, she closed them tightly in metal cans and glass jars and put them in the kitchen safe with her other staples. Later on

Grandmother's method of drying herbs, vegetables and fruits

she used them in old-fashioned dishes that are, to me, the highlights of her simple county-style cookery. Dried apples tasted best in stack cake and fried pies, dried peaches made the best pie, and corn pudding made with dried corn was everyone's favorite.

Dried-Apple Stack Cake

Cook 4 cups dried apples in water to cover until tender. Sweeten with ½ cup sugar and set aside. Add 1 teaspoon cinnamon and ¼ teaspoon nutmeg, if desired.

In a mixing bowl, combine 1 cup pure lard, room temperature, and 1 cup sugar and mix well with a mixing spoon. Add 1 egg and beat well. Add 1 cup sorghum molasses, 1 cup buttermilk, 1 teaspoon baking soda, 3 cups flour, and ½ teaspoon salt. Mix well.

Grease and flour two iron skillets (9 × 2½ inches), and pour the batter into the pans. Bake in a moderate oven (375°F.) for 35 minutes or until a broomstraw or toothpick inserted in the center of the cakes comes out clean. Split each cake in half crosswise. Spread the dried apples between the layers and on top of the cake. Serve with cream or whipped cream.

Half-Moon Pies

Cook 4 cups dried apples or dried peaches in water to cover until tender. Sweeten with ¾ cup sugar. Set aside.

Make a pie dough of 3 cups flour, 1 teaspoon salt, 1 cup lard, and about ⅓ cup water. Divide the dough into 6 portions. Roll out and cut into circles around a medium-sized plate. Put some of the dried, cooked fruit onto each round of dough, moisten the edges with water, and fold over to make a half-moon shape. Press the edges together with the tines of a fork. Fry the pies in ½ inch of hot fat for about 5 minutes on each side. Do not crowd pies together in skillet.

But the old-time flavor that truly harks back to the days of remembered summers is in the dish of leather breeches beans.

Leather breeches beans are dried until they look, and some say *taste*, like khaki colored leather breeches. Some folks called them leather britches beans or shuck beans. For drying, whole fat, tender, green beans had to be strung on strings with a large needle, like popcorn and cranberry strings were strung for the Christmas tree. That was something I liked to do and I often helped string the beans. When the beans were hung clothesline fashion in the attic or behind the kitchen stove, they really looked like a row of men's britches hanging on a clothes line on Monday morning.

When the beans were dry and leathery, they were

cooked in a kettle with a ham bone for flavor. This is how the wintertime dish of leather breeches beans was cooked:

Leather Breeches Beans

Soak one pound of dried leather breeches beans in water to cover for at least two hours, or overnight. The next morning, parboil the beans slowly for about 1 hour with ½ teaspoon baking soda. Drain the beans and cover them with fresh water. Add 1 large meaty smoked ham bone to the kettle, or a piece of salt pork, and boil the beans slowly for about 2 or 3 hours, until they are soft and tender. Add water to keep the beans from boiling dry during cooking. Do not cover the kettle with a lid. Add salt and pepper or use a pod of red pepper.

When I visited my other grandmother's house on a typical winter Saturday, there would likely be a savory kettle slowly cooking on her kitchen range, too, but Grandma Marshall's would contain dried navy beans, not leather breeches beans. My father was reared in a family with sixteen children and his mother did not find it practical to string enough leather breeches beans to feed her multitude. Think of the quantities of food that had to be provided to set a meal before eighteen people, three times a day! Canned peaches by the gallon, sour milk biscuits by the dozens, smoked bacon by the slab, fruit pies by the half dozen, yeast bread loaves by the oven load, jellies by the quart, fried green tomatoes by the crock full, butter by the pound, and giant-sized kettles of beans vanished when the high-spirited Marshall ménage sat along both sides of the long table at mealtime.

But one fact is well known in our community. The many Marshall children of that unique family, in spite of their number, were always well clothed, housed, educated, and well fed. My father always proudly stressed the point that the food served in his boyhood home was abundant and good.

"We had plenty of good food to eat, there's no question about it. Dad and Mom spent all of their time seeing to it that we would have enough. Dad would start out by planting an acre of potatoes. Then after he had cut the rye, he plowed the stubble under and planted an acre or two of beans. Those were the navy beans and red kidney beans— your grandmother planted cornfield beans in among the corn so that the vines would run up the corn stalks instead of having to have sticks for them to climb on.

"We ate the cornfield beans for green snap beans during the summer. We ate the kidney beans and navy beans in the winter. We let those mature until the pods were full and turning yellow. Then we pulled them, bush and all, and took them to the barn to finish drying on the haymow.

"If we hadn't raised a very big crop, all of the boys would beat the beans with sticks and flail them out of their pods. But we usually hulled them when the threshing machine came to hull our cowpeas and soybeans. It was too big a job to do by hand! It took six or seven 50-pound lard cans full of shelled dried beans to do us for a winter.

"I'll tell you, we ate a lot of beans in those days. Most folks did. And your grandmother could cook a pot of beans that made the finest eating in the world. She would soak those dried beans in water overnight and then the next morning she would put them on the stove in a big black iron kettle with a piece of salt pork in with them, and they would cook along *very slowly* until they were tender, but not mushy. Along about noontime, she would mix up a pan of cornbread. Now that was a pan that measured two feet long and a foot and a half wide and it took up one entire rack of the oven. And, by gollies, when dinner was over, there wasn't enough left over to feed the old dog, Strongheart. Those beans and cornbread made a meal as nourishing as a meal of meat.

"Yessir, they would have had a hard time feeding all of us without dried beans."

This is how Grandma Marshall cooked dried beans, as remembered by Aunt Grace. A recipe for cooking beans was not one that was written down.

244

Grandma Marshall's Navy Beans

"It took about two teacupfuls of dried beans to feed all of us. Mom would soak the beans overnight in cold water. The next morning she poured that water off and covered the beans with fresh water. Then she would lift off one of the caps of the kitchen stove and set the black iron pot directly on the fire, if she wanted to hurry up the beans. When the beans boiled hard, she drained the water off and covered them with fresh water. Sometimes she parboiled the beans twice. Then, when the beans came to the boil again, she slid the pot to the back of the stove or wherever she wanted it, and let them cook slowly all morning. That was what made the beans so good, the slow cooking. If she had salt pork, she would put that in. Sometimes she cut peeled Irish potatoes into large cubes and cooked them with the beans during the last half hour of cooking."

My mother cooked dried beans only about once a week, on washday usually, and our family needed just one small canful of shelled matured dried beans to make enough to last us through the winter. Putting by our supply of dried foods for winter was a small task compared with canning the fruits and vegetables, and it was one that gave variety to the regular canning chores.

General Instructions

HOW DRYING PRESERVES FOOD

Drying preserves food because it removes most of the moisture in food and microorganisms that cause decay and spoilage require moisture to grow.

Foods that are "dry" still contain 5 to 20 percent moisture, but this is not enough moisture content for spoilage microorganisms to flourish. Reducing the moisture content of food directly inhibits the action of molds, yeasts, and bacteria. There is no danger of botulism poisoning from dried foods that have been properly stored and reconstituted.

Enzymes are also responsible for food spoilage. The preliminary blanching necessary for most fruits and vegetables before drying stops enzyme development. Also, the temperature used to dry vegetables and fruits is usually about 140°F, which is adequate to check enzyme activity.

NUTRITIVE VALUE OF DRIED FOODS

By eliminating moisture and reducing bulk of foods in drying, the caloric content per cup of dried foods is increased.

Almost all dried produce will have higher protein, fat, and carbohydrate concentration per cup than food that is not dried. Fiber content of foods is not affected by drying.

As in all methods of food preservation, certain vitamins are preserved in dried foods and others are lost or reduced in potency.

Vitamin A is destroyed by the sun's rays if the food is sun dried, but it is retained for a time in foods dried by controlled heat. Vitamin A gradually disappears in dried foods.

The B vitamins—thiamine, riboflavin, and niacin—are preserved in varying amounts according to the pretreatment of the food before drying and the storage conditions after the food is dried. Thiamine is destroyed by heat or sulfuring. Riboflavin is preserved if the food is stored in a dark place. Niacin is unaffected by drying procedures or storing. The B vitamins are water soluble so the foods containing B-complex vitamins should be served in the water in which they are cooked or rehydrated.

The sulfuring, which destroys thiamine in dried foods, helps to preserve vitamin C that is present. It also helps preserve the color of carbohydrate-rich foods. The fruits that discolor badly when exposed to air must be treated with sulfur, salt, ascorbic acid (vitamin C), or other substances that prevent darkening.

Blanching is necessary to stop enzymatic action in foods being dried but a portion of the minerals and vitamins in the food will leach out into the boiling water or will be destroyed by its heat. Care in blanching will keep the unavoidable losses at a minimum. Steam-blanching conserves water-soluble vitamins and minerals that are lost by water-blanching.

Vitamins are conserved if food is dried quickly after harvesting. The dried product will have better color and flavor and more nutritive content if enzyme changes are halted promptly by drying or by blanching prior to drying.

Dried foods have the best flavor, color, texture, and nutritional value if they are used within a year after drying. Naturally there is a gradual loss of quality the longer dried foods are kept before use. But it is possible to keep dried foods much longer than a year. As an extreme example, one manufacturer of a home food dehydrator has kept dried foods up to 26 years and maintains that they still have good appearance and flavor. While this is an amazing record, it is questionable that dried food stored so long would have much food value left.

WHEN IS FOOD "DRY"?

Home dried foods still contain 5 to 20 percent water. Vegetables may contain 5 to 10 percent water; dried fruits may contain 10 to 20 percent water because their sugar content helps to preserve them.

Weighing the food can be a helpful check to determine if enough water has been evaporated from it. If a cupful of food weighed 10 ounces before it was dried, it should weigh between 1 and 2 ounces when dry, allowing it to contain 10 to 20 percent water.

The texture of dried food is the usual index to judging its state of dryness. The instructions for drying each food, appearing later in this section, gives specific visual and textural characteristics of each fruit and vegetable when it is "dry." To generalize, a dried food is reduced in size and is firm. Fruit is dry when it feels dry and leathery on the outside and slightly moist on the inside. Vegetables are dry when they are brittle, tough, and rattle on the trays.

METHODS OF DRYING FOODS AT HOME

Prepared foods may be dried in the sunshine, in the oven, or in a food dehydrator. Some foods, such as herbs and legumes, are air dried in an attic or outdoors in the shade on a hot, dry day.

Dried foods are dehydrated in the sense that water is removed from them to accomplish drying. The terms, dried and dehydrated, are used interchangeably. But, technically, dehydration refers to a more thorough process than drying, in which all but 2.5 to 4 percent of a food's water content is removed. Dehydrated foods are prepared commercially because home drying cannot duplicate the conditions required to dehydrate foods. When the term dehydrated is used in this book, it is used as a synonym for dried foods and does not refer to foods containing only 2.5 to 4 percent water, unless noted. Home food dehydrators referred to in this book do not duplicate the commercial food-dehydrating process but are suited to home drying of foods which leaves a moisture content in the dried foods of 5 to 20 percent.

EQUIPMENT NEEDED FOR HOME DRYING FOODS

For any home-drying project you will need at least some of the special equipment listed here. Check the instructions for the specific food you are drying for just which items will or will not be required.

- An oven or food dehydrator
- Drying trays
- Plastic wrap and cooking parchment
- A food slicer for making uniform slices
- A vegetable blancher
- Cheesecloth netting or discarded mesh curtain without holes to cover trays outdoors
- A thermometer that registers below 150°F and up to 250°F or higher, such as an oven, deep fat, candy, dairy, or fish-tank thermometer
- A sulfuring box
- Packaging materials and containers
- A small electric fan for oven-drying
- The kitchen utensils needed for regular preparation of food, such as paring knives, colanders, bowls, and kettles

TRAYS FOR HOME DRYING OF FOODS

Commercial food dehydrators are fitted with their own removable trays. Drying trays can also be bought separately (see the Sources section in the back of the book), or they can be built by the home carpenter according to the directions below.

Ready-made trays have wire mesh or woven surfaces which allow for air circulation around the food, top and bottom. If the spaces of the mesh are large and allow shreds or small pieces of food to slip through, cover the tray surfaces with cheesecloth. If fruit leather or jerky is being dried, spread it on a layer of plastic wrap or cooking parchment placed on the tray surface.

Homemade drying trays should be constructed of dry wood containing no pitch. Plywood or other composition board is fine. The drying surfaces can be made of various materials—wood strips, nongalvanized window screening, stainless steel hardware cloth, metal mesh, or nylon screening—provided it will withstand high temperatures. Or the bottom of the tray may be constructed of string and netting according to the directions supplied by the United States Department of Agriculture (see page 352).

Trays for sulfuring foods must have slatted wooden bottoms with no wire surfaces because sulfur cannot be used with metal. Wooden fruit trays with lathing strips for bottoms may serve the purpose, or the wooden lids from lug boxes used for packing foods.

If trays are constructed for use in the home oven, they must be 1½ inches smaller on all sides than the measurements of the inside of the oven to allow for air circulation.

Do not use galvanized screening because it has been treated with zinc and cadmium, substances not safe to use with food. Also avoid using fiberglass screening, unless it has been coated to make it safe for food use.

If there is ample room for the drying project on the two racks that come with the stove oven, layers of screening made of food safe material cut to size could be placed on each rack to keep the drying foods from falling through the spaces of the oven racks. Each rack could be covered with a layer of cheesecloth as well, but if used, it must be watched carefully to make sure the cloth does not catch on fire. Be sure the oven heat is kept very low and the temperature indicator is accurate, to avoid combustion. If a fire should occur, douse it with baking soda and close the oven door until it burns out. Naturally, the food being dried would be destroyed and unfit for use.

Convenient oven-drying racks are available for a modest price. See Sources section at the end of the book.

SELECTING FOODS FOR DRYING

The same criteria that are used in selecting fruits and vegetables for canning and freezing apply in selecting them for drying. Produce should be at its peak of color, taste, and freshness. Foods should be dried on the same day they are picked, preferably immediately after harvesting. Wilted or overripe foods will not produce good quality dried foods.

Blemished or bruised fruits and vegetables are susceptible to spoilage, just as they would be if canned. Decay or mold on one slice of fruit can spoil the taste of an entire trayful.

Drying does not improve food quality—it only preserves the level of quality that is already there. So dry only choice fruits and vegetables.

Virtually every food can be dried, but some fruits and vegetables seem better suited to drying than others. Home drying is not as good a method of preserving melons, cucumbers, radishes, and asparagus as other methods. It is especially well suited to preserving apricots, peaches, apples, figs, fruit leathers, legumes, herbs, onions, and parsley.

PREPARING FOODS FOR DRYING

In general, food is prepared for drying in the same ways as it is for table use or for freezing, except that it must be cut into pieces of uniform size. The smaller the pieces or the thinner the slices, the quicker the drying is accomplished.

Most foods to be dried should be briefly blanched in boiling water or by steam. Steam blanching is preferred over water blanching for foods to be dried.

251

Foods that tend to darken during preparation benefit from pretreatment with an antidarkening agent before drying. This treatment is not mandatory, but helps to preserve color and vitamins in the food. The same treatments that are used for preparing foods for freezing may be used when drying foods. In addition, pretreating foods with sulfur is especially suited to drying foods because it helps to preserve vitamins C and A, prevents darkening, and speeds up the drying process. The sulfuring treatment consists of either dipping, soaking, or steaming the food in a sulfur solution, or of exposing the prepared food to the fumes of burning sulfur in a closed box.

PRETREATMENT OF FOODS TO PREVENT DARKENING

Apples and light-colored fruits darken during preparation, drying, and storage if they are not treated with an antidarkening agent before drying.

The usual methods used in preventing darkening of foods when preparing them for the table, for freezing, or for canning, are used for drying foods as well. These methods include the use of ascorbic acid, citric acid or lemon juice, and vinegar. Some fruits and vegetables are dipped or held in salt water and others may be precooked. Some fruits are blanched in syrup to hold their color and to add flavor.

But the most effective pretreatment of fruits before drying is by sulfuring. Sulfuring not only preserves the color of fruits, but helps to preserve vitamins A and C during drying and storage. Foods that have been treated with sulfur require less time to dry than untreated foods.

There are two ways to use sulfur to treat fruits and some vegetables. One way is to expose the food to the fumes of burning sulfur. The other way is to use a sodium bisulfite solution for dipping the fruit pieces before drying or to use the same solution for steam blanching the fruits. (See the following section.)

Foods can be dried without pretreating to prevent oxidation, but they will be dark and unattractive, and many will continue to darken during storage.

SULFURING

Sulfuring is a method of pretreating foods to prevent darkening by oxidation during preparation and storage. It also helps to preserve vitamins A and C, shortens drying time, and destroys insects and many micro-organisms.

The best-known way of sulfuring is to expose the prepared food, usually fruit, to the fumes of burning sulfur. The substance used is known as "Flowers of Sulfur" and it is food-grade elemental sulfur that may be purchased at most pharmacies. The disadvantage to this method is that the fruit must be treated and dried outdoors because the fumes stink and irritate the nose and eyes, to say the least. A special box must be used for sulfuring.

The easier way to sulfur fruits, if you can obtain the substance needed, is to dip the fruit pieces before drying in a sodium bisulfite solution, or to use the same solution for steam blanching the fruits.

An argument against sulfuring is that, while it helps preserve vitamins A and C, which occur significantly in fruits, it destroys thiamine, or vitamin B_1. However, it should be pointed out that fruits are not a major source of thiamine. Meats, cereals, and legumes, which are good sources of thiamine, need never be subjected to sulfuring.

SULFURING WITH SULFUR FUMES Treating foods with sulfur fumes produced by burning "Flowers of Sulfur" prior to drying, protects them from insects and preserves their color, flavor, and certain vitamins. Since fumes of burning sulfur are unpleasant to breathe, sulfuring has to be done outdoors within a sulfuring box. Drying must also be done outdoors, after sulfuring, because the fumes which would arise from oven drying or dehydrator drying of the sulfured fruit would be unpleasant to breathe.

The prepared fruit is placed on trays for sulfuring and the trays are stacked and enclosed in an airtight box with the burning sulfur so that the fumes can penetrate the fruit

253

Cut-out portion for purpose of illustrating inside of sulfuring box

for a time, from a few minutes to a few hours, depending on the requirement.

A cardboard carton such as the one shown in the accompanying illustration, will serve as a sulfuring box so it can be burned after you are finished with it.

If you wish to have a sulfuring box on hand from year to year, a wooden box of the same dimensions as the cardboard carton sulfuring box can be used. It must be airtight so that the fumigating will be efficient, but two closeable openings are necessary to create a draft and to circulate the fumes as needed.

Trays for holding the prepared fruits must have wood-slat bottoms rather than metal or wire bottoms because sulfur reacts with metal.

The procedure is as follows:

1. Spread prepared fruits in a single layer on wooden trays* with the pit cavity or cut surface up and space between each piece of fruit. Each tray will hold about 10 pounds of fruit. Process from 1 to 4 trays at a time.

2. Stack the trays 1½ inches apart, separated by spools or wood blocks placed at the corners, with the bottom tray placed on two fire bricks or concrete blocks arranged far enough apart to support the stacked trays. Place the trays outdoors in a place where the sulfur burner will not damage nearby plants or the surface where it is placed. A gravel driveway is a good location.

3. Cover the stack of trays with a heavy cardboard box that is about 1½ inches larger all around than the stack of trays. Cut two openings in the box as shown in the illustration. A draft will be created when the slashes are opened and the sulfur fumes will circulate. Pack dirt around the bottom edge of the box to keep fumes from escaping.

4. Measure out 1 tablespoon of Sulfur Flowers (U.S.P. standard) for each pound of fruit. Place it in a 1 pound coffee can or on an aluminum baking tray. Lift the box off the stack of trays and place the sulfur burner under the stack of trays near an edge between the fire bricks. Light the sulfur and place the sulfuring box over the stack of trays with the bottom opening near the container of burning sulfur.

5. Start timing. As soon as the sulfur is burning well, close the openings in the box. The amount of time the sulfur burns will depend on the ventilation, the shape of the box, and the weather. The sulfuring is completed when the fruit appears bright and glistening and there is a small amount of juice in the cavity.

6. Remove the sulfuring box from the stack of trays and arrange the trays in single layers in a suitable place outdoors in the sunshine to finish drying the fruits. Cover the trays with cheesecloth to protect the fruit from insects. Turn the

---

Wooden Trays must be used for sulfuring fruits. There should be no metal on the tray to come in contact with the sulfur. Trays can be constructed of narrow lathing strips or the wooden lids from lug boxes can be used.

fruit often and bring the trays inside at night.* Or transfer the sulfured fruits to the trays of a dehydrating cabinet and finish drying the fruits in the food dehydrator placed outside the house, in the garage or on the patio. Sulfured fruits give off a strong odor and should not be dried in the home oven or inside the house.

7. When the fruits are dry, cool them and place them in the freezer for 48 hours before packaging, if dried in the sun. In spite of precautions, sun dried fruits may contain insects. If the foods were dried in a food dehydrator, cool them and package them at once. Store dried fruits in a cool, dark, dry place.

Do not use metal lids on containers used to store sulfured dried fruits unless plastic wrap is placed between the fruit and the lid to prevent reaction between the metal lid and the sulfur.

SULFURING BY DIPPING OR STEAM-BLANCHING Whenever sulfuring is the recommended treatment for fruits, a solution of sodium bisulfite may be used for dipping the fruit instead of treating the fruit with the fumes of burning sulfur. Another alternate method is steam blanching over boiling water containing sodium bisulfite.

While sodium bisulfite is the most common substance called for in directions for sulfuring by dipping, you may find directions calling for sodium sulfite or sodium metabisulfite. All three substances are essentially the same as they are made by reacting soda ash and sulfur, but their molecular structure differs.† These three substances may be used interchangeably. (Do not confuse sodium *bisulfite* with sodium *bisulfate*, which is a toxic solution.)

Drying Fruit Should be Brought in at Night to protect it from dew, rain, or night marauders unless you have a place that is protected. If the temperature does not drop more than 20° lower than the daytime temperature, it is not harmful to leave the fruit outside at night, but cover it with a tarpaulin.

†Molecular formulas are as follows: sodium bisulfite is $NaHSO_3$; sodium sulfite is Na_2SO_3; and sodium metabisulfite is $Na_2S_2O_5$.

To make a cold sulfite solution for dipping fruits before drying, combine from 1½ to 3½ tablespoons (depending on the strength needed or wanted; use the smaller amount for a minimum effect, the larger amount if you wish to achieve the maximum effect) of sodium bisulfite, sodium sulfite, or sodium metabisulfite, whichever is available, with 1 gallon of water. Dip fruits in the solution for a brief time, about 1 minute, unless the directions specify soaking for a longer time for more effectiveness. Drain fruits on paper toweling and arrange on drying trays. Dry the fruit outdoors. Any taste or odor evident in the dried fruit will disappear during cooking.

To steam blanch fruits with sodium bisulfite (or sodium sulfite or sodium metabisulfite), add 1 to 2 teaspoons of the substance to 2 cups of water. Steam the fruit pieces over the solution for a few minutes, according to the instructions, blanching only until the pieces are translucent. Do not rinse the food in cold water after blanching; the sulfite solution loses its effectiveness after 15 or 20 minutes. Drain and proceed with the drying outdoors. Vegetables may also be steam-blanched over a sodium bisulfite solution.

IS SULFURING SAFE? Many of us who resist food additives and chemical preservation of foods will question the use of sulfur to pretreat foods before drying. These points may be considered in making the choice to sulfur or not to sulfur.

- Homemakers, as well as commercial fruit dryers, have used sulfur for years to preserve quality of dried fruits.
- Vitamins A and C are preserved by sulfuring.
- Sulfurous acid that forms on fruit during sulfuring is gradually lost during drying and storage, and the remainder is driven off by cooking.

- The amount of sulfur consumed from home-dried foods is thought to be too small to have any discoverable harmful effect.

A minor argument against sulfuring is that, while it

257

helps preserve vitamins A and C which occur significantly in fruits, it destroys thiamine, or vitamin B_1. However, it should be pointed out that fruits are not a major source of thiamine.

OTHER METHODS OF PRETREATING FOODS TO PREVENT DARKENING

Salt water may be used for dipping or briefly soaking fruits and vegetables that tend to darken. The salt-water bath, made of 4 to 6 tablespoons salt to 1 gallon water, should not be used for more than 20 minutes or there will be loss of nutrients.

Vinegar and salt, at the rate of 2 tablespoons salt and 2 tablespoons vinegar to ½ gallon of water, may be used for dipping or briefly soaking fruits and vegetables that tend to darken during preparation and drying. Submerge the food in the vinegar-salt-water solution for 10 minutes.

Lemon juice added to water used for blanching or holding fruits retards darkening. Use ¼ cup lemon juice to 1 quart water.

Ascorbic acid and water, in the proportion of ½ to 1 teaspoon ascorbic acid to 1 quart of water, may be used to hold fruits and vegetables prior to drying or for blanching.

Syrup blanching will prevent darkening of fruits during drying and adds flavor. Fruits such as apricots and peaches can be simmered for 10 minutes in a syrup made of 1 cup sugar to 3 cups water, or sweeter, if desired.

Precooking without sugar until just tender, except for apples, deters darkening of certain fruits during drying.

Each of these methods is better suited to some fruits and vegetables than to others. The instructions for drying specific foods, which appear later in this section, recommend the best methods for each.

BLANCHING FOODS BEFORE DRYING

Blanching in boiling water or by steam is a standard procedure for preparing most vegetables for drying. A few, notably horseradish, mushrooms, okra, onions, parsley, peppers, pimentos, and herbs, require no treatment.

Some fruits are blanched before drying as well, but blanching is usually an alternate method of preparing fruits for drying. Sulfuring is the preferred method of pretreating fruits for drying because the product is more attractive and nutritious.

Blanching stops the action of enzymes that cause vegetables to lose color and flavor during drying. It also kills spoilage microorganisms that are destroyed by boiling temperatures, such as molds, yeasts, and some bacteria.

Directions for blanching foods in hot water or by steaming are given in the section on Freezing Vegetables and Fruits, beginning on page 194. The times for blanching foods are the same for freezing as for drying, except that foods cut in smaller pieces or shredded for drying require less blanching time. Take care not to overcook foods during blanching.

Blanched foods do not need to be cooled before drying, but cooling prevents overblanching by stopping the cooking instantly. Blanched foods should be drained on paper toweling to blot up excess moisture before proceeding with the drying process.

Steam-blanching is preferred over water-blanching for most foods to be dried because less water enters the produce.

RESIST THE TEMPTATION TO SKIP BLANCHING

As in freezing, there is the temptation to skip blanching or pretreating certain vegetables. It seems so simple just to slice the vegetables and pop them in the dehydrator or oven. They dry attractively and taste fine. So why not?

Not only does blanching shorten the drying time in most cases, but it kills microorganisms that cause spoilage, such as molds, which might not be killed by a drying temperature of 140°F or less. So blanching helps preserve food by preventing spoilage.

Blanching also stops enzymatic action that eventually causes loss of food quality. While foods dried without blanching might not show these losses immediately after drying, it is important for long storage of food that it be blanched. Drying temperatures are not high enough to stop enzymatic action, although it will be slowed down. Enzymes are most active at 85° to 120°F; their progress is slowed at about 140°F, and halted by brief boiling at 212°F.

SYRUP-BLANCHING FRUITS TO BE DRIED

Fruits that tend to discolor when being prepared or dried can be blanched in a sweetened syrup to prevent discoloration. The syrup can be light, medium, or heavy, depending upon the sweetness wanted in the finished product.

Apples, apricots, peaches, nectarines, pears, plums, figs, prunes, and bananas can be treated by syrup blanching.

Combine 1 cup sugar with 1 cup water for heavy syrup, 1 cup sugar with 2 cups water for medium syrup, or 1 cup sugar with 3 cups water for light syrup. Bring the mixture to a boil while stirring, drop in the prepared fruits, and simmer them gently for 5 to 15 minutes, depending upon the size of the pieces. Remove from heat and let the fruit stand in the hot syrup for a few minutes more. Drain the fruit in strainer, then on paper toweling to remove as much moisture as possible. Reserve the syrup for the next batch of fruit. Proceed with drying as directed for the specific fruit.

Corn syrup or honey can be substituted for part of the sugar in syrup-blanching.

Syrup-blancing tends to lengthen drying time. Syrup-blanched fruits will remain sticky when "dry."

PRETREATMENT OF CERTAIN FRUITS IN A LYE SOLUTION

Some fruits, notably prunes, may be dipped in a lye solution to facilitate peeling and to make them dry faster.

Place 2 level tablespoons of lye in 1 gallon of cold water, using an unchipped enamelware container or a stainless steel vessel. Stir the mixture with a wooden spoon or a clean stick. Bring the mixture to a boil. Dip the fruit in the boiling solution, being careful to avoid getting the lye water on your skin. Leave the fruit in the lye water for 5 to 30 seconds, until many small cracks are formed in the skin of the fruit when it is washed. The time required depends upon the size of the fruit and the toughness of its skin.

Rinse the fruit thoroughly in cold water to remove all traces of lye.

Caution: To dispose of lye solution after use, pour it carefully down the sink drain and rinse the sink thoroughly with cold water. Rinse the utensils used in cold water also. Use rubber gloves when handling lye; wash off any lye that contacts the skin with cold water; and use extreme caution to keep lye water from splashing into the eyes. *Do not pour hot water into lye. Never use lye with any metal other than stainless steel or unchipped enamelware.*

TEMPERATURES FOR DRYING FOODS

The temperature needed to dry food when using an electric heat source is about 140°F. Too-low a temperature (below 95°F) allows the food to sour or mold before it is dried. Too-high a temperature (165°F) will scorch the food.

If food is dried in the sun, the thermometer must register temperatures in the high nineties, for the best results, for several consecutive sunny, cloudless days with low relative humidity. The temperature should be fairly constant, at about 95° to 100°F. If the air temperature is not quite that high, but the day is sunny and warm, say—85°F with low humidity—the food can be placed where reflected heat will raise the temperature to 100°F or higher. Such suitable places might be a metal roof, or a surface behind a pane of glass or Plexiglas, or the food to be dried may be placed on a sheet of aluminum foil or solar reflecting material.

Air circulation is almost as important as heat in drying foods. Fans are used in oven drying and in electric dehydrators to provide constant air flow over and around the food. Natural draft dehydrators are designed so that air circulates properly around the trays of food. Since heat and moisture rise, rotating and turning the trays help maintain an even drying rate.

With controlled heat drying, it is often recommended that the drying be begun at the lowest temperature setting, 120°F or lower, then gradually increased after an hour or two to about 140°F, then turned back to lower heat at the end of the drying time to avoid scorching the food. The drying temperature should never exceed 165°F.

PROCEDURE FOR OVEN DRYING

1. Prepare and pretreat the fruits or vegetables as directed in the instructions for individual foods later in this section.
2. Place the prepared food on clean trays in a single layer using 1 to 2 pounds per tray. Do not dry more than 6 pounds of food in the oven at one time. More than one kind of vegetable may be dried at one time but odorous foods such as onions must be dried separately. Sulfured fruits should not be dried indoors in the oven.
3. Place the first tray on the lower oven rack set about 3 inches from the bottom of the oven. The second tray can be placed on the second rack set just far enough above the first to allow for two trays to be stacked between them. If more than two trays are to be dried in a two-rack oven at one time, place two trays of food on each oven rack. Separate the trays on the racks with blocks of wood to keep them 3 inches apart. Leave at least 3 inches between the top tray and the top of the oven.
4. Place a thermometer in the oven, toward the back, and keep the temperature at about 140°F during the drying process. Prop the door to the electric oven open about 4 inches; prop the door to the gas oven open about 8 inches at the top. Adjust the opening of the door as necessary to keep the oven at the proper temperature. Be certain that the flame of a gas stove does not go out when turned very low. Do not leave the drying project unattended.
5. Place a small fan outside the oven in a position that directs the air through the oven door opening and across

the interior of the oven. Change the position of the fan frequently during the drying period to vary the circulation of the air.

6. Rotate the trays every half hour and stir or turn the pieces so that they will dry evenly. Regulate the heat carefully at the end of the drying period when food will scorch easily. The amount of heat needed to maintain the temperature of 140°F is less as the drying progresses.

7. When the food seems dry, take a sample, cool and test it according to the dryness test listed in the instructions for each fruit or vegetable.

8. After the foods are dried, remove them from the oven, cool, and package. Store in a cool, dry, dark place as directed in the section on storage of dried foods.

DRYING FOODS IN A FOOD DEHYDRATOR

Several types of food dehydrators can be bought which work very well for home drying of foods. Surprisingly, drying foods in a food dehydrator takes much more time than drying in either the home oven or the sun, but it is very convenient and produces high quality dried foods. The drying temperature can be regulated and controlled; the air circulates evenly throughout the cabinet and ensures even drying.

I have two brands of food dehydrators in my kitchen and there are slight differences between them. One is very quiet-running but has no options for setting the temperature higher or lower than 140°F. It has an automatic timer, which turns off the dehydrator according to the setting. The other operates with more noise, comparatively, but has optional settings at low, medium, and high. It must be turned off manually. Since neither has a temperature indicator, a thermometer must be placed inside the dehydrators to determine the exact temperature being maintained during the drying process. If you are considering the purchase of a dehydrator, consider all of its features very carefully.

Plans for home-building a food dehydrator are available (see the Sources Section at the back of the book). If you can build one yourself, or have someone build one for you, there will be a considerable cash savings. Naturally the home-built ones are bulkier and not so attractive and streamlined as the commercially made dehydrators, but they are designed to do the same work.

The times suggested in the directions for home drying of fruits and vegetables in a dehydrator are based on the times given in Home and Garden Bulletin Number 217, published by the United States Department of Agriculture. These times can only be used as guidelines in determining the time needed to dry foods in the home food dehydrator because of the variables that exist. There is a 6 to 12 hour leeway in many of the times given, which seems very generous, but it is difficult to be more specific. The size of the pieces of the food being dried, the amount of moisture in the individual foods, the type of pretreatment used, the temperature at which the dehydrator is set—all of these factors affect the time required to dry the food.

Home drying of foods is not as exact a procedure as home canning or freezing. Although drying is the oldest method of food preservation known, the use of home food dehydrators is relatively new. While certain foods seem better suited to home drying than others, the trend in using food dehydrators seems to be to dry literally *everything*. Your particular food dehydrator will probably have a booklet accompanying it that will give you reliable information that can be used with it. If you wish to dry a food not included in your dehydrator's instructions, you will have to be experimental in your approach and follow the best general instructions you have available. When you find out what specific instructions best fit your machine, you can keep notes to refer to for future use.

PROCEDURE FOR DEHYDRATOR DRYING

1. Prepare the fruits or vegetables as directed in the instructions for individual foods later in this section. Pretreat to prevent darkening if recommended.
2. Place the prepared food on clean trays in a single layer, leaving space between each piece of food to allow for air circulation. As the drying progresses and the food shrinks, the contents of the trays can be combined to free space for more undried food to be placed in the dehydrator. If the food to be dried is shredded, spread no thicker than ½ inch deep.
3. Preheat the dehydrator before placing the trays in the unit. Maintain a temperature of about 140°F all during drying unless directions accompanying dehydrator recommend otherwise.
4. Stir shredded food often and turn pieces of food during drying. Keep a thermometer in the dehydrator if there is not a temperature indicator. Let the dehydrator run continuously all during the time required for drying, if possible.
5. When the food appears to be dry, remove a sample, cool

265

it, and test it for dryness according to the instruction for the specific food you are processing.

6. Cool the dried food and store it in a cool, dark, dry, place in packages or containers that will protect it from light, moisture, air, and insects.

DRYING FOODS IN THE SUN

In order to sun dry foods, there must be several consecutive days of hot sunshine with temperatures ideally above 90°F and low relative humidity. When the air temperature is not that hot, the foods can be placed where the reflected heat will be in the mid-to-high nineties, which is ideal for drying—a metal roof is such a place. Or the trays could be placed behind a pane of glass or Plexiglas which is propped up above the drying trays to prevent collection of moisture back of the glass.

Too-low temperatures while drying, high humidity, and long interruptions of sunshine by clouds will result in uneven drying and molding before the food dries.

Some areas are not consistently good for sun drying foods. In humid regions, such as our area here by the Ohio River, we must reserve sun drying for those rather in-

Sun-drying in a home-built solor dehydrator

266

frequent periods of suitable weather. Sometimes it is September before we have hot days without humidity. Even then, we are prepared to finish a sun drying project indoors in the oven. In other regions, such as some in California and Arizona, sun drying can be relied upon as a regular, easy method of preserving various foods.

Foods dried outdoors in the sunshine must be protected from dust. A cheesecloth tent will keep a normal amount of dust from settling on the food but the location chosen for the drying should be one where dust is not stirred up.

PROCEDURE FOR SUN DRYING FOODS

1. Prepare the fruits or vegetables as directed in the instructions for individual foods later in this section. Pretreat as recommended.
2. Place the prepared food on clean trays in single layers. Cover the trays with a cheesecloth tent to keep insects out. Arrange the cloth so that it does not touch the food being dried.
3. Place the trays outdoors in full sunshine on a table or surface above the ground. Do not stack the trays.
4. Turn the fruits or vegetables at least once each day to ensure even fast drying. Bring the trays indoors at sundown to protect the food from dew, unexpected rain, or night marauders.
5. Drying will be completed after several (3 or 4) days of drying under ideal conditions, depending upon the size and moisture content of the food. If rain or cloudy weather interrupts the drying, finish the process in the oven (see page 262). If the temperature is not in the high nineties, place the food where it will absorb reflected heat.
6. When the food appears dry, test for dryness according to the characteristics given in the instructions for individual foods.

OTHER METHODS OF DRYING FOODS

Herbs and grains can be air dried in a hot attic or other

place inside the house where the conditions are right. The ceiling above a heat register or the mantel above the fireplace might be such a place where herbs could be hung; or garlands of leather breeches or apples strung on a string could be hung from ceiling rafters in a warm room.

An area with a fairly constant temperature of 95°F to 100°F can be used to dry foods inside the house. A spot over the top of the refrigerator, near the furnace, or on a rack suspended over a wood range or heating stove might be such a place. Racks or hanging devices must be rigged up to suit the situation so that a fairly constant temperature is maintained and so that the drying food has good air circulation around it.

Some drying trays that I bought are suspended in rope hangers, much as hanging flower pots are hung in macramé holders, so that they can be hung from a bracket or ceiling hook over the heat source. These drying trays can be used in the attic and outdoors, as well. (See the Source Section at the end of the book.)

Stacked drying trays might be placed under a floor lamp or heat lamp, or over a heat register in the floor, to dry certain foods, or to finish a sun-drying project that is interrupted by rain. If a heat lamp is used, remember to stir the food often and to rotate the trays regularly. If the heat from a floor register is used, make sure it is clean so that dust is not blown up on the food, or cover the register with cheesecloth.

CONDITIONING AND STERILIZING FOODS AFTER DRYING

Individual slices or pieces of a food that has been dried may contain varying amounts of moisture because they have dried unevenly and are of different sizes. To equalize the amount of moisture in all of the pieces of dried fruit or vegetable, remove them from the trays and combine them on a clean surface or in a container such as the enamelware canner. (If the dried food has been sulfur-treated, however, *do not place it in or on metal at any time*.) Cover the container loosely to protect the dried fruit and vegetables from dust and insects, but do not make the container airtight. Stir the food several times a day for 2 to 10 days.

After conditioning, sterilize the dried food by heating it briefly in the oven. Spread the food loosely on trays or flat pans. Heat for 10 to 15 minutes in a preheated oven at 175°F. Cool the food before packaging.

PACKAGING AND STORING DRIED FOODS

Dried foods must be cooled before packaging, but once cool they must be packaged without delay. Food not promptly packaged in an airtight container may pick up moisture or be infested by insects in the interim.

To preserve their quality and nutritional value, dried foods must be protected from heat, moisture, light, insects, and rodents. Mold will form on inadequately dried foods or those not protected by proper packaging. Foods dried in the oven or in the food dehydrator should be free of insects or insect eggs, but they are subject to reinfestation if not stored immediately in an adequate container. Foods dried outdoors in the sun, no matter how carefully shielded or handled, are apt to have insects or insect eggs on them. To rid sun-dried foods of possible insect infestation, store them in the food freezer for 48 hours after drying and before packaging.

Tightly sealed plastic bags, filled and closed so that *no air remains inside*, are the best packages. Also, use several smaller containers rather than one large one that must be opened frequently to remove the food. Heat-sealable baggies are ideal: The seal is perfect and the portions small. The clear-plastic bags will admit light, however, so they should be put into another container that shuts out light, insects, and mice, such as a metal lard can or a lidded crock or jar. If the storage jar is glass and will admit light, block out the light either by wrapping the jar in lightproof material, or placing the produce inside a brown paper bag before putting it into the jar. Dried fruits and vegetables look so attractive in pretty glass jars that you may be tempted to store your foods in full view. But resist the temptation; light will fade and reduce the general quality of any unprotected foods that are not used within a short time.

Glass canning jars can be used for storing dried foods. Jars not suitable for canning, such as mayonnaise or coffee jars, are also fine. If old jar rings are used with the lids to make the jars airtight, use two to make the seal tighter if it seems necessary.

All glass and metal containers used for storing dried foods should be washed and scalded before placing the sterile dried foods inside them. Molds, yeast, or bacteria in nonsterile containers could cause spoilage.

There are waxed-paper cartons with lids and bags available that are made especially for storing dried foods. These can be sealed with a warm iron or sealer to make them moistureproof. But since insects and mice are attracted to dried foods stored on a shelf, it is best to place sealed paper packages inside a metal or crockery container with a close-fitting lid.

Dried foods, like canned foods, should be stored in a cool, dry, dark place, where the average temperature is below 72°F. A low storage temperature extends the life of dried food. In fact, if you have space, freezer storage is recommended if a dried food is to be kept longer than a few weeks. Dried foods stored in moistureproof materials in the freezer are safe from all elements that can cause spoilage. And if cereal weevils are a problem at your house, freezer storage may be a necessity.

Some dried foods keep longer than others. Cabbage, onions, and carrots have a shelf life of about 6 months, while tomatoes and mushrooms are at their best for only about half that time. Most kinds of food, however, if properly dried, packaged, and stored, will keep at top quality for at least a year, and often longer, though with a gradual diminishing of quality.

Examine the stored dried foods regularly, especially in the beginning. If any sign of moisture appears, reheat the food in a preheated oven at 150°F for 15 minutes, or return the food to the dehydrator and dry briefly again before cooling and repackaging in a new, moistureproof package. If signs of mold or spoilage appear on food, throw it out.

TO RECONSTITUTE DRIED FOODS

Since drying greatly reduces the bulk of foods, use one-fourth to one-half as much of the dried food as you would of the fresh food.

Cover the dried food with cold water, using about half as much water as food to begin with, and soak until the original texture is regained as closely as possible. Add water as needed.

About 2 hours are required to rehydrate dried foods. Shredded foods may require less time than whole or large pieces of food. Dried food may be soaked overnight in the refrigerator, if convenient. Recipe requirements may direct the amount of liquid used to reconstitute the food.

Avoid throwing away the liquid used to reconstitute the dried food. It contains nutrients and should be used in cooking, if possible, or may be added to other foods.

Some vegetables and fruits can be added directly to soups and other dishes where they will absorb the liquid used in preparing the dish.

Many vegetables and fruits are used dried, without re-hydrating. Remember that dried foods are concentrated and less can be eaten in the dry form than in the fresh state if you are counting calories. One needs to increase the intake of drinking water if dehydrated foods are eaten in quantity, as well.

Fruits that are not eaten in the dried state are soaked in water for several hours, then eaten, or stewed for several minutes until tender. Sugar may be added, if wanted, after the fruit becomes tender.

Dried fruits soaked in brandy or appropriate liquor, or in fruit juices, have added flavor and varied uses. Dried apple slices that have been rehydrated in apple cider are quite a different subject than apples soaked in plain water. Dried fruits plumped up with wine or liqueurs can be used to garnish a plain dessert.

Certain vegetables in the dried form, such as beets, zucchini, and cucumbers, can be used as snacks for dipping in sauces instead of potato chips.

Dried fruits can be made into jellies and butters, using recipes adjusted for their use.

DRIED FOODS AND SURVIVAL

There has been much attention given dried foods by individuals and groups who are concerned about preparing for survival in case of catastrophe, either temporary or extended. The Mormons recommend safely storing away enough food and supplies to last one year, including dried foods and seeds. Cautious motorists who must travel in remote areas or where there is danger of being marooned in a blizzard carry a packet of dried foods in the automobile. Campers and hikers find dried foods ideal for carrying along because dried foods weigh little and provide concentrated energy. Even the astronauts were provided with dehydrated foods.

It has been demonstrated that dried foods are practical for preparations of this sort as well as for normal home use. For those persons who do not themselves preserve foods by drying, a survival food pack equipped with dehydrated and concentrated foods in 2 month, 4 month, and 12 month portions, is available on the market. The rations for a family of four are packed in vacuum sealed cans in cardboard cartons that take up an amazingly small space.

TIME REQUIRED TO DRY FOOD

In drying foods, there can be no absolute time stated in which a food will dry in the sun, or in the oven, or in a food dehydrator. The times suggested in the instructions are only approximate, to be used as guidelines. There are so many variables that affect food drying—the size of the food pieces, the amount of moisture in the air or in the food, the method used for pretreating the food, the temperature used for drying, the method of drying used—that only approximate times can be suggested.

Home Drying of Fruits

INSTRUCTIONS FOR DRYING FRUITS

Apples

Preparation: Wash, peel, core, and section into rings, wedges, or slices about ⅛ inch thick.

Pretreatment: Sulfur fumes: 45 minutes; steam-blanch: 5 minutes; sulfur dip: 1 to 3 minutes; or alternative method.

Drying time: Sun: 3 to 4 days; dehydrator: 6 to 12 hours; oven: 5 to 7 hours.

Dryness test: Soft, pliable, springy, with no moist area in center when cut.

Rehydration: Presoak 1 cup dried apples in 2 cups cold water until plump and moist. Simmer, covered, for 15 minutes or until tender. Sweeten or use in recipe as needed. Or presoak in apple cider.

Apricots

Preparation: If steam-blanching or sulfuring, wash, pit, and halve. Leave whole if water-blanching and pit and halve after blanching.

Pretreatment: Sulfur fumes: 2 hours; steam-blanch: 3 to 4 minutes; water-blanch: 4 to 5 minutes; syrup-blanch: simmer until tender in syrup made of 1 cup sugar to 1

or 2 cups water, as preferred; alternative treatment: hold in ascorbic acid solution, 1 teaspoon ascorbic acid to 1 quart water, for 2 or 3 minutes, drain, and arrange fruits on drying trays, or use sulfur dip (see page 256).
Drying time: Sun: 2 to 3 days; dehydrator: 24 to 36 hours; oven: 9 to 15 hours.
Dryness test: Soft, pliable, leathery, with no moist area in center.
Rehydration and preparation: Add 2 cups cold water to 1 cup dried fruit and refrigerate overnight. To stew, add water to cover and simmer for 15 minutes or until just tender. Sweeten after cooking or use as desired.

Bananas

Preparation: Peel ripe bananas, ones whose skins are still yellow but flecked with brown, and slice evenly into slices ¼ inch thick or into lengthwise quarters.
Pretreatment: Hold 2 to 3 minutes in solution of 1 quart water and 1 teaspoon ascorbic acid, drain, and arrange fruits on drying trays. Or blanch in heavy syrup for 2 minutes.
Drying time: Oven: 5 to 6 hours; dehydrator: 12 to 24 hours.
Dryness test: Firm, chewy, and leathery texture.
Rehydration and preparation: Soak 1 cup bananas in 2 cups cold water for 2 hours before using, or eat dried, without rehydrating.

Berries (firm types)

Preparation: Firm berries such as blueberries, cranberries, gooseberries, currants, and elderberries should be washed and drained after removing stems, if any.
Pretreatment: Plunge prepared berries with tough skins into boiling water for 15 to 30 seconds to crack skins, then into cold water to cool rapidly, and drain. Less-tough-skinned varieties may be steam-blanched for ½ to 1 minute or dried without pretreatment.
Drying time: Oven: 2 hours at 120°F, then 140°F about 2 hours more, or until dry. Dehydrator: 2 hours at lowest heat, then increase gradually and dry at 140°F 4 to 8

hours more, depending upon fruit, until dry. Sun: 1 to 2 days.

Dryness test: Fruits rattle when tray is shaken.

Rehydration: Cover with water and store in refrigerator overnight. To cook, simmer in water to cover until tender, then sweeten or add flavorings.

Cherries

Preparation: Wash, drain, and pit. Bing cherries may be halved. Or leave cherries whole and unpitted.

Pretreatment. Dip in ascorbic acid solution after pitting: use 1 teaspoon ascorbic acid to 1 quart water. Drain and blanch in syrup (see page 260). Drain again. Place on drying trays and proceed as for firm berries.

Instead of syrup-blanching, light-colored cherries may be sulfured for 20 minutes before drying.

Dates

Preparation: Wipe dates clean with a damp cloth. Do not wash. Leave whole or cut into cubes.

Pretreatment: No pretreatment is necessary.

Drying time: Low heat must be used in controlled-heat dryers to prevent scorching. Oven: Method 1—Preheat oven to 225°F, turn heat off, then place dates in oven and leave until oven cools. Repeat process next day and the next until dates are as dry as wanted. Method 2—Place dates on trays in oven and dry at 120°F for 2 to 3 hours. Sun: 2 to 8 days, depending on fruit and temperature. Dehydrator: low heat, 100°F to 120°F for 4 to 6 hours.

Dryness test: Leathery, pliable, and slightly sticky because of high sugar content.

Rehydration: Use dried without rehydration.

Figs

Preparation: Let figs become two-thirds dry on tree, if possible, or pick when fully tree ripened. Wash and drain. Leave whole or cut into halves.

Pretreatment: No pretreatment is necessary but the figs may be blanched in syrup, if desired.

Drying time: Sun: 4 to 5 days; dehydrator: 12 to 20 hours; oven: 4 to 7 hours.
Dryness test: Center is dry; flesh is pliable and slightly sticky, but not wet.

Grapes (seedless varieties)

Preparation: Wash and stem grapes, drain.
Pretreatment: No pretreatment is necessary. Drying time may be shortened, if desired, by either dipping whole grapes into lye water for 10 seconds (see page 260); or blanching in water or steam, ½ to 1 minute.
Drying time: Sun: 3 to 5 days; dehydrator: 12 to 20 hours; oven: 5 to 8 hours.
Dryness test: Raisinlike appearance with no moist center.
Rehydration: Use dry, or soak in boiling water for 5 minutes before adding to recipe. Or soak in rum before adding to rice pudding or cake. Or soak in lemon juice to rehydrate.

Peaches and nectarines

Preparation: Wash, drain, and peel full-flavored just-soft fruit. (For easy peeling, scald the fruit in boiling water, then plunge it into cold. The skins can then be easily removed.) Or, if desired, leave unpeeled. If the fruit is to be sulfured, remove pits and halve. If fruit is to be blanched, leave whole until after blanching, then pit and halve.
Pretreatment: Drop fruit as it is peeled and halved into a solution of ascorbic acid and water, using ½ teaspoon ascorbic acid to 1 quart of water. Drain and treat with sulfur fumes for 2 to 3 hours, or steam-blanch for 8 minutes, or water-blanch for 8 minutes.
Drying time: Sun: 3 to 5 days; dehydrator: 36 to 48 hours; oven: 10 to 12 hours.
Dryness test: Same as for apples.
Rehydration: Soak in an equal amount of liquid, using water, fruit juice, ginger ale, or your choice. Chill before serving. To stew dried peaches, simmer 1 cup

dried peaches in 2 cups water until tender; sweeten or season at the end of the cooking period.

Pears
Preparation: Pick pears while still firm, wrap in paper, and allow to ripen gradually. Wash, peel, core, and cut into halves or slices.

Pretreatment: Drop fruit as it is peeled and halved or sliced into a solution of 1 quart water and ½ teaspoon ascorbic acid. Drain. Treat with sulfur fumes for 5 hours or steam-blanch for 6 minutes.

Drying time: Sun: 5 days; dehydrator: 24 to 36 hours; oven: 5 to 7 hours for small slices, 10 to 20 hours for large pieces.

Dryness test: Same as for Apples.

Rehydration: Use dried, or cover with an equal amount of water and refrigerate overnight. To stew, simmer 1 cup dried pears with 2 cups water until tender, or about 10 to 20 minutes. Sweeten after pears are tender.

Persimmons
Preparation: Cultivated American and native American varieties: Select fully ripe fruit without a puckery taste. Remove dried calyx and rinse, if necessary. Put through the medium disk of food mill to remove pulp, or press through a colander. Add ⅛ teaspoon ascorbic acid per quart fruit and make into persimmon leather (see page 278).

Japanese: Wash soft-ripe persimmons, peel, and slice.

Pretreatment: No pretreatment is necessary but color is improved if fruit is sprinkled with ascorbic acid dissolved in a small amount of water. Use ½ teaspoon per quart of fruit.

Drying time: Sun: 5 to 6 days; dehydrator: 18 to 24 hours; Oven: 5 to 7 hours. Persimmon leather: Dry until leather lifts up from surface on which it is dried and is not tacky in center, about 24 to 36 hours.

277

Pineapple

Preparation: Select ripe, slightly soft, fragrant pineapples. Wash the fruit, remove the spikes, and peel. Cut out the eyes and slice, dice, or cut into thin strips.

Pretreatment: None is necessary, but ascorbic acid or a cold sodium bisulfite dip may be used. The pineapple may be blanched in syrup, if desired.

Drying time: Sun: 3 to 4 days; dehydrator: 24 to 36 hours; oven: 10 to 12 hours.

Dryness test: Firm and dry to the center.

Rehydration: Eat in the dried state, or soak for several hours in the refrigerator in water to cover.

Plums and Prunes

Preparation: Wash and drain. If small, leave whole; if large, cut into halves and pit, or cut into slices. If sulfuring, pit and halve.

Pretreatment: Dip whole fruit in boiling water for 30 seconds to check skins; or dip in boiling lye-water solution for 5 to 30 seconds (see page 260). Rinse in cold water and drain. Sulfuring is optional but produces good flavor; sulfur halves and slices for 1 hour. For oven drying, rinse whole fruits in hot tap water or steam-blanch halves for 15 minutes, slices for 5 minutes.

Drying time: Sun: 4 to 5 days unless dipped in lye-water, then 3 to 4 days; dehydrator: 24 to 36 hours; oven: 9 to 15 hours.

Dryness test: Pliable and leathery; springy; if left uncut, pit will not slip when squeezed.

Rehydration: Use dried, or soak overnight in water or liquid to cover. To cook, simmer in water to cover until tender, then sweeten to taste.

MAKING FRUIT LEATHERS

Making fruit leather has long been a favorite method of drying fruit pulp for winter use. In the years before canning and freezing became widespread, housewives made "leather" out of strawberries and other berries, grapes, native persimmons, peaches, apricots, apples, and whatever other fruit there was on hand. It was stored in rolls, stacked up like firewood on their cupboard shelves, until fruit was needed. Then it was soaked in water and made into pies, puddings, cakes, or eaten as a confection.

To make fruit leathers, select ripe or overripe but sound fruits. Prepare the fruit as for the table. Remove stones or pit, peel if peelings are tough, and cut into chunks or pieces of the right size to puree in the blender or to cook before pureeing.

Most fruits are pureed in the raw state. Lemon juice or ascorbic acid is added to those that tend to darken. Use 1 tablespoon lemon juice or ½ teaspoon ascorbic acid to each quart of fruit. Apples and Concord grapes are cooked until tender and made into a sauce, which is then dried to make leather.

Since the natural sugars in the fruits are concentrated by drying, little if any extra sugar is needed in the leather. Honey may be added, if desired, but the leather may remain a bit sticky if honey is used.

Line a cookie sheet or the drying tray with plastic kitchen wrap. Pour the puree onto the sheet in a thin layer about ¼ inch deep. Distribute evenly by tilting the tray.

Place the tray, covered with cheesecloth, in the sun for 2 or 3 days, depending on the humidity and temperature. In the dehydrator, drying will take 5 to 12 hours at 140°F. Oven drying will take about 6 hours.

The leather is dry when it can be removed from the plastic wrap easily and the center is not tacky. Dust both sides of the leather with confectioners' sugar or a light film of cornstarch as desired. Place the leather between two sheets of waxed paper or plastic wrap, roll it up, and store the rolls in a large jar with an air-tight lid. If wanted, the leather can be cut into smaller pieces, about 3 inches by 3 inches square, and then rolled up in smaller portions suitable for individual servings.

If stored in the refrigerator or the freezer, the fruit leather will keep indefinitely. If properly dried and stored, the shelf life of fruit leather at room temperature is about 6 months.

Fruit leathers can be made of a combination of fruits.

Applesauce makes a good base for fruits that taste a bit strong if made into leather alone. Fruits that are seedy, such as strawberies, will seem to have more seeds when dried. If this is objectionable, the leather will be more pleasing if made of a fruit combination such as applesauce-strawberry.

A touch of spice might be added to applesauce, peach, or other fruit leather, if desired. Nuts and seeds can be added to fruit leathers, but their addition shortens the shelf life of the leather.

Home Drying of Vegetables

INSTRUCTIONS FOR DRYING VEGETABLES

Asparagus
Preparation: Wash thoroughly. Sort stalks according to thickness. Halve large stalks or cut into small pieces.
Pretreatment: Water-blanch: 2 to 4 minutes; steam-blanch: 3 to 5 minutes. Drain.
Drying time: Dehydrator: 6 to 10 hours; oven: 3 to 4 hours; sun: 8 to 10 hours.
Dryness test: Leathery to brittle.
Rehydration: Soak 30 minutes in unsalted cold water, using 2 cups water to 1 cup vegetable. To cook, simmer in boiling water until tender, then season.

Beans (Green, Snap, and Wax)
Preparation: Wash, drain, snip off ends of, and remove strings from tender young beans. Cut into short pieces or French-cut.
Pretreatment: Water-blanch: 2 minutes; steam-blanch: 2½ minutes. Drain.
Drying time: Dehydrator: 8 to 14 hours; oven: 3 to 6 hours; sun: 8 hours.
Dryness test: Dry and brittle.

Rehydration: Soak in cold water to cover until plumped. To cook, simmer in water with seasonings until tender.

Broccoli
Preparation: Remove outer leaves, trim and split stalks lengthwise to make uniform pieces. Remove insects by soaking 20 minutes in salted water (4 teaspoons salt to 1 gallon water). Rinse and drain.
Pretreatment: Water-blanch: 2 minutes; steam-blanch: 3 minutes.
Drying time: Dehydrator: 12 to 15 hours; oven: 3 to 4½ hours; sun: 8 to 10 hours.
Dryness test: Brittle and crisp.
Rehydration: Soak in cold water until plumped, 30 minutes or more. To cook, simmer in boiling water until tender, then season.

Cabbage
Preparation: Remove outer leaves, wash, quarter, and core. Cut into shreds ⅛ inch thick.
Pretreatment: Water-blanch: 1½ to 2 minutes; steam-blanch: until wilted.
Drying time: Dehydrator: 10 to 12 hours; oven: 1 to 3 hours; sun: 6 to 7 hours. Cabbage tends to scorch during the last part of the drying period; reduce controlled heat accordingly.
Dryness test: Tough to brittle.
Rehydration: No soaking necessary. To cook, drop shreds into boiling water and simmer until tender, about 15 minutes.

Carrots
Preparation: Remove tops, scrub, and scrape or peel. Cut into uniform slices or strips ⅛ inch thick, or thinner, if possible.
Pretreatment: Water-blanch: 3 minutes; steam-blanch: 3½ minutes.
Drying time: Dehydrator: 10 to 12 hours; oven: 3 to 5 hours; sun: 8 hours. Paper-thin disks will take less time.

Dryness test: Tough and leathery.
Rehydration: Soak larger-cut carrots in water for 2 hours. For shredded carrots, cover with water for 15 minutes, then simmer until tender. Season at the end of the cooking period.

Celery

Preparation: Trim stalks, wash thoroughly, and drain. Slice stalks as thin as possible. Mince celery leaves and dry separately, following directions for Parsley.
Pretreatment: Blanch in water or steam: 2 minutes.
Drying time: Dehydrator: 12 to 15 hours; oven: 3 to 4 hours; sun: 8 hours.
Dryness test: Brittle.
Rehydration: Soak larger celery pieces in water for 1 hour, using 1 cup celery to 2 cups water. Use the dried celery leaves for seasoning as you would an herb.

Corn

Preparation: Select freshly picked corn with milky kernels. Husk, remove silks, and trim.
Pretreatment:
Method 1: Blanch corn on the cob in boiling water for 2 to 2½ minutes, plunge in boiling water, drain, then cut kernels from cob. Steam blanch for slightly longer time, just until the milk is set in the kernels.
Method 2: Cut the corn from the cob with a sharp knife immediately after picking. Do not scrape the cob. Do not blanch.
Drying time: Dehydrator: 6 to 10 hours; Oven: 2 to 6 hours; Sun drying: 6 to 8 hours.
Dryness test: Corn is dry and brittle, and rattles when trays are shaken.
Rehydration: See special recipes beginning on page 288.

Cucumbers

Preparation: Peel and cut into slices ⅛ inch to ¼ inch thick.
Pretreatment: None is necessary. Sprinkling lightly with salt will draw out some of the moisture and produce a tastier chip.

Drying time: Dehydrator: 10 to 12 hours; oven: 4 to 6 hours; sun: 6 to 8 hours.
Dryness test: Crisp and dry.
Rehydration: Use dry as a chip with prepared chip dips.

Eggplant

Preparation: Wash, peel, and slice firm, ripe eggplant into ¼-inch slices.
Pretreatment: Drop prepared slices into salted water, using 4 teaspoons salt to 1 gallon water. Water-blanch: 1½ minutes; steam-blanch: 2½ to 3 minutes.
Drying time: Same as for Summer Squash.
Dryness test: Leathery and dry.
Rehydration: Cover with water for 2 hours, drain, and use in a recipe.

Herbs

See the special section on drying herbs; page 287.

Leather Breeches Beans

Wash, drain, and remove the strings and ends from tender green beans. Thread a large-eyed needle with a length of coarse cotton thread or white cotton carpet warp. Push the needle through the center of each bean and thread one after another on the length of string until it is filled, leaving little space between each bean. Hang the string of beans in a warm, airy place to dry, but not in direct sunlight. An attic, outside in the shade, or near a source of warm air inside the house, such as above a wood-burning stove, would all be suitable places. Let the beans hang until dry and leathery. Store them in brown paper bags for longer storage.
To cook leather breeches beans: See the recipe on page 243.

Mushrooms

Preparation: Wash well and drain. Discard tough stalks. Slice into profiles ⅛ to ¼ inch thick, or small pieces.
Pretreatment: None is necessary. White-flesh mushrooms may be kept from darkening during preparation by slicing them into a solution of 2 tablespoons

vinegar to 1 quart of water, or by holding briefly in ½ teaspoon ascorbic acid dissolved in 1 quart of water. Drain.

Drying time: Dehydrator: 8 to 10 hours; oven: 3 to 5 hours; sun: 6 to 8 hours. Mushrooms may also be threaded on a string, as described for Leather Breeches Beans, and dried indoors in a warm, airy place.

Rehydration: Add to soups or sauces without rehydrating. Or soften in warm or cool water for 20 to 30 minutes before using.

Hint for storage: Peppercorns added to packages of dried mushrooms will keep bugs away.

Onions

Preparation: Wash, remove skins, and trim off roots and tops. Cut into slices ⅛ to ¼ inch thick. Separate rings and spread on drying trays.

Pretreatment: None is necessary.

Drying time: Dehydrator: 10 to 20 hours; oven: 3 to 6 hours; sun: 8 to 11 hours.

Dryness test: Crisp and brittle.

Rehydration: Cover with water and soak 1 to 2 hours. Use both the soaking water and the onions to flavor other dishes.

Parsley

Preparation: Wash carefully and drain. Trim off coarse stems. Leave leaves in small clusters or mince.

Pretreatment: None is necessary.

Drying time: Dehydrator: 1 to 2 hours; oven: 2 to 4 hours; sun: 6 to 8 hours. Drying at about 100°F will achieve the best quality.

Dryness test: Crisp and flaky.

Dehydration: Use for seasoning as you would an herb.

Note: Herbs that touch metal when drying will be darker than those dried on cheesecloth or non-metal surface.

Peppers and Pimientos

Preparation: Wash, stem, core, and remove seeds and

membranes. Cut into circles ⅛ to ¼ inch thick, or into pieces ⅜ inch square.

Pretreatment: None is necessary.

Drying time: Dehydrator: 8 to 12 hours; oven: 2½ to 5 hours; sun: 6 to 8 hours.

Dryness test: Brittle.

Rehydration: Soak a portion of the dried vegetables in 2 to 3 times that amount of water for 1 hour.

Pumpkin

Since pumpkins keep well over a whole winter in a cool, dry place, there is really little point in going to the trouble of drying them. If, however, there is some reason you wish to anyway, follow the directions for Hubbard Squash.

Pumpkin circles were hung from the ceiling beams in old homesteads and dried by the rising heat of the fireplace.

Squash

Preparation:

Banana: Wash, peel, and cut into sices ¼ inch thick, or strips.

Hubbard: Wash rind and pat dry. Cut into halves, remove seeds, and scrape cavity. Cut squash into 1-inch-wide strips and peel off rind. Cut peeled strips into small, uniform pieces about ⅛ inch thick.

Summer and Zucchini: Wash, trim, and cut into ¼-inch slices. If squashes are large, peel and remove seeds.

Pretreatment: Water-blanch: 1 to 1½ minutes; steam-blanch: 2½ to 3 minutes.

Drying time: Dehydrator: 10 to 16 hours; oven: 4 to 5 hours; sun: 6 to 8 hours.

Dryness test: Tough to brittle.

Rehydration: Cover with water and soak for 1 hour. Simmer until tender or use in a recipe.

Zucchini Chips

Preparation: Slice into ¼- to ⅛-inch thickness. Peel, if desired.
Pretreatment: None is necessary.
Drying time: Same as for Cucumbers.
Dryness test: Same as for Cucumbers.
Rehydration: Use as cucumber chips.

DRYING HERBS

Herbs should be cut on a sunny morning after the dew or rain has dried. They are at their height of flavor just as they are beginning to bloom. Cut them with a length of stem, swish them through cold water if necessary, shake off the moisture, and lay them on a terry towel to drain.

The herbs can then be tied in small, loose bunches and air dried in one of several ways. Hang the bunches from the rafters of a hot, airy, dustfree attic (darkened, if possible) and leave them until the leaves crumble and can be easily stripped off their stems. Or cut air holes in brown paper bags and place the hebs, heads down, inside the bags, gathering up the tops of the bags and tying them with strings. Hang the bags in the attic, as above, or on a clothesline in the shade on a hot, breezy day. Do not place the bags in the sun, and bring them indoors at night. If the conditions are good for drying in your kitchen, nothing looks more decorative or smells as good as herbs drying in clusters hanging from the ceiling.

Microwave ovens can be used for drying herbs. Follow the general directions given and the times suggested in the manual accompanying the microwave oven.

Dehydrator drying is a good method for preserving the color and oils of flavorful herbs. Use a temperature setting of 100°F, and strip the leaves off the larger stems as soon as they are dry enough to remove easily. The larger leaves of basil and comfrey may be removed from their stems before being spread on the trays.

Herbs are dry when the stems are brittle and the leaves crumble. The dried herbs can be stripped from the stems and stored in coarse leaf form, or powdered by rubbing them with a mortar and pestle or whirling them in the blender. Light fades the color of herbs so they must be dried and stored away from the light. When storing herbs, use airtight containers and keep them away from a direct heat source.

The color of dried herbs seems to be brighter if they are not in contact with metal while drying.

SOME DRIED CORN RECIPES

To Make Dried Corn from Frozen Corn

Spread a two pound package of frozen corn in a single layer on a drying rack, or a large shallow pan. Place the corn in a low oven, 150°F with the door ajar. Sprinkle the corn with 2 teaspoons sugar. Stir the corn frequently during the drying period, bringing it in from the edges to the center of the pan. Dry until it is brittle and as dry as popcorn.

To use, soak in water overnight. Bring to a boil, then simmer slowly in the same water for 1 hour, or until tender. Add more water, if needed. When the corn is almost tender, add 2 tablespoons butter, 1 teaspoon salt, 1 tablespoon sugar, and ⅛ teaspoon pepper. Add cream, if desired.

Colonists' Dried Corn

To each 8 pints of raw sweet corn, which has been cut off the cob but not blanched, add 6 tablespoons brown or white sugar, 4 teaspoons pure salt, and ½ cup sweet cream. Simmer in a heavy pan for 15 to 20 minutes, stirring constantly. Spread the mixture on drying trays and dry in the oven at 150°F with the door ajar, or in an electric food dehydrator at 140°F, until the kernels are crisp. Stir often as the drying progresses, and lower the heat at the end of the drying period to avoid scorching. When the corn is dry, cool it, then tie it in brown paper bags and hang it in the attic, or the driest warm place available. When the corn rattles inside the sacks, store it in glass jars with airtight lids and away from the light. This corn does not have to be soaked before cooking; simply simmer in milk or cream and add butter.

Dried-Corn Fritters

To 1 cup dried corn, add 3 cups boiling water and let soak for 2 hours. Then, using the same water, bring the mixture to a boil, and simmer for 30 minutes. Drain and cool.

To the cooled corn, add 2 teaspoons sugar, 1 teaspoon salt, 1 beaten egg, 1 teaspoon baking powder, and 2 tablespoons flour. Mix well and drop by spoonfuls into hot deep fat, 365° to 375°F, until golden brown. Or sauté in shallow hot fat until browned. Serve with syrup or honey butter.

Baked Dried Corn and Oysters

Soak 1 cup dried corn in 3 cups of boiling water for 1 hour or longer. Add 2 teaspoons sugar, and salt and butter to taste. Simmer for 30 minutes.

Make a white sauce of 2 tablespoons butter, 2 tablespoons flour, and 1 cup milk. In another bowl, combine 1 cup bread crumbs and ⅓ cup melted butter.

In a greased baking dish, alternate layers of the simmered corn, white sauce, buttered bread crumbs, and fresh oysters, using 1 cup or more, as desired. Top with bread crumbs and bake at 350°F until golden brown and bubbling, about 30 minutes.

Dutch Dried-Corn Dish

Cover the amount of corn to be cooked with boiling water and let stand overnight. Add salt in the proportion of 1 teaspoon salt to each 2 cups dried corn.

The next morning, add enough water to cover again, and cook slowly until the liquid has almost cooked away. Add more water and cook until nearly dry twice more. Then add 2 heaping tablespoons of dark brown sugar and 2 tablespoons butter for each cup of corn cooked. Add milk to cover the corn halfway, salt to taste, and simmer until the corn is hot.

Dried-Corn Pudding

In a blender grind 1 cup dried corn and transfer it to a bowl. Pour 2 cups scalded milk over the corn and let the mixture stand for 1½ hours. Stir in 2 eggs, lightly beaten, ½ cup heavy cream, 3 tablespoons brown sugar, and ½ teaspoon salt. Transfer the mixture to a buttered 6 x 10 x 2-inch baking dish, and dot the top with 1 tablespoon softened butter. Bake the pudding in a preheated moderate oven (350°F) for 30 minutes, or until it is puffed and golden.

PART V

---•---

Some Specialties Preserved by Fermenting, Wining, and Brining

GRANDMOTHER'S
MINCEMEAT

In our family making mincemeat was an occupation that accompanied the winter ritual of butchering, which took place as soon as the weather was cold enough to preserve the meat safely and whenever the steer was fatted for the slaughter. With equal parts of foresight and good fortune, the two events coincided closely enough to ensure mince pies both for the holiday feasting and throughout the winter.

The making of the Thanksgiving mincemeat was one of Grandmother's projects. She welcomed visitors in the kitchen whenever special preparations were under way and to me her kitchen was but an extension of Mother's, for my maternal grandparents lived just across the road. I spent my days running between the houses, carrying a message or a borrowed cup of sugar, and sniffing out the most compelling activities. So when Grandmother began shredding the firm white suet and chopping the boiled lean beef, I was there, perched on a chair beside the table, to turn the handle of the meat grinder. Small girls were allowed to have a hand in apple paring, as well. I impaled red Baldwins on the prongs of the wobbly apple peeler that was attached to the edge of the kitchen table, and turned the handle that turned the rotating blade that made one long red curl of each apple peel. Then Grandmother quickly went through the mound of peeled apples, slicing off bits of peeling left behind by the peeler and cutting out cores with a sharp knife.

And before I took the panful of peelings out to the horses—for a treat—Grandmother could be coaxed into a bit of kitchen fortune-telling. When I tossed a long red curled apple peel over my left shoulder, Grandmother could see the initial of my beau in the shape made by the peeling when it fell on the floor.

Grandmother always had time for a diversion between chores, even when the crescendo of activity was increasing. Out came the chopping board, a large worn slab of hard maple wood that showed the scars of years of mincing crisp apples, raisins, citron, suet, and dried fruits. She scattered a handful of cut apples on its surface, then starting at one side of the board, wielded the sharp long-bladed knife with staccatos of rapid chops—and the apples were minced! Grandmother used the tip of the tapered knife blade as a pivot and it stayed down close to the board while the rapid chopping movements advanced the back of the blade across the board, leaving a fan-shaped swath of minced apples behind it. Then she swept the chopped apples off the board into a large wooden bowl. I was given a curved-blade chopper, with a handle that kept my fingers safely above its sharp blade, and I chopped it up and down in the bowlful of apples, mincing them even finer, while Grandmother cut up the rest of the mincemeat ingredients on the chopping board.

When all of the ingredients were minced, Grandmother mixed them together in the big chopping bowl—the apples, meat, suet, raisins, citron or pickled watermelon rind, and spices. Other contributions were made with some variation. Perhaps she might add a jar or two of the tart juicy cherries she had put up in June or a generous amount of melted damson plum jelly or dark honey from the autumn nectar flow. But the most flavorful inundation was boiled cider. In October, just before the cider began to ferment, Grandmother boiled quantities of it to the consistency of syrup and bottled it, and the resulting sweet-tart liquid made her mincemeat extraordinary.

Grandmother kept the mincemeat for the most immediate use in the cold pantry in a brown stoneware pot topped with a lid of apple brandy. This was the extra special mincemeat that she used for our Thanksgiving pie. The rest of the winter's supply was canned in glass jars and stored in the cellar until it was needed. The mincemeat-making, as all of the chores that came with butchering, was a cooperative project between our two families and Grandmother made enough for all of us.

When the kettle of mincemeat was finally simmering on the kitchen range, filling the air with meaty, spicy scents, it was my chore to stand on a stool and wash the canning jars in a dishpanful of hot sudsy water—as always. When the mincemeat was cooked down and the fruits were tender, it was transferred to the clean canning jars, lidded, and boiled for hours over a hot fire. This was the way we canned foods containing meat in the days before we owned a pressure canner.

Grandmother's mincemeat recipe was one of the few she wrote down, not one of the many she kept in her mind. She copied the recipe in her lacy old-fashioned handwriting on a slip of paper that today is foxed by age and shows faded stains made by her fingers. It was kept in a latticework wall pocket along with a few other special recipes, the OLD FARMER'S ALMANAC, the weekly church publication, greeting cards, letters, and accumulated household and farm receipts. I remember Grandmother rummaging in that fascinating collection of papers, looking for the recipe, when we were making ready for mincemeat-making. But after the preliminary review of the recipe, it was stuck into the papers at the front of the cache and seemed thereafter not to be all-important to the actual concoction of the mixture. Grandmother proceeded with the ingredients she had at hand and improvised on her written recipe if she felt inclined to do so.

This is the recipe Grandmother used as a guide when she was making our mincemeat:

Mincemeat for Pies

Finely mince two pounds of lean boiled beef, and half as much of clear white suet, and twice as much of firm, tart apples. Baldwins, Yorks, or Winesaps do nicely. Use bought citron, about ½ pound, or preserved citron melon; if neither is to be had, use pickled watermelon rind, nicely chopped. Also, 1 pound sugar, or more, 2 cups boiled cider, 1 pint canned pie cherries, 1 pound seeded raisins, picked over, or may use some currants, and 2 jars good tart jelly, currant or damson. Spice well with 1 grated nutmeg, some cinnamon, mace, cloves, and salt. Use beef broth or cider for cooking the mincemeat. Keep a slow fire until it is done. Last, put in a good measure of apple brandy, but not until the mince is cool. Put away in a stone crock in a cold pantry. Keeps all winter.

A batch of mincemeat lends itself well to variations. There are several basic ingredients that must be included in the recipe and a number that are optional. By making choices from the optional additions and choosing the basic ingredients according to availability or personal preference, one can make a successful, unique mincemeat mixture. Following is a summary of suggestions and a few simple proportions that might provide guidelines for your own mincemeat improvisation.

The basic ingredients of mincemeat are meat, suet, apples, raisins, sweetening, liquid (fruit juice or broth), and spices. Currants, citron, and liquor or wine are almost always included, as well.

The list of optional ingredients is long. Mincemeats may include other dried fruits, such as dates, or dried apricots, pears, or peaches. Candied fruit peels and the grated fresh peel of lemon and orange are also used. Glacéed fruits may be added, too. Sometimes canned peaches, pears, pineapple, or sour red cherries are added, either to the mincemeat when it is prepared, or directly to the pie. Cooked sweetened cranberries may be used similarly.

A jar of marmalade or a tart jelly is often added for sweetening and flavoring, as is a small amount of fresh lemon or orange juice. Angostura bitters give a distinctive flavor to mincemeat. A small amount of vinegar or the syrup drained from spiced pickled fruits is sometimes added to sharpen the flavor. A cup of strong coffee may be added to darken the mincemeat.

My grandmother's frequent substitution for candied citron, which was an extravagant luxury in a simple country kitchen such as hers, was sweet pickled watermelon rind. My most inspired addition to mincemeat was the winey syrup and fruits from a crock of tutti-frutti.

The sweetening used in mincemeat may be either sugar or syrup, or both. Light or dark brown sugar, white sugar, raw sugar, or maple sugar may be used along with maple syrup, honey, sorghum syrup, molasses, or corn syrup.

Broth and sweet cider are most often used to moisten the mincemeat during cooking, but boiled cider, orange juice, grape juice, or leftover fruit juices from canned fruits may be used.

Nutmeats are added after the mincemeat is cooked or just before use. If a spirituous liquid is used for flavoring or to preserve the mincemeat, it is added after the mincemeat is cooked. Here the choice may be made according to personal taste or appropriateness—wine, brandy, hard cider, rum, or liqueur.

Obviously, a certain restraint must be used in choosing the optional ingredients to combine with the basic ones, or the mincemeat will be less than a brilliant improvisation. The proportions given in the following recipe can serve as guidelines.

Mincemeat Improvisation

In a large bowl combine 1 measure boiled minced or ground lean beef, venison, or beef tongue, 2 measures peeled, chopped tart apples, ¼ to ½ measure ground beef suet, 1 measure raisins or raisins and currants combined, ¼ measure chopped citron, 1 measure sweetening combining sugar and syrup, 1 measure liquid, and a combination of spices chosen from cloves, cinnamon, mace, allspice, and nutmeg and amounting to at least 1 teaspoon of combined spices per quart of mincemeat mixture. Add ¼ teaspoon salt per quart of mincemeat and mix well.

Transfer the mixture to a heavy kettle and simmer, stirring often, for at least 1 hour or until the apples are tender and no excess liquid separates from a spoonful of the mincemeat placed on a saucer. If the mixture becomes too dry during the cooking period, add liquid as needed.

If optional ingredients are wanted, judiciously choose a total of 1 measure of dried chopped fruits, or chopped candied fruits and fruit peels, or chopped canned fruits, or a mixture of these, and add to the mincemeat mixture before it is cooked. After the mincemeat is cooked and cooled, chopped nutmeats; glacéed cherries or pineapple; jam, jelly, or marmalade; and brandied fruits may be added, but do not exceed a total of 1 measure of these. When the mincemeat is complete, a generous amount of liquor or wine may be added, using about 1 pint to the gallon of mincemeat, or to taste.

Cover the mincemeat and let it ripen in the refrigerator for about three weeks before using.

Venison Mincemeat

Put about 2 pounds of lean boiled venison through the medium blade of a food grinder. Measure out 5 cups of ground venison and put it into a large bowl along with 1 cup ground beef suet (¼ pound of suet before grinding), 10 cups tart apples, peeled, cored, and chopped, 4 cups seedless raisins, 1 cup currants, 1 cup chopped citron, and 1 teaspoon each of ground cloves, cinnamon, mace, nutmeg, allspice, and salt. Combine the mixture well. Stir in 3 cups maple syrup and 2 cups brown sugar, or more, according to tartness of apples. Add 1 quart of sweet cider. Put the mixture into a large, heavy kettle, preferably enameled iron, and simmer for 1 hour. Stir often to prevent sticking and add more cider if needed. Makes about 6 pints mincemeat.

TO CAN MINCEMEAT

Pack cooked mincemeat while still hot into hot sterilized

jars, leaving 1-inch head space. Adjust caps. Process pints or quarts 20 minutes at 10 pounds pressure, following directions accompanying the pressure canner for processing and cooling.

TO FREEZE MINCEMEAT

Pack mincemeat, cooked and cooled, into rigid pint or quart freezer containers, leaving ½-inch head space, and freeze quickly at 0°F or at sub-zero temperatures, preferably −10°F.

Uncooked mincemeat may also be frozen if the meat in the mixture has been previously cooked.

TO KEEP MINCEMEAT FOR SEVERAL WEEKS

Place cooked mincemeat in a covered stoneware or glass container and pour at least 1 pint of wine or liquor over each gallon of the preparation. Store in the refrigerator until used. Uncooked mincemeat can be ripened this way, too, provided the meat in the mixture is cooked.

The mincemeat jar can be replenished throughout the winter, like a rum pot, with the addition of bits of cooked beef, fruits, and leftover juices. Be sure the added ingredients are fresh and have been brought to a boil and cooled before mixing with the original mincemeat. More of the liquor can also be added during the storage period.

Pear Mincemeat

Peel, quarter, and core about 12 pears, using Anjou, Bartlett, or another firm variety. To prevent them from darkening, sprinkle over the peeled pears a solution of ¼ teaspoon ascorbic acid dissolved in 2 tablespoons water. Cut 1 orange and 1 lemon into quarters and remove the seeds, but do not peel. Grind the pears, orange, and lemon in a food chopper, using the coarse blade. Add 2 cups seedless raisins, 2 cups sugar, ½ teaspoon each of mace, cinnamon, and allspice, and ¼ cup crystallized ginger, chopped fine. Combine all together in a heavy kettle and bring to a boil while stirring. Reduce the heat to medium and cook, stirring constantly, until the mixture is glossy and thickened, about 30 minutes. Remove from the heat and stir in ¼ cup Grand Marnier and 4 drops Angostura bitters.

Store until used in the refrigerator, freeze until needed, or can. This mincemeat makes a good filling for pies, cakes, or brown-bread sandwiches.

TO KEEP PEAR MINCEMEAT IN THE REFRIGERATOR

Pack the cooled mincemeat in a glass or crockery jar and cover with additional Grand Marnier, using 3 tablespoons or more. Cover and keep cold until used.

TO FREEZE PEAR MINCEMEAT

Pack cooled mincemeat into freezer containers, leaving ½-inch head space, and store at 0°F until needed.

TO CAN PEAR MINCEMEAT

Have ready 3 hot sterilized pint jars and fill them to within ¼ inch of the top with the boiling-hot, cooked mincemeat. Wipe the top of each jar with a clean, damp cloth as soon as it is filled and close the jar immediately, using a screw band and self-sealing lid closure. Process the packed jars for 10 minutes in a boiling-water bath. Remove the processed jars from the canner and cool for 12 hours on a folded cloth. When cool, check the seals and store in a cool, dark, dry place until used.

Green-Tomato Mincemeat

Wash and core 1 quart firm green (unripe) tomatoes and put them through the coarse blade of a food chopper. Sprinkle the chopped tomatoes with 1 teaspoon salt and let stand 1 hour. Drain and add boiling water to cover. Let stand for 5 minutes and drain again. Add the grated rind and pulp of 1 orange, ¼ cup chopped beef suet, ½ cup raisins, 1 cup brown sugar, ½ cup tart apples, peeled, cored, and chopped, ¼ cup apple cider, ½ teaspoon cinnamon, ¼ teaspoon each of cloves and nutmeg, and ⅛ teaspoon ginger. Mix together well and simmer in a heavy pan until the apples are tender and the mixture thickened, stirring often. Cool and refrigerate for later use. Stir in ¼ cup light rum, if desired. This amount will make 1 pie.

Dried-Fruits Mincemeat

Using a sharp knife, cut into thin slices 1 cup dried apricots, ½ cup seeded dried prunes, and ½ cup dried peaches. In a bowl, combine the sliced dried fruits with ½ cup raisins, ½ cup currants, and ½ cup Amaretto liqueur. Cover and let the fruits stand overnight to absorb the liqueur.

In a kettle simmer 1 beef tongue in water to cover until tender. Remove from the broth, and cut away and discard the outer layer. Put the trimmed meat through the food chopper, using the medium blade. In a large bowl combine 2 cups chopped tongue and 4 cups dried apples which have also been put through the food chopper using the medium blade. Add the 3 cups of dried fruits (above), 4 cups light brown sugar, 2 cups boiled cider, and 4 cups sweet cider. Combine well and transfer to a large heavy kettle. Simmer over low heat for about 1 hour, or until the fruits are tender, stirring often. Near the end of the cooking time, stir in 1 teaspoon mace and 1 cup of chopped candied fruits and peels including orange peel, lemon peel, citron, and candied pineapple. Remove from the heat, cool, and stir in 8 ounces orange marmalade, ½ teaspoon Angostura bitters, and 1 cup sliced almonds. Transfer the cooled mincemeat to the container in which it will be stored and pour ¾ cup Amaretto or Grand Marnier on to the top of the mincemeat. Store in the refrigerator, covered, until used. This mincemeat is excellent in cakes and cookies as well as pies. Makes about 3 quarts of mincemeat.

Preserving Fruits in Spirituous Liquids

An old-new method of preserving fruits is to store them in spirits. Insects, mold, and bacteria cannot live in alcoholic liquids.

Raw fruits can be preserved in spirituous liquids by adding sugar and allowing the fruits to ferment and make their own alcohol. Or liquors can be added to raw fruits in quantities sufficient to preserve them. Also, liquor can be used as a preserving agent for certain cooked foods, as in brandied peaches and mincemeats.

Brandied fruits, melanges, tutti-frutti, and rum pots are all elegant ways to preserve choice fruits. Only the simplest ingredients are necessary—the fruit combinations, sugar, liquor, and spices. No special equipment is needed except a suitable container for fermenting or storing the fruit in its liquor.

In earlier days, imported brandy, rum, homemade cider, and homemade wines were plentiful commodities in colonial households. Fruits steeped in these liquids were safe from spoilage and could be used long after their seasons had passed. The only other method used at that time to preserve fresh fruits was drying. It was not until the early 1800's that a way to successfully preserve foods by heating them in a sealed bottle was discovered by a Frenchman named Nicholas Appert. Before that, the only methods of preserving were by salting, smoking, drying, and fermenting foods.

Some of the most fashionable fruit desserts and beverages of today's gourmets were "everyday" recipes of the colonists that were devised to preserve the perishable fruits of summer. Brandied fruits, especially peaches, were popular and easily preserved. The fresh peaches were placed in a crock, covered with brandy, put in the cellar—or even buried in the ground—to age until needed.

Following are some old recipes for brandied fruits taken from old cookbooks and some that have been adapted to modern measurements and wordage.

TUTTI-FRUTTI

A stone jar is best for making tutti-frutti, and a tight cover is an absolute necessity. If your jar has no lid, cover the top with a china plate and fit a piece of heavy aluminum foil down over the plate. Then tie a string around the jar top to keep the foil where it belongs. When a stone jar is not available, use a large mason-type jar with its own lid. Cover the outside of the glass jar with aluminum foil to keep the light from fading the fruit.

Wild strawberries gathered in early June are the magic ingredient in an old-fashioned stone jar of tutti-frutti. Take the first quart of tiny, sweet berries and cover them with an equal amount of sugar. Let the strawberries plump up with sugar for about an hour, then pour one quart of good brandy over the sugared fruit. Put the brandied fruit into the jar, cover it, and place it in a dark, cool cellar corner. As the different fruits of summer ripen, add a quart of each, with an equal amount of sugar, to the jar. No more brandy will be needed. After the addition of each new fruit, stir the tutti-frutti every day until the sugar in the bottom of the jar dissolves, which takes a week or more. Between times, stir the sauce as often as you think of it, or daily if you can remember.

The following fruits, as they come into season, may be added with equal amounts of sugar to the tutti-frutti: red or black cherries, stemmed and pitted; red raspberries; wild blackberries; currants; gooseberries; sliced, peeled peaches, apricots, nectarines, and fresh pineapple; and green-gage, purple, and red plums, peeled and seeded. Fruits with tough skins, such as grapes or apples do not brandy well. The same is true for very soft fruits, such as bananas and melons. Too many small seeds are also objectionable; black raspberries are omitted for that reason and because they darken all the other fruits. Oranges, if added, should be seeded carefully.

Spices and interest to tutti-frutti. According to taste, stick cinnamon, orange or lemon peel grated fine, whole allspice, and whole cloves may be added as the jar fills. To give it the flavor of almonds, add a few blanched peach kernels.

The last of the fruits should be added around September. Then, when the golden peaches go under the brandy, the jar is sealed well and put aside to mellow until Thanksgiving or Christmas.

Traditionally, the tutti-frutti makes its grand debut on the festal board as the finishing touch to pudding, chiffon pie, or ice cream, or as a dark, rich sauce to accompany the meat course. At our house, the tutti-frutti jar is hidden in the darkest corner and stirred in secrecy lest the nontraditionalists discover it to spoon over French vanilla ice cream long before holidays arrive. When tradition triumphs, favored friends find small jars of tutti-frutti under their Christmas tree.

The winey syrup on tutti-frutti, of which there is always an excess, makes excellent pudding sauce. Dilute it with a little water and thicken it with cornstarch. Tutti-frutti syrup is superb, too, on waffles and pancakes.

The tutti-frutti jar can go on indefinitely. Refresh it in wintertime, when local fruits are not in season, with fruits shipped in from warmer climates. Add canned crushed pineapple and packages of frozen fruit, thawed and sweetened. Small amounts of leftover fresh fruit may be added, too.

If your house has no cellar and you don't want a fermenting crock (with the accompanying fruit flies) in your kitchen all summer, make space for it in the refrigerator.

Go into it whenever conscience permits for bright, delicious brandied fruit to enhance ice cream, puddings, or chiffon pies. Then, when the weather cools, about the time the last peaches are added, take the tutti-frutti from the refrigerator and store it in a cool room or enclosed porch. Fermentation will occur as soon as the crock is removed from the refrigeration, and its wine sauce will "make" in time for the holiday season.

BRANDIED PEACHES

Select 4 pounds of the best quality peaches, either yellow freestone or white clingstone varieties. The peaches should be table ripe. Plunge a few peaches at a time into boiling water, then into cold water, drain, and remove the skins. In a kettle, combine 6 cups sugar and 1½ cups water. Stir until the sugar dissolves and boil the syrup for 5 minutes. Drop in a few peach halves or whole peaches at a time and simmer until the fruit is just tender when pierced, but not soft. Lift the peaches out and drain them in a colander, reserving the liquid. When all the peaches are cooked, combine all the juice—that which has drained from the cooked peaches plus that remaining in the kettle—and boil it until it thickens, or about 10 minutes. Pour the syrup over the cooked peaches and let them stand in the syrup until cool. Remove the peaches from the syrup with a slotted spoon and place them in hot sterilized jars. Heat the syrup to boiling and pour over the peaches in the jars, filling the jars half full with syrup. Finish filling each jar with good brandy, leaving ¼-inch head space. Adjust lids. Store in the refrigerator until used, or process for 10 minutes in a simmering-water bath. Makes 2 quarts.

Options: If peaches are to be served with meat, two whole cloves may be inserted into each peach. Unspiced peaches may be served with ice cream, puddings, and chiffon pies.

BUSHEL OF BRANDIED PEACHES

Scald and skin 1 bushel of firm, ripe Alberta freestone

peaches. Place in a 5-gallon earthenware crock. Add 6 pounds sugar, cover the crock with a plate or lid, and tie a cloth down over the top. On the second and third days, stir the mixture gently to help dissolve the sugar. On the third day, add 1 cake of yeast which has been dissolved in a small amount of peach juice. Place a plate with a weight on it down inside the crock on top of the peaches to hold them submerged in their own fermenting juice. Then cover the crock and keep it at room temperature or in the cellar. Open the crock and stir every two days. When the peaches sink to the bottom of their own accord, they may be taken from the crock and used, or sealed in glass jars.

TO SEAL BRANDIED PEACHES IN JARS

Lift the peaches from the liquid in the crock with a slotted spoon and place them in hot sterilized jars, cut side down and edges overlapping. Fill the jars to the neck with peaches. Heat the liquid from the crock, almost to boiling. Do not allow it to boil or the alcohol will evaporate. Pour the hot liquid over the peaches, filling the jars to within ¼ inch of the top. Clean the rim and apply a self-sealing lid and screwband. Process in a boiling-water bath for 10 minutes to ensure a seal.

APRICOTS IN BRANDY   (Old recipe)

Take freshly gathered apricots not too ripe; to half their weight of loaf sugar, add as much water as will cover the fruit; boil and skim it; then put in the apricots and let them remain five or six minutes. Take them up without syrup and lay them on dishes to cool; boil the syrup till reduced one half; when the apricots are cold put them in bottles, and cover them with equal quantities of syrup and French brandy. If the apricots be clingstone, they will require more scalding.

PEACHES IN BRANDY   (Old recipe)

Get yellow soft peaches, perfectly free from defect and newly gathered, but not too ripe; place them in a pot, and cover them with cold, weak lye; turn over those that float frequently, that the lye may act equally on them; at the end of an hour take them out, wipe them carefully with a soft cloth and get off the down and skin, and lay them in cold water; make a syrup as for the apricots, and proceed in the same manner, only scald the peaches more.

VINTAGE FRUIT SAUCE

This recipe was originated by a yeast company. It is an instant tutti-frutti, maintained on the order of a sourdough starter. When some of the fruits are taken from the jar, more are added to keep the supply going indefinitely. New batches of fruit sauce can be started with a portion of the fermented fruit taken from the original sauce.

To make the original fruit sauce: In a glass jar with a loose cover, such as an apothecary jar, combine ¾ cup drained canned peaches, cut into pieces, ¾ cup drained pineapple tidbits, 6 maraschino cherries, cut into halves, 1½ cups sugar, and 1 package active dry yeast. Let sauce stand at room temperature. Stir the sauce several times the first day, then stir once each day. The sauce is ready to use at the end of two weeks. Use as much of the sauce as needed but save 1 cup to make the foundation for the next batch of sauce. Repeat the fruit and sugar every two weeks thereafter, regardless of how much sauce is used, always leaving a minimum of 1 cup of sauce in the jar.

To remake the sauce using "Starter": Combine 1 cup of fermented fruit sauce from the original recipe, ½ cup drained canned peaches, cut into pieces, ½ cup drained pineapple tidbits, 6 maraschino cherries, cut into halves, and 1 cup sugar. Let stand at room temperature and stir once each day. This sauce can be served after one week; repeat the fruit and sugar every two weeks.

Sauerkraut and Turnip Kraut

I liked the change in the usual routine of canning season that came with the making of sauerkraut. Sometime in July the cabbages would reach their full size all at once, and it suddenly became urgent to get them worked up into sauerkraut. If the heads grew too large, they burst. Then, if rains came, the heads might sour and be wasted or the cracks might be invaded by voracious cabbage worms. Even the sight of the small white cabbage butterflies, which preceded the invasion of the caterpillars, was enough to incite my mother to action.

The sauerkraut was fermented in a dark-brown earthenware crock that held ten gallons. There was a round wooden board that fitted inside the neck of the crock and had been made especially by Grandpa to hold the kraut down under its liquid. This was weighted with a rock my grandfather had selected at some time or other, making sure it was not limestone. These items were carried out of the smokehouse anteroom into the sunshine, where they were scrubbed, scalded, and aired. The kraut cutter, too, had to be brought out of storage in the attic, and it was washed and the blades carefully dried. The kraut cutter was set over a washtub, which was also carefully scoured and scalded.

When all the equipment was ready, Mother took a

sharp knife and a bushel basket and we went into the garden to cut the cabbage heads. The outside leaves were stripped off and left lying in the row, and the heads were washed clean under the stream of water at the backyard cistern. The cabbage was quartered and trimmed and then shredded on the kraut cutter until the tub was almost brimful of thin, uniform shreds no thicker than a dime.

The whole process of shredding, salting, and packing the cabbage into the large crock captured my interest. It was fun to be on hand when the sauerkraut was made. But later, when the crock of cabbage began to ferment and the smell of souring juices filled the cellar, I would dash down the steps holding my nose and quickly run back up again after completing an errand. How could anything that smelled so bad in the making taste so good later on when cooked with potatoes or used as stuffing for a fat baked hen?

SAUERKRAUT

Sauerkraut is fermented, salted cabbage. The cabbage is cut into thin shreds, salted down, and allowed to ferment in its own juice. It is not difficult to make and is a good way to preserve surplus cabbage. Sauerkraut has its own distinctive noncabbage flavor. It is the basis of many delicious dishes and is a good source of vitamin C.

Kraut can be fermented in a large crock or other suitable container, or it can be fermented in quart-size glass canning jars.

Cured sauerkraut should be packed into canning jars and processed in a boiling-water bath if it is not to be used within a few weeks. For short-term storage, cured sauerkraut can be kept in a cool place or in the refrigerator.

If sauerkraut is to be made in quantity, one should have a kraut cutter made expressly for the purpose of cutting cabbage for making sauerkraut. The cabbage shreds should be no thicker than a dime. A knife can be used to cut cabbage for kraut, or a vegetable shredder, but nothing works so well as an old-fashioned kraut cutter. Old ones are plentiful in antique shops for reasonable prices and new ones are still being made. (See the Sources section in the back of the book.)

Turnips are also made into "kraut" by a similar method to that of making cabbage kraut. Turnip kraut is sometimes called "sauer rüben." If turnip kraut is to be made, finding a turnip kraut cutter is not as simple as finding a cabbage kraut cutter. There are a few old ones to be found in antique shops from time to time, but the prices are high because turnip kraut cutters are a novelty. In my area, there are a few people who make new turnip kraut cutters, but they are also expensive and limited in supply. So, you will have to devise the best way you can to cut the turnips into julienne strips if you are not fortunate enough to have access to a turnip kraut cutter.

MAKING A SMALL AMOUNT OF SAUERKRAUT

1. Remove the outer leaves of firm cabbages, wash, and drain. Cut the cabbages into quarters, core, and shred with a kraut cutter or sharp knife, making pieces no thicker than a dime. Weigh the cabbage. Two pounds of shredded cabbage make one quart.
2. Sprinkle pure granulated pickling or canning salt over the shredded cabbage, using 3 tablespoons salt to each 5 pounds of cabbage. Combine the cabbage and salt and mix well. Let stand for a few minutes until the cabbage is slightly wilted.
3. Pack the salted cabbage into sterile quart jars, pressing it down firmly into the jars with a wooden spoon. Brine will form and cover the cabbage. Fill the jars up to the neck with cabbage.
4. Place a pad of clean, white cheesecloth in each jar, directly on top of the packed cabbage, to cover it completely. Hold the cloth in place by inserting two wooden strips, cut to size from Popsicle sticks, so that they catch under the neck of the jar on each side.
5. Close the jars with suitable lids, leaving them slightly loose.
6. Set the jars in a shallow pan so that the overflow during

310

fermentation will spill into the pan. Keep the jars at a constant room temperature of about 70°F for the next 10 days. There should be no scum formed on the top of the cabbage but the progress of fermentation should be watched. If scum forms, remove it and replace the cheesecloth pads with clean, dampened pads and insert the wooden sticks, as before.

7. After about 10 days, the brine level will drop noticeably. This indicates that the fermentation is almost over. Remove the cheesecloth pads and wooden strips from the jars. Fill the jars to within ½ inch of the top with a 2½-percent brine solution (1 ounce salt to 1 quart water.) Press the cabbage down to release gas bubbles. Clean the rims of the jars and apply clean lids.

8. For short storage, place the cured sauerkraut in a cool place and use within a few weeks.

9. For long storage, process the filled jars in a boiling-water bath for 30 minutes. Remove the jars from the boiling water after processing, complete seals, if necessary, cool the jars, and store.

MAKING A LARGE AMOUNT OF SAUERKRAUT

Follow Steps 1 and 2 for Making a Small Amount of Sauerkraut, combining cabbage and salt in the same proportions, using 3 tablespoons salt to each 5 pounds of shredded cabbage.

3. Pack a layer of salted, shredded cabbage firmly and evenly into a large, clean crock and press the cabbage down firmly with the hands or a wooden potato masher until its juice flows and comes to the surface. Add another layer of shredded and salted cabbage and repeat, packing until the cabbage fills the crock to within 3 or 4 inches of the top.

4. To prevent growth of film yeast or molds, cover the cabbage so that the surface is protected from exposure to the air, using one of these two methods:

   a. Cover the cabbage with a clean, thin, white cloth, such as unbleached muslin, and tuck the edges down against the inside of the container. Cover the cloth with a heavy plate or a round paraffined board that just fits inside the container so that the cabbage is not exposed to the air. Put a weight on the plate or board so that the brine comes to the top of the cover, but not over it. A glass jug or jar filled with water serves the purpose of a weight. During the fermentation period, replace the cloth every day, or as needed, with a clean one that has been dipped in boiling water and wrung out. Remove daily any scum that forms.

b. Fill a large, heavyweight, food-use plastic bag with water and place it directly on top of the fermenting cabbage. The water-filled bag keeps the air from the surface of the cabbage. Put just enough water in the bag to make enough pressure to keep the cabbage covered with brine. To protect the bag from accidental leakage, put it inside another plastic bag before filling it with water.

5. Keep the crock of cabbage at a temperature of 68° to 72°F for 5 to 6 weeks until the fermentation is completed. Formation of gas bubbles indicates that fermentation is taking place. Remove daily any scum that forms.

6. To store cured sauerkraut: Remove the kraut from the fermenting crock, heat it in its own juices to simmering, and pack it hot into clean, hot jars. Cover the sauerkraut with its own hot juice, leaving ½-inch head space. Adjust lids. Process in a boiling-water bath, 15 minutes for pints, 20 minutes for quarts. Start counting processing time as soon as hot jars are placed into actively boiling water. Remove jars from canner after processing, complete seals, if necessary, and cool jars upright on a folded cloth or wire rack.

CARAWAY SAUERKRAUT

If the flavor of caraway is wanted in the sauerkraut, add caraway seeds to the shredded cabbage during the fermentation process, or to the cured cabbage when it is being heated prior to packing it into canning jars for processing. Use about 2 teaspoons seeds to every 3 quarts, or 6 pounds, of cabbage, or to taste.

COMMON CAUSES OF SPOILAGE IN SAUERKRAUT

Off-odors, off-flavors, pink or dark kraut, and soft texture all indicate spoilage in sauerkraut.

Soft kraut may be caused by too little salt, too high temperatures during fermentation, improper packing, or uneven distribution of salt through the cabbage.

Pink kraut is caused by certain yeasts, which grow if there is too much salt or an uneven distribution of salt, or if the kraut is not covered or weighted properly during fermentation.

Rotted kraut is found at the top of the cabbage where it was not covered properly during fermentation.

Dark kraut may be caused by improperly trimmed or unwashed cabbage; too little brine during fermentation; an uneven distribution of salt; exposure to air; high temperatures during fermentation, processing, or storage; or an overly long storage period.

If there is any sign of such spoilage, the whole crockful must be thrown out.

MAKING TURNIP KRAUT

Peel young, juicy turnips and shred them to a size that resembles fine shoestring potatoes. If a turnip-kraut cutter is used, the pieces will come out in long strings, thicker than spaghetti; the kraut is best when the turnips are cut this way. Without a turnip kraut cutter, improvise a way to make the longest julienne strips possible, such as with a shoestring potato cutter or the coarse side of a kitchen grater-shredder.

Put a layer of shredded turnips in the bottom of a stoneware jar and sprinkle with salt, using 2 tablespoons of salt to every gallon of shredded turnips.

Some cooks believe in adding a little sugar to the turnips, so if sugar is to be added, sprinkle it on each layer of turnips with the salt, using 2 to 3 teaspoons of sugar per gallon of shredded turnips.

Take a wooden potato masher and firmly tamp down the salted layer of turnips to make the turnip juice begin to flow. Then add another layer, sprinkle with salt (and sugar, if desired), and again tamp down that layer. Repeat until the jar contains as much kraut as you want to make. Cover the top of the turnips with a clean cloth, pushing it down around the sides of the jar. Put a plate, upside down, on top of the cloth and a weight on top of the plate to keep the turnips under their juice. Let the jar stand for 3 or 4 days, but remove the cloth each day and exchange it for a clean cloth.

On the fourth day, sterilize pint or quart jars and put the kraut into the jars, covering it with the brine which has formed in the jar. Fill the jars up to the neck of the jar, making sure that the kraut is covered with brine. If there is not enough brine on the turnips to fill the canning jars, add water to finish filling them. Clean the rims of the jars and put on lids, preferably zinc lids with rubber rings. Fasten them down as tight as possible. Check the jars every day to be sure that the lids have not loosened, and if they have, tighten them again. If the juice from the jar runs out, just retighten the lid. Let the canned kraut stand for 2 or 3 weeks (some cooks recommend 6 weeks) before eating.

Turnip kraut can be eaten just as it comes from the jar, chilled, like cabbage kraut, or it can be drained of brine and cooked for about 20 minutes in a small amount of water. Season cooked turnip kraut with bacon fat.

To keep the turnip kraut for a short time, store in a cool place, preferably the refrigerator, until used.

To keep for long storage, fill the jars to within ½ inch of the top with a 2½-percent brine (1 ounce salt to 1 quart water), if needed. Clean the rims of the jars and apply clean lids. Process the filled jars in a boiling-water bath for 30 minutes. Begin counting the time as soon as jars are placed in actively boiling water.

PART VI

Storing Unprocessed
Foods

GRANDPA'S OUTDOOR CELLARS

A group of special smaller buildings was clustered around my grandparents' tree-shaded 1890's farmhouse. They were built of white-painted weatherboards in the same architectural style as the farmhouse, and their small-paned windows were outlined with dark green paint of the color used on the house shutters. Ornate wooden scrolls and carved moldings trimmed the eaves and cupolas of the smaller buildings to match the white Victorian-style decorations of the farmhouse. The outbuildings on a farmstead such as my grandparents' were important appendages to the farmhouse and they were as necessary to the production and preservation of the family's food as Grandmother's kitchen.

Grandpa was handy at carpentry and he had planned all of the companion buildings about the house and barn for the greatest possible convenience. There were nearly a dozen of these small outbuildings near the house, not including the barn buildings such as the corncrib and granaries. Many of these were on my daily rounds because I kept the path hot between my grandparents' house and our own next door. We children were not permitted to play in these irresistible buildings as a rule, but with good timing, I could manage to be on hand whenever Grandpa was in the milk house separating the cream from the milk with the

317

grand new DeLaval separator, or when the baby chickens were hatching out of their shells in the chicken house, or when Grandmother went down into the dark, spooky storm cellar to bring up a basket of apples and potatoes to use in the kitchen.

It was just good thinking to pay a visit to Grandmother to see what plans she had for the apples she brought in from the storm cellar. Grandmother made wonderful apple pies and cobblers and she always made enough for visitors to sample.

Grandmother's Apple Cobbler

Peel and slice enough apples to fill an 8 x 10-inch baking pan almost to the rim, or about 5 cups. Sweeten the apples with 1 cup sugar and sprinkle them with 1 teaspoon cinnamon, ½ teaspoon nutmeg, and 2 tablespoons flour. Dot the apples generously with butter, using about 2 tablespoons butter.

Make a rich biscuit dough: sift together 2 cups flour, 4 teaspoons baking powder, ½ teaspoon salt, ½ teaspoon cream of tartar, and 2 tablespoons sugar. Cut in ½ cup butter until the mixture looks like coarse meal. Stir in about ⅔ cup milk and roll dough out to ¼-inch thickness. Cover the apples with the dough and trim the edges; cut a vent in the top to allow steam to escape during baking. Sprinkle the top of the dough with additional sugar, about 2 tablespoons, and bake the cobbler in a hot oven (400°F) about 45 minutes, or until the crust is browned and the apples tender. Serve warm with rich cream.

Grandpa's storm cellar was used principally for the storage of apples and root vegetables, but it was truly built with the idea of providing safe shelter in the event of a tornado. With his practical turn of mind, Grandpa built it to serve well for either purpose.

Only one tornado ever swept through our community during my childhood. But often in summer when stormy skies threatened, we children were hurried across the yard into the dark safety of Grandpa's storm cellar where we huddled among the freshly dug potatoes until the storm blew over, just in case. To this day, the particular earthy scent that surrounds new potatoes recalls to me the spectacular flashes of lightning and loud startling thunderclaps that were characteristic of those summer electrical storms that sent us flying into the safe haven of the storm cellar.

Grandpa's storm cellar was built like those on other farmsteads in our community. The lower half of the structure was built in an excavation dug out of a small earth bank near the house. The framing was of strong timbers and the underground walls were sided with large flat stones from the creek bed. The portion of the cellar that extended above the excavated earth bank was topped with a strong flat roof. After the cellar was finished with storage bins and shelves built along the walls, a sturdy door hung at the entrance, and a ventilating chimney installed through the roof, the entire structure was buried under the soil that had been excavated from the earth bank. The soil covering over the storm cellar provided natural insulation that kept the temperature inside the cellar cooler in summer and warmer in winter than the outside temperatures.

In winter, Grandmother moved the jars of vegetables and fruits that had been stored there in the summertime and autumn to the inside of the house so they would not freeze during the last cold months before spring. The fruits and vegetables that were stored in the bins inside the storm cellar, snug in coverings of straw, sand, or dry leaves, were safe from freezing. In fact, some fruits and vegetables kept better if the temperature in the cellar could be kept almost at the freezing point.

Grandpa hung a long thermometer just outside the door of the storm cellar and another one inside the cellar. On certain days, after consulting both thermometers, he opened the louvered panels in the front wall of the storm cellar. I always knew when Grandpa had let the outside air into the storm cellar because a sweet, ripe, fruity odor wafted out of the ventilating chimney on top of the cellar which could be smelled all the way across the yard.

The smells drifting out of Grandmother's kitchen in the middle of winter were just as distinctive as those escaping from the vent in the roof of the storm cellar. I could tell, as soon as I opened the kitchen door and smelled the cabbage cooking, that Grandmother was making a boiled dinner.

Before the severe cold of winter set in, usually around Christmas, Grandpa regularly began digging up the various strawlined pits and mounds he had made around the garden for the storage of vegetables that were not put into the storm cellar with the apples and potatoes, lest the apples taste like cabbages. The carrots, turnips, rutabagas, beets, and cabbages could not be kept forever in pit storage and, as the winter drew on, Grandpa went out more frequently with spade and basket to dig the snow and straw away from the root pit, to bring in still another mess of cold, firm, earth-scented vegetables that needed to be used. The root vegetables made their appearance regularly on Grandmother's table, one by one, creamed, stewed, scalloped, steamed, and fried. But the boiled dinner made use of everything Grandpa could bring in all at once.

Grandmother's boiled dinner began with a large brisket of beef which she put on to cook, submerged in cold water, in a large, heavy kettle. All morning the pot simmered on the back burner of the kitchen range, until the meat broth was rich and amber colored and the meat tender, but not quite tender enough to pierce easily with a long-tined fork. Now and again, while the meat was simmering, Grandmother added a bunch of celery and a few onions for flavoring, some pepper, salt, and a leaf of fragrant herb for seasoning, or skimmed off a spoonful of scum or excess fat that rose to the top of the rich broth. Finally it was time to add the scrubbed and peeled vegetables from Grandpa's root pit. Those that required the longest cooking were put in the kettle first, about forty-five minutes before dinner time; first the scraped carrots, then whole white onions, a few turnips, some sweet parsnips, a lot of large white peeled potatoes, and last, the wedges of cabbage were

320

placed on top of the cooking vegetables where they would steam until the vegetables were done.

By today's standards, the cabbage in Grandmother's boiled dinner would be considered overcooked. By the time the vegetables were fork-tender, the wedges of cabbage barely held their shape and the leaves were pale and tender, and sometimes tinged with pink. But the homely, honest flavor of the cooked cabbage in the boiled dinner, as well as the strong, sweet, steamy cabbage smell in the kitchen, gave its character to the dinner which Grandmother served on a huge ironstone platter. The brisket of beef was carved in thick juicy slices and placed in the center of the platter, with the cabbage and other vegetables from the root pit arranged around the sides. For Grandpa, who liked it, there was horseradish to go with the boiled beef. For me, the boiled dinner needed only fresh warm bread and butter to supplement it and apple cobbler to polish it off.

Storing Fruits and Vegetables

Many fruits and vegetables can be kept over the winter by storage in basements, cellars, outbuildings, or pits as long as the average outdoor temperature is below freezing from mid-November to mid-March and the proper ventilation and temperature are maintained inside the storage area.

WHICH VEGETABLES AND FRUITS MAY BE STORED?

More vegetables than fruits may be kept in cool dry storage at home. Most commonly, apples may be kept through the fall and part of the winter. Pears, grapes, and citrus fruits may be stored for a few weeks to a couple of months. Potatoes, onions, sweet potatoes, pumpkins, squashes, parsnips, turnips, and other root crops may be stored during the winter. Cabbage and celery will keep all winter, while cauliflower, peppers, endive, and green tomatoes will keep several weeks.

Dry beans and peas will keep as long as wanted or until they are used.

Each fruit and vegetable has its own storage requirements of temperature, humidity, and ventilation, as shown on the chart on page 332. Sometimes vegetables and fruits with the same requirements can be stored together in the same place; but for others, individual storage must be arranged.

SELECTION OF PRODUCE FOR STORAGE

Only vegetables and fruits that are picked in their prime and are of choice quality should be stored. The old saying, "One bad apple spoils the barrel," sums it up. Any damaged, decaying, bruised, crushed, insect-infected, diseased produce placed in storage along with perfect specimens will ruin the whole lot. Select only the best produce available and handle it carefully during harvesting and storage.

Vegetables and fruits that are brought in from the garden may be warm and moist from the sun and weather conditions. Do not place them in storage until they have dried and cooled.

TEMPERATURE AND HUMIDITY OF THE STORAGE AREA

Maintaining the proper temperature within the storage area has much to do with the length of time produce will keep in storage. To regulate the temperature for the maximum storage time, you will need to place one thermometer outdoors and one inside the cellar, outbuilding, or basement so you can make adjustments to keep the temperature as required.

Outdoor temperatures of 32°F or lower are required to cool the air inside the storage area to 32°F and to maintain that desirable temperature. Once the temperature inside the storage area reaches 32°F, it is regulated by opening and closing the doors, windows, and ventilators, usually daily. The temperature inside the storage area will rise when the ventilators are closed, even when the temperature outside is quite cold, but the danger of overventilating during subfreezing weather must be guarded against.

A study conducted by a leading university showed that full ventilation day and night was required when the outdoor daytime temperature ranged between 18°F and 30°F and the nighttime temperature was as low as 10°F. A minimum temperature of 8°F at night, or a windy 12°F night, will drop the temperature inside the storage area to 30°F after a few hours.

Without the proper humidity, the stored vegetables and fruits will shrivel and lose quality. There are several ways to provide humidity inside the storage area. One way is to sprinkle water on the floor, or to lay wet straw or sawdust on the floor. Another way is to place containers of water where the incoming air passes over it. Another method is to store the produce in polyethylene bags or box liners. A few small holes must be cut in the sides of the bags or box liners to permit air to enter. Tie the bags and fold over the box liners, but do not make them air tight.

Another method is to install a humidifier in the storage area or to use a cold-vapor humidifier, if the area is small.

The general conditions for humidity are given in the chart on page 332. In the book, *The Buying Guide for Fresh Fruits, Vegetables, Herbs, and Nuts* (See Sources), the ideal relative humidity for storage of various fruits and vegetables is given. If you can control the humidity of your storage area and have a method of measuring it, you may be able to keep the humidity at the exact percentage considered ideal for your produce.

STORAGE AREAS

The area used for winter storage of root crops, other vegetables, and fruits may be any place where the temperature is constantly cold, between 32°F and 40°F during the storage period, and where there is enough moisture, between 70 and 95 percent humidity, to keep the produce at its best quality. The area should be free of drafts, dark, and protected from rodents. The ground surrounding the storage area should be well drained.

A root cellar was once considered a necessity for a well-managed household, along with a smoke house, a springhouse, and other useful outbuildings, and one was usually constructed at the time the house for the family was built. Some of us who own older buildings still have the root cellars that were built into a hillside or have cold cellars under houses that originally did not have central heating. Lacking those, a suitable place must be built or improvised if one is to keep fruits and vegetables over the winter by "root cellaring."

Besides the outdoor root cellar and the unheated cellar under a house, there are several other areas around the home that may be prepared or adapted for winter storage of fruits and vegetables. A room may be partitioned off in a heated basement, or the produce may be packed in barrels or baskets and buried under a mound of earth, or it may be stored in a pit insulated by dirt and straw. Some vegetables may be left in the ground over the winter.

If the basic requirements for good root cellar storage can be met, more unusual areas can be adapted for cold storage of fruits and vegetables—in the attached woodshed, the crawl space under the house, or a garage separate from the house where a space can be insulated and protected from overventilation.

THE OLD-FASHIONED OUTDOOR ROOT CELLAR

Grandpa's root cellar was partly underground and partly buried under a mound of dirt. A pit was dug about half as

deep as the cellar was to be, then the sides and top were constructed of timbers and field stones. Soil was mounded up against three sides of the structure and the top of the root cellar was also covered with soil. A roof was put over the soil on top of the root cellar so that the layer of insulating earth would not become water soaked and heavy. A door was put in the exposed side of the root cellar and there were about three steps leading down to the door. Inside, the root cellar was a dirt floor, covered with bricks, and shelves and bins lined the sides and back wall of the cellar.

An opening was left somewhere in the root cellar for the intake of air and a chimneylike ventilator was extended up through the roof or just under the eve of the roof to draw the air out and provide circulation. After several months, the aroma of the fruits stored inside could be smelled at a good distance from the root cellar.

Sometimes the doors leading down to the root cellar were placed almost flat on the ground over the stairway leading down to the root cellar, and to open them you laid them over on the ground.

BUILDING OUTDOOR UNDERGROUND CELLARS Plans for an underground cellar, entirely covered with soil except for the door, are available from your agricultural agent or your State Extension Service at the agricultural college of your state. The plan is identified as Plan 6209. This cellar can be used for food storage and as a storm cellar or as a protective shelter against radioactive fallout.

A description article, giving good details about constructing an underground root cellar with railroad ties as the main building material, appeared in issue No. 29 of *The Mother Earth News.*

BASEMENTS

A well-ventilated basement with a furnace in it may provide a place for short term storage of potatoes, sweet potatoes, onions, and for ripening tomatoes. But for long-term storage in such a basement, a special insulated room with outside ventilation is necessary. It can be partitioned off

Air duct box placed over opened window in room in basement partitioned off from furnace

away from the furnace and its ducts on the north or east side of the basement in an area where there is at least one outside window.

The storage room should be kept dark. If an air duct box is placed over an opened window, the box will darken the room. The room itself may be divided into two compartments to provide for the separate storage of fruits and vegetables to prevent one from absorbing the odor of another. The shelves and flooring of the storage room should be slatted flooring, if possible, so that water or dampened materials can be placed in the room to provide humidity, if needed. Bins or wooden crates and boxes can be used for storing the produce.

An unheated basement or cellar with a dirt floor and an outside door or window makes an ideal cold-storage room for fruits and vegetables.

CONSTRUCTING OUTDOOR STORAGE MOUNDS

Cone-shaped mounds, or "pits," for storing apples, pears, cabbages, and for storing root vegetables such as carrots, beets, potatoes, turnips, salsify, and parsnips may be used in areas where the outdoor temperatures in winter stay below freezing.

The pit may be built at ground level or a hole several inches deep may be dug where the mound is to be located. Spread the area to be covered by the mound with a layer of straw, hay, or other bedding material. A layer of hardware cloth may be spread on the bedding to deter rodent invasion. On top of the bedding, or hardward cloth, if it is used, make a mound of the vegetables or fruits to be stored. Do not store vegetables and fruits together. Then cover the stacked vegetables or fruits with a layer of straw or bedding, making a cone-shaped mound. Cover the entire pile with 3 or 4 inches of soil. Tamp the soil down over the mound with a shovel. If the temperature of the area is generally mild, no other covering is necessary. A top layer of bedding will further protect the mound if severe temperatures are expected. Mound storage is not adequate to protect the fruits and vegetables in climates where temperatures remain far below 0°F for extended periods.

A shallow drainage ditch must be dug all around the pit to keep water from standing around the mound. To pro-

A cone-shaped mound for outdoor storage with an air vent at top

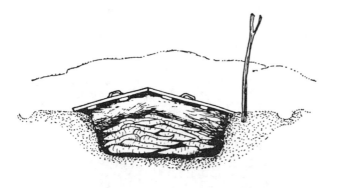

A pit constructed below the frost line for outdoor storage

vide for ventilation of the interior of the mound, leave a small air vent at the top of the earth covering of the mound and let the interior bedding extend through the opening. To keep rain from penetrating the straw and reaching the vegetables or fruits inside, cover the air hole with a board or piece of metal held down with a rock.

Several mounds, each containing a few bushels of vegetables or fruits, may be built. This is practical because the entire contents of the mound must be removed from the mound once it is opened. Several vegetables can be stored in the same pit together, separated by layers of straw, but apples and pears must be stored in their own separate pits. Cabbages also require separate storage.

A large mound may be built if there is storage space for the vegetables in a suitable place indoors after they are removed from the outdoor pit. For example, potatoes might be stored in an earth mound until room has been made for them in the potato bins of the regular root cellar.

A barrel, large drainage tile, large box or old refrigerator body, or other suitable container can be filled with vegetables or fruits with bedding material surrounding and separating them, and then buried in an earth mound.

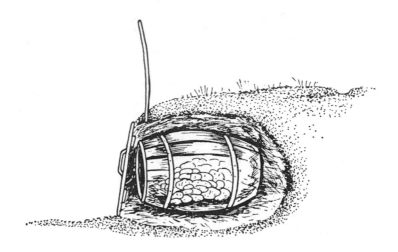

The locations of the mounds or boxes should be well-marked by stakes if the area is one in which heavy snows could camouflage them. The location of the openning or the barrel, or the lid of the box, should also be marked.

Pits should not be built on the same spots in following years. Move their locations each year to avoid contamination. Use the bedding material for compost or mulching after the pit is dismantled.

IN-THE-GARDEN STORAGE

Certain crops can be left in the ground just as they grew, without harvesting, until needed. These vegetables may be harvested from the ground throughout the winter and spring. Some are more flavorful after a period of ground storage. Vegetables that can be left in the ground until harvested are carrots, garlic, horseradish, Jerusalem artichokes, leeks, beets, parsnips, radishes, salsify, and turnips.

The vegetable rows and surrounding area should be covered with a thick layer of mulch, 12 to 18 inches thick, after the ground freezes. Hay, straw, dried leaves, or similar bedding may be used for mulching. The rows in which the crops are left should be marked so that they can be located beneath the mulch when the vegetables are to be dug. Snow and frozen ground will complicate the digging during the winter, but a bucketful of hot water poured on the ground after the mulch and snow are scraped aside will facilitate the digging.

Some green vegetables that grow above ground are hardy and withstand frosts well. If protected by mulch, they can be kept green and growing for some time after cold weather sets in. Some, notably kale and Brussels sprouts, are enhanced by cold and frosting. Other green vegetables that can be left in the garden under a mulch of hay or other bedding are broccoli, cabbage, Chinese cabbage, parsley, Swiss chard, mustard greens, endive, and peas. If these crops are to be harvested late in the fall, after cold weather begins, they must be planted in mid-summer to assure a crop.

Mulch the green vegetables with about 18 inches of bedding as soon as it begins to frost. Do not wait until after a hard freeze, as with the below-ground crops.

SPECIFIC RECOMMENDATIONS FOR EACH VEGETABLE AND FRUIT

The text that follows gives specific recommendations on how best to store each kind of food to achieve the maximum possible storage period.

The accompanying chart sums up the information for quick reference.

FREEZING POINTS, RECOMMENDED STORAGE CONDITIONS, AND LENGTH OF STORAGE PERIOD FOR VEGETABLES AND FRUITS

Commodity	Freezing Point (° F)	Place to Store	Storage Conditions		Length of Storage Period
			Temperature (° F)	Humidity	
Vegetables					
Dry beans and peas	—	Any cool, dry place	32° to 40°	Dry	As long as desired
Late cabbage	30.4°	Pit, trench, or outdoor cellar	Near 32° as possible	Moderately moist	Through late fall and winter
Cauliflower	30.3°	Storage cellar	Near 32° as possible	Moderately moist	6 to 8 weeks
Late celery	31.6°	Pit or trench; roots in soil in storage cellar	Near 32° as possible	Moderately moist	Through fall and winter
Endive	31.9°	Roots in soil in storage cellar	Near 32° as possible	Moderately moist	2 to 3 months
Onions	30.6°	Any cool, dry place	Near 32° as possible	Dry	Through fall and winter
Parsnips	30.4°	Where they grew or in storage cellar	Near 32° as possible	Moist	Through fall and winter
Peppers	30.7°	Unheated basement or room	45° to 50°	Moderately moist	2 to 3 weeks
Potatoes	30.9°	Pit or storage cellar	35° to 40°	Moderately moist	Through fall and winter
Pumpkins and squashes	30.5°	Home cellar or basement	55°	Moderately dry	Through fall and winter

Root crops (miscellaneous)	—	Pit or storage cellar	Near 32° as possible	Moist	Through fall and winter
Sweet potatoes	29.7°	Home cellar or basement	55° to 60°	Moderately dry	Through fall and winter
Tomatoes (green, mature)	31.0°	Home cellar or basement	55° to 70°	Moderately dry	4 to 6 weeks
Fruits					
Apples	29.0°	Fruit-storage cellar	Near 32° as possible	Moderately moist	Through fall and winter
Grapefruit	29.8°	Fruit-storage cellar	Near 32° as possible	Moderately moist	4 to 6 weeks
Grapes	28.1°	Fruit-storage cellar	Near 32° as possible	Moderately moist	1 to 2 months
Oranges	30.5°	Fruit-storage cellar	Near 32° as possible	Moderately moist	4 to 6 weeks
Pears	29.2°	Fruit-storage cellar	Near 32° as possible	Moderately moist	See text

Source: United States Department of Agriculture, Home and Garden Bulletin No. 119.

PARSLEY

One way to keep parsley protected from the weather so that it may be harvested from the bed after cold weather sets in is to cover it with an inverted basket that has been filled with straw, hay, or leaves.

Another way is to cover the parsley bed with a thick layer of mulch (hay, straw, or leaves), 12 to 18 inches thick.

DRY BEANS AND PEAS

All kinds of dry beans and peas will keep in any cool, dry place inside the home. They need only be thoroughly dry and protected from weevil and moth destruction.

To harvest the beans and peas, either pick them as soon as they are mature and have them in a suitable place until they are thoroughly dry, or pull the entire bean plant after most of the pods are dry. Shell the beans from the pods, or flail the beans from the pods and winnow out the trash, and finish drying, if necessary.

After the beans and peas are thoroughly dry, give them either a heat or freezing treatment to destroy any insects or insect eggs that might be present. Either place the beans in the freezer at 0°F for 3 or 4 days, or heat them in a 180°F oven for 15 minutes.

Store the dried beans and peas in closed jars until used. If there is any sign of weevil infestation, treat the beans again with heat or cold.

CABBAGE

Cabbages that mature late in the season may be kept through late fall and into the winter if stored properly in an outdoor storage cellar, in a pit or trench, or in a mound.

The cabbages must not touch each other during storage. If they are stored in a cellar, it should be away from the house because the odor of the stored cabbages will permeate the surroundings and other vegetables and fruits. Place the cabbages on shelves.

The cabbages are harvested by pulling them out of the ground with the root attached. They are stored upside down in a ground-level mound, and root-side down when buried in a trench or pit.

Cabbages stored in a cellar require moderately moist humidity. They freeze at about 30°F and keep best as near 32°F as possible.

CELERY

Late-maturing varieties of celery may be kept for a month or two by leaving the plants in the garden where they are growing. Leave their roots in the soil and at the end of their growing season throw an extra bank of soil around the base of the plants. Then, before freezing, build up the earth bank to the top of the plants and cover the banked celery with straw or corn stalks held down by boards.

Another way to store celery is in a trench. Dig up the mature plants with a clump of soil around the roots, and pack the celery plants in a trench 2 feet deep and 1 foot wide. Water the plants as they are put in the trench, but do not cover the trench until the plant tops are dry. Then make a roof for the celery trench by placing a board, 12 inches wide, on edge beside the trench and banking it with soil. Then use boards or other material to cover the celery tops, propping them up off the celery by resting them on the edge of the upright board. Cover the board roof with straw or hay, or other light material. Instead of digging a trench, an existing hotbed can be packed with celery in the same manner and the top covered over with boards and straw.

If space is available, celery may be stored on the floor of an outdoor storage cellar or a basement storage room. Dig up the celery including a ball of soil around the roots. Set the plants on the storage-room floor, packing them together tightly. Water the celery as it is stored and keep it moderately moist during storage. Do not store celery near turnips or cabbage because the celery will pick up the odor of strong-flavored vegetables.

ENDIVE

Endive may be kept in a storage cellar in the same manner

as celery for as long as 2 or 3 months. Endive keeps well at around 32°F and freezes at 31.6°F.

To promote blanching, tie the leaves together during storage.

ONIONS

Onions must be mature and dry to keep well over the winter. The tops of onions fall over when mature. They should be cured for several days in the garden after harvesting, or dried in a warm, well-ventilated place before storing. Do not store onions with green tops or wide necks.

After the onions are cured, they will keep best in a cool dry place at about 32°F. Onions freeze at about 30.6°F and must be protected from freezing during storage.

Onions keep best if stored above the floor. Hang them in mesh bags from rafters or braid them together in bunches that can be hung from overhead hooks. Or place the onions in slatted crates and place the crates on crossbars so that there is good air circulation around the containers. Do not store onions in the cellar. They will keep well in an unheated room or a well-ventilated attic.

PEPPERS

Green bell peppers that are harvested just before freezing can be kept for 2 or 3 weeks if properly stored.

Pick the peppers when they are mature, firm, and dark green. Wash them and sort for maturity and firmness before storing in polyethylene bags or box liners. Keep at a temperature of 45° to 50°F. Lower temperatures will cause earlier decay.

Hot peppers should be dried and stored. Either pull the entire plant and hang it up until the peppers are dry, or pick the peppers from the plant and thread them on a coarse thread to dry. Use a large needle and punch the hole for the thread in the upper third of the pepper. String the peppers and hang them from a ceiling hook in a warm, dry place with good air circulation until they are thoroughly dry. Then store peppers away from the heat until used, but do not store in a cellar. An unheated attic or room makes a good storage place. The string of peppers currently being used can be hung decoratively in the kitchen.

Do not let the peppers touch each other on the string while they are drying. After they are dry, they can be arranged in a tighter cluster.

POTATOES

Potatoes must be handled carefully when they are harvested to prevent damage that could shorten their storage life. The potatoes should be dug when the soil is dry enough to fall off the potatoes. Mud clings stubbornly to potatoes that are dug when the ground is wet and makes the potatoes unpleasant to peel all winter long. The potatoes must not be allowed to lie in the sun after they are dug. Sunburn causes potatoes to discolor and may turn the skins green. Wind is also damaging to newly dug potatoes.

After the potatoes are dug, they should be spread out in a protected place, such as on a sheltered porch, and allowed to cure for 1 to 2 weeks at 60°F to 75°F. Curing allows the tiny cracks and skinned places to heal over and prevents decay from setting in later on. Any potatoes that are badly cut or bruised should not be put into storage; use those up as soon as possible.

After the potatoes are cured, place them in baskets or bins and store them indoors in the basement, in an outdoor root cellar, or in pit storage. They must be kept in the dark or they will turn green. If there is green on the skin of a potato, be sure to peel deeply to remove it during preparation. The green substance, selenium, makes the potatoes bitter and is thought to be harmful if eaten in quantity.

Potatoes require moderate moisture or they will shrivel. If sprouts appear, they should be removed. If the potatoes begin to sprout soon after storage, the storage area is too warm and moist. They will sprout naturally as spring approaches when kept between 40° and 60°F. Potatoes keep best at 35° to 40°F for long term storage but they will keep quite well for some time at 60°F. Potatoes that are stored for several months at 35°F will sweeten and should be brought out of storage and placed in the kitchen at about 70°F for a week or so before use.

If potatoes are kept in an indoor cellar or basement where other fruits and vegetables are stored, keep the apples and potatoes separated to protect the apples from a certain mustiness they tend to pick up from potatoes stored nearby.

Late-crop potatoes are better for long-term storage than early potatoes because cool storage temperatures are difficult to maintain when early potatoes must be harvested. But in areas where the summer temperatures are mild, the potatoes can be left in the soil until fall. When the temperatures are unexpectedly high and the rainfall is heavy, the potatoes cannot be left in the ground for later harvesting without rotting.

PUMPKINS AND SQUASHES

Pumpkins and squashes with hard rinds can be kept for several months.

Harvest the pumpkins and squashes when their rinds cannot be pierced with the thumb nail and leave a piece of stem on the plant. Cut the stem; do not pull it from the vine.

Cure the pumpkins and squashes for 10 days at warm room temperature, about 80° to 85°F. Place them in a warm attic or near the source of your heat to achieve this temperature. Curing will harden the rinds and heal small cuts. Do not store pumpkins and squashes with serious mechanical injuries or insect injuries, however.

After curing the pumpkins at about 80°F, store them in a dry place at 55° to 60°F. When stored below 50°F, pumpkins and squashes gradually dry out and become stringy. It is best to spread the pumpkins out for storage, but if space limitations require that they be piled, examine them regularly for signs of mold or rotting.

Acorn squash can be stored in a dry place at 45° to 50°F for one month, or more. They do not require curing before storing. If kept too long or at too high a temperature, the acorn squashes will lose their dark-green color and the rind will turn orange.

Pumpkins and squashes must not be stored in pits or outdoor storage cellars.

SWEET POTATOES

Sweet potatoes cannot be handled roughly during harvesting because they are easily bruised and cut. They should be dug when the earth is dry enough to brush off easily, then put directly into baskets or other storage containers.

Place the sweet potatoes in their containers in a place where the temperature is 80° to 85°F, with high humidity, for 10 days to allow them to cure. These temperatures can be obtained if the potatoes are placed near the furnace or heating stove, and the humidity can be supplied by covering the baskets of potatoes during curing with plastic or tarpaulin. If temperatures less than 80° are maintained during the curing period, lengthen the time to 2 to three weeks. After curing, move the sweet potatoes to a cooler place in the house where the temperature will be about 55° to 60°F and the sweet potatoes will not be chilled below 50°F or subjected to freezing temperatures. As with squashes and pumpkins, sweet potatoes will suffer damage if chilled below 50°F. They require a moderately dry storage place. Do not store them in outdoor pits or in cellars where there is dampness.

In a house without central heating, the sweet potatoes can be kept near a warm chimney or near a heating stove. The upstairs rooms of some houses provide the necessary environment.

TOMATOES

Tomatoes that are harvested just before the first severe frost can be stored where they will gradually ripen. Fresh tomatoes for the table can be provided for 4 to 6 weeks after frost.

Pick all of the tomatoes, green and partially ripened ones, as well, and wash and dry them well. Remove all of the stems from the tomatoes and sort them according to degree of ripeness. Store the tomatoes showing red in containers separate from the green tomatoes. Pack the tomatoes in shallow boxes or on trays, one or two layers deep, for ripening. Wrap each tomato separately in newspaper or tissue paper.

Keep the tomatoes at 55° to 58°F in a well-ventilated room for the most gradual ripening. Mature green tomatoes will ripen in about 1 month. At a higher temperature, 65 to 70°F, mature green tomatoes will ripen in about two weeks.

There must be moderate humidity in the room or the tomatoes will shrivel. Too much moisture will encourage decay.

The tomatoes should be sorted periodically to remove the decaying fruits and to separate the redder ones from the ones that are still green. If a large table, covered with newspapers, can be spared for the ripening, the best attention can be given to the tomatoes as they are spread out on the table.

Do not use tomatoes that have ripened in this manner for canning purposes unless they are acidified by the addition of lemon juice or citric acid (see page 92).

PARSNIPS, SALSIFY, HORSERADISH, JERUSALEM ARTICHOKES

These vegetables can be left in the ground until needed. The flavor is improved by freezing, but alternate freezing and thawing damages them.

Root crops to be left in the ground should be mulched lightly at the end of the growing season. Then when the outdoor temperature is consistently low, remove the mulch so that the root vegetables can freeze and remulch them deeply enough to keep them frozen.

These vegetables may also be stored like other root crops in outdoor root cellars or in pit storage, except for Jerusalem artichokes, which keep best in the ground.

ROOT CROPS

Various root vegetables, such as beets, carrots, celeriac, kohlrabi, rutabagas, turnips, and winter radishes should be left in the ground until the weather is cold enough to store them at their best storage temperature, which is 32° to 40°F. These vegetables are not harmed by autumn frosts and can be left in the garden longer than other vegetables.

Turnips, especially, can withstand hard frosts but will be harmed by alternate freezing and thawing.

In the late fall when immediate storage can be arranged, dig the root crops and cut the plant tops one-half inch above the crown. Harvest the crops when the soil is dry enough to brush off the vegetables, or wash the vegetables and thoroughly dry them before storing them. Make sure the roots are cool when put into storage.

Do not store turnips or rutabagas in the basement or cellar under the house as their strong odors will permeate the living quarters above. Store them and other root crops in an outdoor cellar or in pit or mound storage.

All root crops except turnips or rutabagas can be stored in the basement storage area or unheated cellar. They should be separated from each other by placing packing material such as sand, peat, sphagnum moss, straw, or other suitable material between the layers of vegetables. If bedding is not available, use polyethylene bags or box liners with ventilating holes punched in them. Root crops stored in crates or other containers without bedding or polyethylene will eventually lose their moisture.

Outdoor pit or mound storage can be used for storing root crops if the area is safe from freezing.

If the temperature of the storage area rises above 45°F. for any length of time, the root crops will become woody and sprout new tops. Moist conditions are necessary to keep the roots from withering.

APPLES

The length of time that apples can be kept in cold storage depends on the variety of apple, its maturity and quality when it was picked, and the temperature at which it is stored.

Varieties of apples that are late-maturing, such as the Winesaps, York Imperial, Rome Beauty, McIntosh, and Newtown, are good for home storage. Early-ripening varieties cannot be kept as long.

Apples freeze at about 29°F and keep best at a temperature of about 32°F. Apples that are kept at 50°F will ripen

341

about four times as fast as those kept at 32°F and they will become overripe rapidly at 70°F or above.

Pick apples when they are mature but still hard. Make sure that all apples to be put into storage are free from insect damage and are not injured during handling.

Apples keep best in cellars that can be kept about 32°F. They can also be stored in insulated boxes in a cold climate, in outbuildings, in a haystack, in straw-lined pits, or in soil- and straw-covered barrels. Where the outdoor temperature remains below 10°F for extended periods, apples must be protected from freezing.

Apples need moderately moist humidity in storage to prevent shriveling. Perforated polyethylene bags and box liners are helpful to prevent shriveling of apples during storage.

CITRUS FRUITS

Citrus fruits may be kept from 4 to 6 weeks in a fruit cellar at a temperature close to 32°F. Both oranges and grapefruit freeze at about 30°F.

Moderately high humidity is required for storing citrus fruit.

GRAPES

In sections of the country where late-ripening grapes mature immediately before freezing temperatures set in, grapes can be kept for 1 to 2 months if they are of perfect quality and fully ripe when put into storage.

Grapes absorb odors from other fruits and vegetables and must be stored separately. They freeze at about 28°F and will keep best in a cold (32°F) place with moderately high humidity.

Catawbas keep best, but other kinds can be kept satisfactorily.

PEARS

Most pears should be picked when mature and firm and allowed to ripen off the tree.

The color of the pear fruit will change from deep green to a lighter green when it has reached maturity. The color of the fruit should not be allowed to develop to the yellow stage on the tree, although damaged fruit will ripen early. Another indication that the pears are maturing is the development of tiny brown dots on the surface of the fruit. The seeds also turn from white to brown when the pears mature, and the fruit can easily be separated from the stem.

Mature pears harvested at the correct stage will ripen in a few days if first chilled to 35 to 40°F, then ripened at 60 to 70°F at high humidity (80 to 85 percent).

Pears can be stored for 6 to 8 weeks at a temperature of near 32°F and a moderately moist humidity. The proper humidity can be maintained if the fruit is stored in polyethylene bags with ventilating holes punched in them. The pears can be stored anywhere where the temperature of below 40°F can be maintained, either in a root cellar, or in an unheated cellar, or in the refrigerator if space permits.

Pears may be stored along with apples or under the same conditions.

CHESTNUTS

Harvest the chestnuts that have fallen to the ground. Remove any remaining prickly burrs. Spread the chestnuts in a single layer on a flat surface to dry at room temperature for about a week. Choose a dry airy place such as a porch. Do not sun dry. After 7 to 10 days, the chestnuts can be eaten raw, boiled, or roasted.

To boil chestnuts, cut a gash on the side of each nut. Place the nuts in a saucepan and cover them with water. Boil them for 5 to 20 minutes, depending on how you will use the chestnuts after they are cooked. Drain the chestnuts and shell them as soon as they are cool enough to handle.

To roast chestnuts, cut a gash in the side of each chestnut. Place in a hot oven, 400°F, for about 20 minutes. To be sure when the chestnuts are roasted, one chestnut can be roasted without a gash cut in its side; when it explodes, the chestnuts are done. This method, however, necessitates cleaning the oven.

Boiled or roasted shelled chestnuts may be stored in jars in the refrigerator for a few days, until used. For longer storage, freeze the boiled or roasted chestnuts.

Uncooked chestnuts that have been cured for a week after harvesting, as directed above, may be stored for several weeks in the vegetable crisper of the refrigerator. The chestnuts should be placed in a perforated plastic bag. Or, place the cured chestnuts in a metal can with a perforated lid and store the can in the refrigerator. Line the can with waxed paper or place the chestnuts inside the can in a perforated plastic bag.

HICKORY NUTS, BLACK WALNUTS, AND BUTTERNUTS

The best way to keep hickory nuts, black walnuts, and butternuts after they have been hulled is to crack them as soon as possible after the nutmeats are dry and store the nutmeats in the freezer. Until the nuts are cracked and picked out of the shells, they should be kept in a dry, cool place, such as an outdoor garage, or one connected to the house if it is unheated or partially heated only.

Because of their high fat content, nutmeats will become rancid after they have been cracked and picked out of their shells, and they will become rancid or dry up eventually when left in the shell at room temperature. Nut worms will also develop and eat the nuts if the meats are left too long in the shell.

Nutmeats will keep fresh for several weeks, or even for several months, if packaged in plastic or placed in jars and stored in the refrigerator.

If there is room in the freezer for such space-taking items, unshelled nuts can be stored there in the shell. Some think that the nuts can be cracked and shelled more easily and that the nutmeats can be removed in larger pieces when the nuts are stored in the freezer before cracking them. Any insect contamination will be killed by brief freezer storage.

Nutmeats may be canned for storage. Pack thoroughly dry nutmeats into hot sterilized jars that are dry inside. Do not add any liquid to the nutmeats. Adjust the lids. Process jars in a boiling-water bath for 10 minutes to ensure a vac-uum seal.

PEANUTS

Peanuts should be dug before the tops are yellow to avoid having the majority of the peanuts become over-mature. When the peanuts have been growing for the average number of days required to reach maturity, dig a few plants when the earth is dry, to see if they have reached proper stage for harvesting.

Shake the soil from the pods. Spread the plants on wire drying racks or tie them in small bundles and hang them, with the roots inverted, to cure indoors in a dry, well-ventilated area. After 2 or 3 weeks, remove the pods from the plants and store the peanuts in a wire basket or other container that permits air circulation.

For prolonged storage, keep the peanuts in a cool, dry place. Avoid dampness.

TO ROAST AND SALT RAW PEANUTS Spread the shelled peanuts in a shallow layer on a flat pan and heat in a slow oven, 300°F, for 30 to 40 minutes. Stir the nuts often and check the brownness by slipping the skins from a few nuts from time to time during the roasting. Remove the nuts from the oven and spread them out to cool as soon as they are as brown as desired.

When the nuts have cooled, slip the skins off by press-ing the nuts between thumb and forefinger. Add 1 tea-spoon of butter or margarine for each cup of peanuts and place the nuts in a saucepan over low heat until the butter has melted and the nuts are well-coated and warm. Shake and stir the nuts constantly while heating. Spread on ab-sorbent paper and sprinkle with salt while warm.

Peanuts may also be roasted in the pods, shelled, and then warmed and salted, as above.

Homemade Peanut Brittle

In a heavy saucepan, combine 2 cups sugar, ½ cup water, and 1 cup white syrup and cook to 170°F (use a candy thermometer). Add 2 cups shelled raw peanuts, with or without the red skins, and cook to 300°F, stirring constantly. Remove candy from the heat, add 2 tablespoons butter and 1 teaspoon baking soda. Beat until well blended and foamy. Pour candy onto a cookie sheet greased with butter or onto a greased marble slab. Spread as thin as possible but handle carefully to avoid being burned by the hot syrup. Cool until the underside is set; check by running a spatula under the candy. When the sheet of candy is set enough to hold together, lift and turn the entire sheet. When cold, break into pieces and store in an airtight container.

SUNFLOWER SEEDS

If the sunflower heads are left in the garden after they have become ripe, the birds will eat the seeds or the seeds will fall to the ground.

When the seeds in the sunflower heads are large enough, cut the heads with a foot or two of stem attached. Hang them from a ceiling hook or rafter in a dry, well-ventilated place to finish drying. The heads are dry and the seeds are ready to be removed when they are brown and the stalks are brittle. The seeds should separate easily from the head.

To remove the seeds from the heads, rub them over a surface that provides friction, such as across a coarse metal screen or across a rack from a barbecue grill. Or use a wire brush or curry comb.

Spread the seeds out in a thin layer and allow them to become thoroughly dry before storing them.

Dried sunflower seed should be stored in a cool, dry place in metal containers, such as covered lard cans, to keep them safe from mice. Open the cans and stir the seeds frequently.

To hull small amounts of sunflower seeds by hand, immerse the seeds briefly in boiling water and drain before hulling.

HONEY

Honey may be left in the comb for home storage, or extracted from the comb. It should be kept in a covered container in a dry place at room temperature.

To store honey in the comb, cut the honeycomb into pieces that will fit into a wide mouth jar or syrup bucket, and cover it tightly. Honey left in the comb is already in natural storage as the honey is sealed in the comb. It will not crystallize as long as the comb is capped. But if comb honey is not kept in a closed jar or other tightly covered container, wax moths may invade it, or ants may be attracted to it.

To extract small amounts of comb honey for storage, cut the honeycomb out of the frame and place the pieces in a colander. Press the honeycomb with a wooden potato masher and let the liquid honey drain through the colander. Strain the honey a second time through a fine sieve to remove the small flecks of beeswax.

A honey extracting machine is practical when large amounts of honey must be removed from the comb. Some community canning centers have honey extractors for public use, if one is not available for home use. However, only honey formed on special reinforced foundation comb can be extracted with this equipment.

Pure honey does not need to be kept in the refrigerator. It should be refrigerated only when it has been diluted with water or other liquid, or whipped or creamed. Refrigeration causes pure honey to thicken and eventually to crystallize.

Pure honey will keep indefinitely even though it may crystallize. Crystallization is a natural process and does not injure the honey. It occurs when honey is kept at cold temperatures or when honey has been kept on the shelf for many months. Pure honey does not spoil. Honey that has been diluted with water or other liquid will ferment or mold.

If crystallization occurs, bring the honey back to liquid form by placing the container of honey on a rack in a pan of warm water over low heat. Warm the honey on the lowest heat until the crystals disappear. Do not overheat honey or its color and flavor will be altered.

Creamed or whipped honey may be kept either at room temperature or in the refrigerator. If kept too long or stored at too high a temperature, creamed and whipped products tend to separate.

Honey-butter must be refrigerated and used before the butter becomes rancid.

STORING MAPLE SYRUP

Maple syrup that is sealed when it is made in a tin or jar that is airtight will keep indefinitely, though it may crystallize in time. Once opened, it must be refrigerated or it will mold.

For best results, do not store maple syrup in a partially filled container. The less air space there is in the jar, the lesser the chance for mold formation.

SASSAFRAS ROOTS AND BARK

Sassafras roots and bark for making teas are best kept in a container that is covered to keep the dust off, but not airtight. Sassafras stored in an airtight container will mold because of the moisture in the roots and bark.

Freezing is also a satisfactory way of keeping sassafras. Package the roots or bark in plastic bags and store in the freezer until needed.

KEEPING AN OPENED GARLIC BUD

To keep a partially used bud of garlic from shriveling and drying out or from sprouting before it is used, peel all of the cloves of garlic and cover them with olive oil or vegetable oil. Store in a covered jar on the cupboard shelf. The garlic cloves can be minced or crushed in the garlic press and used like fresh garlic. The oil in which the garlic cloves were stored can be used for flavoring as well.

Epilogue

In late autumn there comes a day when a killing frost finally arrives and even the most tenacious gardeners must bid farewell to summer's bounty. The chilly winds shift to the north, the sky clears, and the raspy voiced cricket's song dwindles to an occasional rusty note. It is time to gather the garden's last gifts: a few red-ripe tomatoes hanging on worn-out straggly vines, a late crop of tender spinach leaves, some dark green acorn squash, Brussels sprouts, ruffly-edged kale just coming to full flavor, late cabbages and okra, and orange pie pumpkins. To its last day the vegetable garden is generous and giving.

We who have spent the summer picking and storing away the season's largesse would not pass by this last offering. One final round of harvesting and preserving brings to an end many hours of canning, freezing, pickling, and jelly making. Jars of pickles and relishes with their vinegary juices have been sealed; packages of ripe fruits and crisp vegetables, carefully frozen. Sweet summer berries in jellied syrups sit on the shelf next to succulent fruits submerged in brandy. Strings of fiery red peppers hang from the mantelpiece, and fragrant faggots of herbs are drying on attic beams. Shredded cabbages are salted down in stoneware jars in the cool cellar, and lively brewages ferment in wooden kegs.

Those who have persisted in the chores of preserving will not be deprived of summer's flavors after vine and bush are wasted by the black frost and the ground is snow-covered. Our reward for hoeing and weeding, for picking, peeling, chopping, and grinding, and for tending the steaming kettle is the feeling of everlasting security that comes with a filled cupboard, a snug root cellar, and a frosty hoard in the freezer. The pleasures of our winter table are ensured.

Sources of Publications and Equipment and Other Useful Information

HELPFUL PUBLICATIONS

Excellent books, booklets, and bulletins on various subjects relating to food preservation are available for a small charge, or free, from sources given below. When ordering, include your name, address, zip code, and the title of the book and/or number of the bulletin. If you are writing for information about ordering, include a self-addressed, stamped envelope. Enclose check or money order with your order if a charge is given below.

The Buying Guide for Fresh Fruits, Vegetables, Herbs, and Nuts. Available from Educational Department, Blue Goose, Inc., P.O. Box 46, Fullerton, California 92632. This is an excellent book for general information about how to select foods of quality. Specific varieties of fruits, vegetables, herbs, and nuts are described, including interesting historical notes and useful food-composition charts. Price: $2.50.

Ball Blue Book: The Guide to Home Canning and Freezing. Available from Consumer Service Division, Ball Corporation, Muncie, Indiana 47302. Price is $1 per copy.

Kerr Home Canning & Freezing Book. Available from Consumer Products Division, Kerr Glass Manufacturing Corp., Sand Springs, Oklahoma 74063. Price: $1.00.

Ball Freezer Book. Available from Consumer Service Division. Ball Corporation, Muncie, Indiana 47302. The price is 75 cents per copy.

United States Government Publications. To order bulletins published by the United States Department of Agriculture, Office of Communication, Publications Division, Room 500-A, 14th Street and Independence Avenue, S.W., Washington, D.C. 20250, enclose your name, address, zip code, the name and number of the bulletin, and the money required.

"Home Canning of Fruits and Vegetables"	Home and Garden Bulletin G8	35¢
"Home Freezing of Fruits and Vegetables"	Home and Garden Bulletin G10	55¢
"How to Make Jellies, Jams and Preserves at Home"	Home and Garden Bulletin G56	40¢
"Making Pickles and Relishes at Home"	Home and Garden Bulletin G92	45¢
"Keeping Food Safe to Eat"	Home and Garden Bulletin 162	35¢
"Storing Vegetables and Fruits in Basements, Cellars, Outbuildings, and Pits"	Home and Garden Bulletin G119	40¢
"Drying Foods at Home"	Home and Garden Bulletin 217	45¢

CONSTRUCTION PLANS FOR DRYING EQUIPMENT

Dry It! You'll Like It! by Gen. MacManiman, published by Living Foods Dehydrators, P.O. Box 546, Fall City, Washington 98024. The price of $3.95 includes detailed plans for the Living Foods Dehydrator.

"Drying Foods at Home," United States Department of Agriculture Home and Garden Bulletin Number 217. For sale by the Superintendent of Documents, U.S. Government Printing Office, Washington, D.C. 20402. Price 45 cents. Includes directions for construction of a natural-draft dehydrator, drying trays, and a portable electric food dehydrator.

Plans for Solar Dehydrator. $1.50. Community Environmental Council, Solar Research Group, 109 E. De La Guerra, Santa Barbara, California 93101.

Build It Better Yourself, by the editors of Organic Gardening and Farming, published by Organic Gardening, 1978, 236 pages. Hardback. Price is $16.95. Includes plans for solar food dryer, fruit press, root cellar. Directions for making a low-cost carboard carton indoor food dryer appeared in *Organic Gardening and Farming*, August, 1975 issue, pages 52–53.

How to Build Food Drying Equipment by John A. Magee, published by California Wood Plans, Box 541, San Luis Obispo, California 93406. Price is $2.00.

Instructions on how to make a cabinet-type dryer appeared in *The Mother Earth News* issue No. 34, pages 36–37.

SUPPLIES AND EQUIPMENT FOR HOME FOOD PRESERVATION

Hydrated lime is packed for Dacus, Incorporated, P.O. Drawer 528, Tupelo, Mississippi 38801 under the label, "Mrs. Wages Pickling Lime." If this product is not found in a store near you, send a self-addressed-stamped envelope to Dacus, Incorporated, for the location of a source nearby. Mrs. Wages Citric Acid, Mrs. Wages Fresh Fruit Preserver, Mrs. Wages Canning and Pickling Salt, and Mrs. Wages Dill Pickle and Bread and Butter Pickle Mixes are also packed for Dacus, Inc.

Hydrated lime suitable for pickling purposes is produced by the Mississippi Lime Company, 7 Alby Street, Alton, Illinois 62002. This product is available in hardware and garden supply stores.

Calcium hydroxide U.S.P., formerly listed as slaked lime, is provided to pharmacies by Eli Lilly and Company, Indianapolis, Indiana.

General equipment and supplies for home food preservation can be ordered by mail from the *Garden Way Catalog*, 1300 Ethan Allen Avenue, Winooski, Vermont 05404, or from the Sears, Roebuck & Company catalog.

Special equipment for food preparation and preservation, such as electric food dehydrators, sun-drying kits and oven-drying kits with drying crystals, steam canners for fruits, food processors and juicers, are available from the

Newburgh Country Store Enterprises, 5577 Grimm Rd., Newburgh, Indiana 47630 (send a self-addressed, stamped envelope for their brochure), and from Hammacher Schlemmer, 147 East 57th Street, New York, New York 10022 (write for their catalog).

Home-canning tools, canning jars and labels, plastic freezer containers, and Ball canning and freezing books are available from Ball Brothers General Store, Box 330, Muncie, Indiana 47302. Brochure available.

COMMUNITY CANNING CENTERS

In a growing number of communities throughout the country, canning centers equipped with heavy-duty washing, peeling, capping, cooking, and cooling equipment have been established for the use of people who need such facilities.

Community canning centers may be operated by private individuals, villages or towns, religious groups, co-operative organizations, or community service organizations. The facilities of the canning centers may be available to persons who wish to use them for a flat fee charged per jar or for the use of the equipment, or the participants may be required to buy a membership in the co-operative, or the use of the canning center may be free when the center is funded by the government or by a charitable organization.

Persons who do not have access to their own home-canning equipment, those who need help or advice about canning procedures, or those who wish to undertake large-quantity canning projects may wish to locate a nearby community canning center.

If the location of the nearest community canning center cannot be easily determined by the usual methods, such as consulting the telephone directory or the public library, or inquiring of public service agencies such as the county Co-operative Extension Service, this information may be acquired by writing to the Director, Ball Food Preservation Program, 345 S. High Street, Muncie, Indiana 47302. Individuals or groups interested in setting up a community canning center can obtain information as to the costs involved (at this writing, about $10,000) by writing to the same address.

KITCHEN METRICS

To convert the U.S. Customary System of measurements of volume and weight to metric measurements, apply these equations:

teaspoons	x 5	= milliliters
tablespoons	x 15	= milliliters
fluid ounces	x 30	= milliliters
fluid ounces	x 0.03	= liters
cups	x 240	= milliliters
cups	x 0.24	= liters
pints	x 0.47	= liters
quarts	x 0.95	= liters
gallons	x 3.8	= liters
ounces	x 28	= grams
pounds	x 454	= grams
pounds	x 0.45	= kilograms

To convert metric measurements to the U.S. Customary System of measurements of weight and volume, apply these equations:

milliliters	x 0.2	= teaspoons
milliliters	x 0.07	= tablespoons
milliliters	x 0.034	= fluid ounces
liters	x 34	= fluid ounces
milliliters	x 0.004	= cups
liters	x 4.2	= cups
liters	x 2.1	= pints
liters	x 1.06	= quarts
liters	x 0.26	= gallons
grams	x 0.035	= ounces
grams	x 0.002	= pounds
kilograms	x 2.2	= pounds

UNDERSTANDING BASIC METRIC TERMS USED IN THE KITCHEN

The fundamental units of the International Metric System are the meter and the kilogram. The meter is a unit of length and the kilogram is a unit of mass or weight. Liquid volume is measured by the liter, a unit of measurement derived from the meter.

Other units of measurement are used to measure the quantity of time (second), electric current (ampere), temperature (degree Kelvin) and luminous intensity (candela).

The size of the unit of measurement is described by prefixes, as listed below, except for the kilogram which is the only base measurement unit that contains a prefix. The gram (or 0.001 kilogram) proved to be too small for practical applications.

These are the metric prefixes most used by homemakers:

mega = one million times
kilo   = one thousand times
hecto = one hundred times
deca = ten times
deci   = one tenth of
centi = one hundredth of
milli = one thousandth of
micro = one millionth of

The approximate U.S. Customary System equivalents of metric units often used in kitchen activities are:

1 meter   = 39.37 inches or 1.1 yards
1 gram   = .0353 ounces
1 liter   = 1.06 quarts
1 kilogram = 2.2 pounds

°F — Temperature of Food for Control of Bacteria

250

240
Canning temperatures for low-acid vegetables, meat, and poultry in pressure canner.

Canning temperatures for fruits, tomatoes, and pickles in water-bath canner.

212

Cooking temperatures destroy most bacteria. Time required to kill bacteria decreases as temperature is increased.

165

Warming temperatures prevent growth but allow survival of some bacteria.

140
Some bacterial growth may occur. Many bacteria survive.

125

DANGER ZONE. Temperatures in this zone allow rapid growth of bacteria and production of toxins by some bacteria. (Do not hold foods in this temperature zone for more than 2 or 3 hours.)

60

Some growth of food poisoning bacteria may occur.

40
Cold temperatures permit slow growth of some bacteria that cause spoilage.*

32

Freezing temperatures stop growth of bacteria, but may allow bacteria to survive. (Do not store food above 10° F. for more than a few weeks.)

0

* Do not store raw meats for more than 5 days or poultry, fish, or ground meat for more than 2 days in the refrigerator.
Source: United States Dept. of Agriculture Office of Communications, 1975.

357

Index

Index

Index

Greens
  frozen, 210
  hot pack, 83

Half-Moon Pies, 242
Head space, 33-34, 203
Heavenly Grape Conserve, 141
Herb Jelly, 132-133
Herbs
  dried, 287-288
  for pickling, 151
  frozen, 210-211
Hickory nuts, 344
Homemade Peanut Brittle, 345-346
Honey, 60, 347-348
  crystallization, 347
  extracting machine, 347
  and jelly, 118
Honey-Grape Jelly with Homemade
  Pectin, 131
Horseradish, 340
Hot pack, 31
  fruit, 62-63
  tomatoes, 94-95
  vegetables, 75-76
Hot-Pepper Jelly, 134
Hot-Pepper Sauce, 177

Ice cream, 11
Indiana Stuffed "Mangoes," 169-170

Jalapeno Jelly, 135
Jams, 113
  recipes, 135-138
Jars
  reheating, 30
  types, 27-28
  washing, 28-29
Jellies, 49, 113
  and acid, 116-117

equipment for, 114-115
extracting juice for, 122-124
failures, 126
jars, 28, 29
and jelling, 124-126
and mold, 46-47
recipes, 128-135
sealing, 127-128
and sugar, 117-118
Jelly bag, 114
Jelly glasses, 115
Jelly-making kettle, 114
Jelly stock, 130-131
Jelmeter, 119
Jerusalem Artichoke Relish, 173
Jerusalem artichokes, 340
Juanita's Frozen Cucumbers for
  Frying, 228
Juice, 68, 219-220
  extracted from fruits, 61-62, 121-124

Kohlrabi, 211
Kosher Dill Pickles, 164
Kraut cutter, 309-310

Labeling (for freezing), 202-203
Leather breeches beans, 243, 284
Lemon Butter Frosting, 234
Lemon Curd, 187
Lemon juice, 220
  to acidify, 93
  as anti-darkening agent, 59, 201, 252, 258
  and jelly, 117
Lemons
  pickled, 180
Lima beans
  frozen, 207
  hot pack, 79
  raw pack, 79

Index

Index

Index